ANDREI TARKOVSKY

A LIFE ON THE CROSS

ANDREI TARKOVSKY:
A LIFE ON THE CROSS
by Lyudmila Boyadzhieva

Translated by Christopher Culver
Edited by Scott D. Moss and Camilla Stein

Image courtesy of Kai Holland, akg-images GmbH

© 2012, Alpina Non-Fiction

© 2014, Glagoslav Publications

www.glagoslav.com

ISBN: 978-1-78267-101-5

A catalogue record for this book is available
from the British Library.

LYUDMILA BOYADZHIEVA

ANDREI TARKOVSKY
A LIFE ON THE CROSS

TRANSLATED BY CHRISTOPHER CULVER

GLAGOSLAV PUBLICATIONS

CONTENTS

ACKNOWLEDGEMENTS

The author would like to thank everyone whose materials and reflections on the work of Andrei Tarkovsky assisted in the writing of this book: Marina Tarkovskaya, Andrei Voznesensky, Nikolai Burlyayev, Donatas Banionis, Andrei Mikhalkov-Konchalovsky, Natalya Bondarchuk, Valentina Malyavina, Alla Demidova, Eduard Artemyev, Vadim Yusov, Neya Zorkaya, Valery Basenko, Lev Annensky, Olga Surkova, Otari Teneyshvili, Mikhail Romm, Mikhail Romandin, Vera Shitova, Ebbo Demant and many others who had the fortune of meeting, working with or writing about Tarkovsky.

A DANCE OF THE FLESH AND SYMPHONY OF THE SPIRIT

TARKOVSKY REVOLUTIONIZED THE WORLD OF FILMMAKING, WORking almost half a century ahead of his time.

He brought a kind of magically arranged film content to life, which the audience was not supposed to understand or even perceive. Emotions and the intellect are only pitfalls in an attempt to understand the human soul. He sought a way to convey deep, mysterious but stirring images from one soul to another, he dreamed of a filmmaking that affected people on a subconscious level, because this would save all mankind. He knew one thing for sure: in order to survive, the world needs a renewed Homo sapiens, developing under the influence of great art, high culture and firm spiritual values, an individual driven exclusively by moral standards, ignoring all the material demands of the base flesh.

Cinema, true cinema, would be the unique means of influencing the transformation of the human race and therefore the most effective medium for saving the world.

Andrei Tarkovsky made seven complete films and left one unfinished. Each of them won the highest acclaim from the international film community. One of his films, *Andrei Rublev*, has been given the title of "film of films", just as the Bible has been called the "Book of books".

A great deal has been written and said about Tarkovsky. His films have been watched and will continue to be watched, uncovering more and more meanings, sparking reflection and debate, at least as long as the controversy between the spiritual and the material finds no definitive solution; as long as there are no answers to the "eternal questions" such as: Who are we? Who sent us into this world? What are we living for? Where do we go afterwards? It is only then that what tormented Tarkovsky, gazing into the abyss of human existence, will seem to us, the omniscient ones, no less naive than the historical disputes over the shape of the Earth.

It seems, however, that the plan of the Creator, combining spirit and flesh into a single creation, does not offer any key. Therefore, the search for the meaning of existence, expressed by the language of cinema, will always be relevant, as long as cinema does not become a quaint exoticism, out of touch with the mankind of a new civilization; when, like old floppy disks, communication by means of a camera and the methods of transferring information available to it become superseded with no going back. Only then will the "damnable questions", debated for centuries, be approached through other means of creativity.

However, something quite the opposite might happen as well. It may be that the magical, not entirely comprehensible essence of Tarkovsky's films will be of particular importance to a world on its way to spiritual collapse. The special properties of his film language are matter, cut open, as if under the dissector's knife, and time caught in a trap by a motionless camera — these transform the slow pacing and the unspoken into "spiritual zones" (like Goa, hidden from civilization), areas for meditative immersion into the depths of self-knowledge, and they will preserve his films in a special niche of wisdom, along with religious teachings and spiritual practices.

Tarkovsky's seven-and-a-half films are a drop of something different in the ocean of commercial and simply bad cinema, whatever its origin. These seven-and-a-half achievements, standing apart in the world of film, are like the small verdant island in the mysterious ocean of Solaris and have become a code word for a person's intellectual and aesthetic maturity, a sort of IQ in and of themselves.

When thinking of Tarkovsky and his work, one main, unanswered question remains, connected to a realm generally inaccessible to human beings: the matter of talent, inspiration, sudden insights, i.e. the presence of some irrational higher power in earthly affairs, in the frail confines of human embodiment, which is often alien to this higher power.

Where did Tarkovsky, not always aware of the workings of his revolutionary output, draw these images, motifs, ways of combining or the joining together of various aspects of creation into a single whole, playing with such concepts as the soul, matter, humanity, history, death and eternity?

He established new worlds out of elements that were occasionally not rationally explainable, studying phenomena and feelings that were not so close to him personally — sacrifice, compassion, love. The paradox of Tarkovsky's personality, marked by an enigmatic complexity, consists in his simultaneous existence in two different worlds, his "double citizenship": the material and the spiritual. Thus in the higher spheres lie the sources of his unique talents, while the mundane level determines one's human nature, something that cannot be confused with talent and often contradicts it. The result of this is the long series of paradoxes which followed all of Tarkovsky's undertakings like a bad omen.

He respected his home country, accepting it with all its drawbacks of full-fledged socialism, with its idiocies, cruelty, hypocrisy and hostility. He wanted to be "understood by his own country", embraced and rewarded by it. However, being far from political and social engagement, lacking an understanding of the backstage workings of the world of cinema, he suffered failure after failure. For the Soviet authorities, the law-abiding, ideologically moderate Tarkovsky remained an outsider, a nuisance due to his obscurity and incapability for mutual understanding. Sniffing out with their hunter's senses his outsider inclinations, the authorities did everything they could to reject his works, excommunicate and annihilate them. Standing distant from ideological rebellion, devoted to his country without any dissident plotting, Tarkovsky virtually became a foreign object, forced to seek refuge abroad.

He thought of himself as a messiah, devoting all his spiritual and creative energy to the refinement of humanity. But the audience for whom he worked often was unable to reach an understanding of what he was preaching. The wide audience of the USSR had no cultural bearings with which to get a handle on Tarkovsky's films. They lacked an intellectual background and subtleness of perception, a familiarity with sophisticated material. "Yes, my films are received with difficulty," Tarkovsky admitted. "But I will not make even the smallest compromise for the masses, make my films more accessible or 'interesting', I will not take even half a step toward being understood by the audience."

He was not going to entertain, or even sustain interest. He feared even the tiniest drop of sentimentality or humor that might sneak into the film. Tarkovsky was absolutely insistent that the reception of his films ought to be a painful act, almost as distressing as the making of a film itself. Only then would someone be able to change something in himself and, subsequently, the world that had sunk into mundane materialism would change.

Tarkovsky rejected other ways of influencing audiences through the medium of cinema. He spoke very negatively in his public statements about the leading figures in the film industry who looked for ways of communicating with the audience that were different from his own principles. The insistence of the "messiah" exasperated the "unbelievers". More and more often they would shout, "Crucify him, crucify him!"

In his films, Tarkovsky depicted love and sacrifice as the primary manifestations of the spirit, holding the universe together. In real life he was unfamiliar with the mystery of love. In fact, he did not feel devoted and self-sacrificing love toward anyone, whether friends, colleagues, children or women. "A woman does not have her own inner world and should not have one. Her inner world should be completely dissolved into the inner world of a man." Such was his unbending insistence.

Unable to love, he could not distinguish authentic feelings from a poor imitation. Though he proclaimed as an artist the importance of loyalty and complete sincerity in a relationship between a man and a woman, he was himself an inconstant partner. His fate was to cheat on women and be cheated on. Any woman who was not ready to dedicate her life to an outcast and martyr could not be his support and his muse, her feelings would go unrequited. In his marriage, Tarkovsky was dealt the role of prey, a puppet in the hands of a stronger, mercenary partner. Consequently, marriage to a woman destroyed his own identity. Probably the worst trap that Tarkovsky's fate set for him was to meet and then spend many years of his life with Larisa Kizilova, later Mrs. Tarkovskaya.

The conditions of the last years of Tarkovsky's life turned him into a bundle of nerves. This was owing in large part to his steady companion, who decided, whatever it took, to "go down in history", to enter an esteemed place among the greats, to get a ticket to the easy life. And the most important thing was to remain for Tarkovsky's descendants the rightful owner of his fame, his guardian angel, his inspiration, who everywhere and always helped this genius to ascend to the throne of demiurge of world cinema. In the union of Mr. and Mrs. Tarkovsky, genius and malice became merged like two halves of an androgynous individual. When he got himself his own personal temping serpent, Tarkovsky began a headlong journey into his own tragic ending.

Tarkovsky was proud, unmercenary, firm in his intentions, madly courageous in defending his own principles. Dignity and a firm adherence to one's principles were his motto. But he then slandered his friends, insulted his colleagues, raised his demands for payment from foreign distributors and scared away those who had offered him a helping hand with his cold disdain.

The majority of people who encountered him in the course of his career reluctantly admitted, "He's a genius, but he is not a great human being."

Stubborn, provocatively direct, far from being sentimental, even with those who unquestioningly executed his ideas, he submitted to a selfish woman and he dealt roughly with his colleagues, friends and relatives, who were not useful to him, that is, he thought them of no practical value.

Perhaps he found it easier to arrange his private things with someone else's help. Perhaps, immersed in his work, he was simply too weak to oppose her.

Tarkovsky, persistently declaring his disdain for material values in the name of spiritual growth, reconstructed his ideal existence in his film *The Mirror*: a poor village from his childhood. At the same time he undertook the construction of an "estate" in Podmoskovye, adorning it with paintings and buying antique furniture. He dreamed of acquiring an old castle in Italy, giving careful consideration to the size of its pool. Keeping on the right course was still managed by the same woman who had taken the biggest role in Tarkovsky's life.

Tarkovsky never had the timid smile of an artist who had reason to doubt his own achievements in cinema and for humanity. He knew his own worth perfectly well, defying authorities as early as in his university years. When he found himself in the "jungle of capitalism", Tarkovsky claimed exclusive rights: general admiration and financial success. He demanded that his revelatory films, which he had "gratuitously given to the people", be generously rewarded. Tarkovsky did not place himself alongside anyone, even his respected elder Bresson, whose win at Cannes he questioned.

A stranger in the land of people who were cynical and mercenary, or simply did not understand him because of his different approach, he struggled, baited by fear and anger, and became stuck in the trap of collisions with the authorities, unsettled financial hardships, and a disconnect between his personal and creative life. The eternal struggle of the spiritual and the material, the investigation of which he believed to be the primary objective of art, became his own fatal battle.

The outcome is a sad one: an incompatibility with everything that he was living for, the endless pressure of a woman driving him like a horse with more and more demands, brought the irreversible disaster nearer. In his last years Tarkovsky, already impulsive enough, was constantly on the verge of a nervous breakdown. His terminal illness — "the disease of my entire life" — was a death sentence, the end. He was worn out and grew weak. He would not believe the news for a long time, just as he refused (so stubbornly refused) to believe in death. "For me there is no such thing as death." By deluding himself, he tried to ward off the inevitable.

He died before he even had the chance to grow old, to fully carry out his work, to finish realizing his many plans, a poor man but renowned worldwide. He died rejected by his homeland, deprived of the legitimate honors and financial independence that he ardently yearned for. He left the world pitifully early, not entirely sure if he was going out as a winner or a loser.

PART I. A feeling of immortality

"*All his life an artist feeds on his childhood and his own memories, the sense of immortality, his keen reflexes and simple happiness.*"

Andrei Tarkovsky

Chapter I.
CHILDHOOD

The brighter one's childhood memories,
the greater one's creative potential.

Andrei Tarkovsky

I.

Andrei Tarkovsky was fortunate with his ancestry. He was fortunate if one looks at the seven-and-a-half films which he managed to bring into the treasury of world cinema, and if we overlook the painful road he was forced to walk. In his genes lay a powerful gift and the elements of a contradictory, complex personality, which predetermined the director's difficult path through life.

Andrei Tarkovsky's father, the famous poet Arseny Alexandrovich Tarkovsky, was born in 1907 in a provincial town in the Kherson Governorate to the family of a clerk at the Elisavetgrad Public Bank. However, the volatile blood of the rulers of Dagestan, who were the root of Tarkovsky's ancestry, showed itself — the fate of its representatives was not easy.

The roots of the Tarkovsky family, according to one version, go back to the "Tarkovsky holdings", as this area, covering almost the whole of Dagestan was called, and only after 1867 was its name changed to the Temir-Khan-Shura district. Shamsudin, the last prince of the Tarkovsky holdings, is considered to be the founder of the Tarkovsky bloodline. The features of the powerful prince can be guessed in the rugged handsomeness and stern character of Arseny Alexandrovich and his son Andrei.

Alexander Karlovich, Andrei Tarkovsky's grandfather, was endowed with an uneasy and restless soul. Apart from his work at the bank, he wrote poems, stories and translated Dante, Giacomo Leopardi, Victor Hugo for his own pleasure. Furthermore, in the 1880s, he took part in a Narodnaya Volya circle, which brought him under police surveillance. He was arrested, imprisoned three times in Voronezh, Elisavetgrad, Odessa and Moscow and exiled for five years to Eastern Siberia. In exile, he took up journalism, working with newspapers in Irkutsk. Alexander Karlovich's first wife died young, leaving behind a young daughter. His second wife, Maria Danilovna, bore her husband two sons, Valery and Arseny. As he was undependable for political reasons, Alexander Karlovich's children were mostly brought up by the family of a relative, the actor and playwright Ivan Karpovich Tobilevich, who was one of the founders of the Ukrainian theater and known in the history of drama under the name Karpenko-Kary.

The family was immersed in literature and theater. Poems and plays, written by lovers of the stage, were performed among friends. At the beginning of the 20th century, drama circles, societies, university and high school student troupes quickly multiplied, encompassing what we might call today the entire youth subculture. Almost everyone wrote poetry: in girls' albums, in local magazines and newspapers; they published collections at their own expense or timidly kept their secret writings in a desk drawer. And most importantly, they read the poems in mellifluous voices at literary evenings, which were held regularly and ended with stormy debates or dancing.

Arseny, writing in secret and only for the eyes of a girl he loved, found great success among his young peers due to his outlook, which everyone compared to the anti-hero Pechorin in Lermontov's *A Hero of Our Time*, and his mysterious, romantic nature. As a young man, he was handsome with a fiery Caucasian beauty, and this alone could evoke sighs and note-passing from the fair sex. And when he recited poetry, it led to walks in the dusk or gardens that had frozen over, kisses, vows, as in the sort of sweet stories that Kuprin, Bunin and Chekhov often wrote.

In the intellectual Tobilevich home, thoroughly in tune with the cultural and artistic trends of the time, one could hear a piano or singing to guitar accompaniment, recitals of poetry or performances of theatrical sketches. How similar was the cherry plush of the Tobilevich living room, the porcelain stove, the cream-colored curtains over the windows to the home of the Turbins, the childhood home of Mikhail Bulgakov. This was an atmosphere in which people were brought up with Romantic bravery, an unshakable sense of duty and a thirst for artistic expression.

While still quite young, Arseny Tarkovsky, together with his father and brother, participated in the literary evenings of some of the capital's celebrities: Igor Severyanin, Konstantin Balmont and Fyodor Sologub. Later the young man came to Moscow to immerse himself in an atmosphere of poetry. It is difficult to imagine that somewhere beside him, in a banquet hall packed with attentive listeners in rows of chairs, shone the short-sighted eyes of a young Marina Tsvetaeva. Perhaps Arseny saw how, with trepidation, she presented Konstantin Balmont with a white peony after one of his recitals, blushing with embarrassment. Perhaps Arseny heard the first recitals of this budding poetess, who, at her own expense, had already published the collection *Evening Album*? Much later, in pre-war Moscow, having returned from the West, Marina Tsvetaeva fell under the spell of this handsome man, no longer young, and even wrote him passionate poems. A year later Arseny, learning of her tragic death in August 1941, wrote an epitaph in verse for the martyred Marina.

The Ukrainian civil war ended with the victory of the Soviet authorities. Arseny's older brother Valery was killed in battle against the ataman Grigoriev in May 1919. People were terrified by the Soviets' seizure of power and hoped that it would not last long. Arseny and his friends, mad for poetry and constitutional monarchy, published an acrostic in a newspaper in which the first letters depicted the head of the Soviet government, Vladimir Lenin in an unflattering light. The young men were arrested and taken to Nikolaev, which in those years was the administrative center of the oblast. Arseny Tarkovsky managed to escape from the train on the way. This son of an intellectual family became a starving beggar, wandering across Ukraine and the Crimean Peninsula. He was forced to try his hand at several professions, working as an apprentice to a shoemaker and in fisheries. He turned out to be a jack of all trades, which proved useful in his later life.

In 1923, Arseny Alexandrovich came to Moscow and called on an aunt, his father's sister. Two years later, he enrolled in the Higher Literary Courses, which had been organized in place of the Literary Institute, closed after the death of Valery Bryusov. After he had observed the students for a while, Arseny noticed a beautiful young woman with a tuft of fair hair on the back of her neck, as if her hair were so heavy that it made her hold her chin up with pride.

"She's the one!" the young poet decided after Maria Vishnyakova's speech in a student auditorium, where she talked passionately and in an inspired tone about the poetry of Blok.

They would soon take long walks along the Moscow lanes, dance to an orchestra in Gorky Park, read poems ceaselessly to each other and kiss in the intoxicating scent of blooming linden trees.

"I started to write poetry already when I was in nappies!" Arseny boasted, a smile in his dark eyes. "Our house was a place for high arts, we organized various events and poetic evenings. I don't even remember any more when I made my debut. I just remember that I had to stand on top of a stool. Only later did I grow tall. As a boy I was quite small."

"At least in my ancestry we are very tough and principled. I don't forgive insults." Maria looked into his loving eyes. She knew that she wasn't the only one dreaming of the handsome young man with the dark looks, but she thought, "Other women's husbands cheat on them, but I'm a special girl!" and said to him, "Remember, Arseny, you are meant for me for life."

"Don't worry, you can rely on me," he said. "If I have fallen in love with you now, it is for life." He embraced Maria, but she pulled away and ran ahead of him, a gauze scarf fluttering in her hand. She hid behind an old maple, pressing her back to its trunk. Arseny caught up with her, kissed her gently on her snub nose, took her in his strong arms. "You won't get away now. I respect people with principles." He buried his face in her warm hair, which smelled of wild strawberry soap. "You are the only one for me. This scent… No one can have a scent like this!" (Under the spell of love, the country's only brand of soap at the time was transformed into a rare perfume.)

"And what do you like most about me?" he asked.

Maria furrowed her brow playfully and answered, "That you know how to make shoes. I'll never be barefoot."

Maria's parents liked him and in 1928 the young couple were married.

The next year, Tarkovsky was granted, in recognition of his excellent studies, a monthly stipend from the state publishing house's foundation for beginning authors. This small sum of money came as a great help to the young married couple. Tarkovsky's first publications — the quatrain "*Svecha*" (The Candle) and the poem "*Khleb*" (Bread) date from his studies in the Courses of Higher Literature. But then the poet's career stalled. He had to wait a long time to issue a collection of his own poems — several decades, in fact.

In the following year, the Higher Literature Courses closed under scandal, the suicide of one of the female students. Tarkovsky was hired by the newspaper *Gudok*, the very one where Bulgakov, Olesha and Ilf and Petrov moonlighted. Tarkovsky reviewed court cases and wrote satires in verse and fairy tales under various pseudonyms. The most popular "author" of Arseny's satires was the rustic character Taras Podkova.

In 1931, Tarkovsky worked as a senior instructor and consultant for an arts program on Soviet radio.

"They took me, dear Maruska, they took me!" he said to his wife as he got home. "Now we'll make the big money. I'll write plays for broadcast over the radio."

"Oh, for radio! You're my hero. That sounds like a promising and progressive career. But the important thing is not to lose your ideological bearings and don't say anything… Well, you know," Maria broke off and looked around furtively, lest someone might have heard the word "anti-Soviet" almost tumbling from her lips. She was making soup from bad fish, part of their rations, on a kerosene stove. "Don't worry, I'm a smart man, I've had some schooling. They've already given me a commission for the radio. The play will be called *Steklo* (Glass). It tells of heroic glassmakers." Arseny scooped up a bit of broth, blew on the spoon and tasted it. "It's like in a restaurant! It's even better that the potatoes are frozen, so they melt in the mouth."

To get acquainted with glassmakers and learn something of the process by which they worked with molten glass, Tarkovsky went to visit a glassworks. The play was produced in a very short time, recorded by the noted actor Osip Abdulov and broadcast by All-Union Radio.

Almost all the inhabitants of the communal apartment gathered around the radio receiver in the kitchen, neatly seated in rows, as if at a theater. After the play finished, the author was congratulated by his neighbors. Maria set the table, welcoming them with her own vinaigrette salad recipe. They read poems, sang and drank to their life becoming completely wonderful as soon as possible.

"Life will be wonderful! You'll become a writer for the stage, and we'll have a son," whispered Maria one night into the shaven but always stubbly cheek of her husband. "Your hair is so coarse, like bristles."

"Huh, what?" his eyes shown in the darkness, he sat up and embraced her in astonishment. "What are you saying, Maruska?! You're expecting a baby boy? That's fantastic!"

"Or a little girl…"

"No, as you promised, first a boy and then later a girl."

The next evening Arseny came home in a somber mood. He sat down and pushed his dinner plate away. "I don't deserve this food. Marusya, your husband is without a job. Oh, what a thrashing the director gave me just now! My ears were burning."

"They didn't like the play?" his wife asked, horrified.

"Worse than that, they called me…" Arseny coughed, "They called me a 'mystic'."

"A mystic? How awful!" Maria collapsed on a stool. "Arsyusha, that's bad, very dangerous even. Where did they find it, this mysticism?"

"Oh, the devil tempted me! I'm just a lover of the pen, I wanted to give life to a play, putting it in the voice of the founder of Russian glassmaking, Mikhail Lomonosov."

"That was a great writing strategy. You showed a link between the generations, a connection with tradition."

"And I told them, 'I used my means as an artist to bring the play to life. And you are all, comrades, a bunch of bores!'"

"Right, they are bourgeois reactionaries," Maria smiled and put her hand over her belly. "He's kicking!"

"Look here, woman," he banged his fist on the breadcrumb-covered tablecloth. "The city with its dust is no place for you with a small child. Write to your family, 'It's settled, we're leaving soon.'"

Maria's mother and stepfather, as soon as they heard about the pregnancy, had flooded the young couple with letters, begging and pleading that they deliver the child at Nikolai Matveyevich's hospital and then come to them in the countryside as soon as possible. Back at the beginning of the 20th century, to save themselves from the hunger ravaging Moscow, the Petrovs had moved to the village of Zavrazhye in the Yuryevetsky District, situated on the left bank of the Volga not far from where the Nemda River joins it.

Maria's stepfather, Nikolai Matveyevich Petrov served as a general practitioner at the local hospital. They rented rooms in a large wooden house. It was a large Volga village with the sound of foghorns, a wide stretch along the river with forests and fields and a five-domed church which the militantly atheist government had not yet destroyed, and it naturally seemed like paradise to a woman expecting a child.

At the end of March, the Tarkovskys set off on the hazardous journey. Their trek was not a short one: it took them around twenty-four hours by train to reach Kineshma, and there, on the dirty square of the train station, shooing away the geese and chickens, they packed themselves into a rickety carriage. They still had thirty kilometers ahead of them, but what a thirty kilometers! The road went along the Volga, then over a river still frozen over but the ice of which would soon begin to crack. It took them from three o'clock in the afternoon until five o'clock in the morning. Arseny held his wife's hand and prayed only for one thing: that she not go into labor at night in this frozen wasteland. Maria fell silent, worryingly listening to the kicking in her womb, and she thought the same thing.

Arseny tried to cheer his wife up, "Marusenka, your date is set for April 20! I think we'll get there in three weeks." He tried to make jokes, but on every bump her heart fluttered, "That's it, it's beginning!"

"Let the Devil take this broken road," the coachman looked back at them. "I'm afraid we'll shake the little woman apart. I'm trying to take it slowly and go around these damn ruts in the road. Where are you going, you stupid animal, you're taking us right into them." He cracked his whip and the carriage jolted at the next icy pothole. Maria weakly squealed.

"Don't be afraid, I'm with you," her husband consoled her, trying to stay cheerful

"Arsyusha, if anything happens, can you manage?" Maria looked at his face, whitened by the reflection of the snow. "Can you deliver a baby?"

"Lord have mercy," he crossed himself. "I've seen a lot of things in my life, but nothing like that has ever come up. But don't you worry. Nekrasov wrote about how Russian women gave birth right in the fields without any help. There's a story of Kuprin about…"

"Oh, please, you don't have to go on about that," she took his warm, sinewy hand in both of hers. "Better," he said, "to recite Lermontov's poem "Alone I set out on the road":"

> *Alone I set out on the road;*
> *Through the mist the flinty path is sparkling;*
> *The night is still. The desert harks to God,*
> *And star talks to star.*

Maria joined in:

> *In the heavens it is solemn and wondrous!*
> *The earth is sleeping in a blue glow…*
> *Why do I feel such pain and troubles?*
> *Do I await something, regret something?*

"Oh, it's passed," she faintly smiled. "With poems I can even make it to the hospital."

But she didn't make it to the hospital. Maria Ivanovna gave birth in her family home on the dining room table, covered with a starched tablecloth. Her mother was so nervous that she forgot where the midwife's house was, but Arseny, energetic and excited, found her. The midwife and Nikolai Matveyevich together delivered the baby.

After everything was over, the doctor, who had been very worried, took a decanter from a cupboard and poured glasses for himself and his son-in-law. He looked at the mother with her crying baby, lying on a clean bed.

"Well, Maruska, you can have the next baby wherever you want! It's very stressful to deliver a baby at a relative's place."

2.

The next day, the young father, with his characteristic impatience, registered the birth of his son Andrei Arsenyevich Tarkovsky with the local authorities and received a birth certificate, "Born in the village of Zavrazhye in the Yuryevetsky District on April 4, 1932".

The parents of the new-born, as literary people and amazed by his birth, began to keep a diary. They wrote nearly every day, together or in turn. Gazing at his tiny wrinkled face, Maria tried to set down in as much detail as possible even the new-born's cloudy eyes: "His eyes are grayish-blue, bluish-gray, grayish-green, narrow, like a little Tatar or a lynx. He stares angrily. His nose is like mine, but it's hard to tell. He has a fine mouth. We'll call him our little Lynx."

There was only one problem: the child cried tirelessly. "April 12," Maria wrote in her diary, "around 10 o'clock in the evening. This night has been a nightmare. He cries and cries, and nothing can be done."

Maria was not worried about her own sleep. It would be all right if the mother alone couldn't sleep, but Nikolai Matveyevich had to see patients at the clinic starting in the morning, then make house calls on his bicycle, and quite often he had to get up at night when someone came to him for help.

But little Lynx kept crying, finally wearing the elderly ones out. They took the young couple to live in the mezzanine of a large laboratory wing, where it was comfortable enough: two smallish rooms with a balcony. Arseny, a jack of all trades, deftly painted the walls and ceiling and set their living area in order. Even though they had only a well outside and had to heat water on a wood stove, such chores came as a joy to Arseny. He was bursting with enthusiasm because of the presence in his life of the little creature, whom he called Lynx or Drilka. Arseny washed his diapers, cradled him to sleep and made up lullabies for him.

Maria wrote in her diary, "Daddy Arseny is a fine dad and a very good nanny."

Arseny found a hundred things to do: he restored books, repaired shoes, darned socks in a virtuoso fashion, and could spend all night taking apart and repairing his typewriter. He liked beauty and elegance, he could create an atmosphere of refinement, humble cosiness at home. He read books and wrote poetry day and night. The only thing that troubled Arseny Alexandrovich were the translations he had to do to make a living. He would put them off until the last minute and would do them frantically just before the deadline.

The warm season came, the earth bloomed in all its colors. They baptized the baby in the local five-domed church and he became somewhat calmer.

Maria and Arseny had a hiding place behind the lilac bushes.

When the lilac blooms, and you dive into it, you feel like you are all alone in the world, and this world is heaven.

"Listen to what I've written," Arseny drew a pre-written sheet of paper from his shirt pocket and, gazing at the blue sky between the heavy, fragrant tufts, he began to recite in a slightly different voice, subdued and solemn:

> *You were a dream and you became music,*
> *Become a name and be the memory.*
> *With your tanned girlish palm,*
> *Touch my half-opened eyes*
> *So that I can see the golden sky,*
> *So that in my beloved's widened pupils,*
> *Like in mirrors, a reflection will appear*
> *Of a double star that guides ships.*

Maria held his hand with tears in her eyes. "You were a dream and you became music…" It was written about her! There was such happiness like no one had ever felt before. He was the only one who she could love and take care of until the end of time…

He was already kissing her, impatiently taking her lace blouse from her hot shoulders.

"Oh, Arsyushenko, Arsyusghenko," she could only whisper. "I want a little girl too."

"We'll have one."

She pressed herself to his chest, listening to the strong and resounding beating of his heart. "Will our children be poets too? Yes, they will! They certainly will! You have enough talent for five people."

"My dear, my dear… This is a mystery." He could suddenly turn into something "great". One moment he was kissing her, and the next he would become quiet. He would sit, not moving at all, and his thoughts would move far away. This was the mystery, God's blessing. Maria fell silent, new poems would now suddenly flow into his soul from heaven.

"You know what you are, you are a great man! Don't argue, you are a first-class poet."

Spring with its fragrance and birdsong were wonderful days for these parents, as well as for their infant son, who would laze in the sun in a cardboard box. For Maria, the world became a sheer delight when the tall, stately man with a chiselled profile walked beside her, reading the poems that he had recently written. Lynx would sleep, lazing in the warmth of his father's arms. The happiness was overwhelming, almost unbearable. But they were worried, very worried; when you hold on to something dear to you, you are always worried. The rich are always anxious, but the poor don't care, because they have nothing to lose.

"Maruska, you are like a white swan, so stately and impressive as you walk chewing on a blade of grass, gathering flowers. But I have to do something, I can't walk around without anything to do. Do we have to fix the roof over the well? I'm almost finished with the bookcase, who will put it together? It's not right. There's a mess, it's not cozy. Maybe you should make some napkins, they would turn out well. I'll put varnish on the wood and you'll bring the lace. Then there will be a place for Tolstoy and Dostoevsky to rest their laurels." Yet again, Arseny encouraged his wife to make their house a nest.

"Forget about the napkins," Maria threw up her hands. "That's bourgeois. They just collect dust." She was a typical person of her time. She could be content with the bare minimum: a cup of tea, a piece of bread, but she despised vases and pictures on the wall. In everyday life she was not demanding, she would collect a bouquet of flowers from the meadow and stick them in a big glass bottle which her mother had kept for cherry brandy. They washed the floors until they shone and this was enough. And really, wasn't it nice!

But what her heart aspired to and could not embrace, was the endless, always-new charms of nature. For Andrei, who was just learning to walk, she would raise a flower to his nose or point to a bird or hairy caterpillar:

"Look, my son, at what a world we live in. What a joy it is."

His mother wrote about forests and fields, clouds and little spiders, nice stories that were loved by her friends. When she was at school, they would jokingly call her "Tolstoy in a skirt". But one day Arseny said offhand:

"Nice, very nice. For a woman's scrapbook."

Maria was not the type to forget an insult. She gathered up her notebooks and threw them into a bonfire behind the shed. She destroyed both her poems and prose. Andrei lay crying in his box next to her, apparently protesting the destruction.

"What are you doing here?" Arseny was surprised to find his wife at this strange activity. "You're going to suffocate the little boy with this smoke." He picked up his son together with his makeshift crib. He looked closer, "Why are you burning paper? I need every sheet I can get!"

"This is my paper. It's destroyed now."

"What do you mean, 'destroyed'?"

"I wrote all kinds of things. Poetry, short stories, it's all burning there."

"Why are you making an *auto-da-fé* of what you've written? Don't cry now, Drilka, you're interrupting your parents." After he had taken his wailing child to the porch, Arseny returned, lifted his wife who was crouched in front of the fire and shook her by the shoulders. "What are you burning your work for?"

She smiled at his morose face. His eyebrows were like black pitch extending from his nose to his temples, a real demon.

"Because," she said caustically, "of a lack of talent," She turned away and went over to the child, ending the conversation. Arseny remained silent, holding back his anger, "What a character she has, stubborn and proud." He only muttered lines that he had recently written:

> *You are still walking in your black dress.*
> *The night will pass, you await the dawn,*
> *You are still awake in the spacious house,*
> *As if living in a song.*

The bell-like wind is blowing
In the domes of the churches by night.
Your unwilling sleep is flying
Past your chamber.

It is good that in the spacious house,
There are no mirrors and no darkness,
So you are still walking in your black dress
And you have forgotten me. (…)

Who had he written it for, who was he thinking about? Would anyone ever understand? He didn't read these lines to his wife.

No matter how well they lived that summer, they became very tired. Thankfully, grandmother made dinners for them. They couldn't get enough sleep, losing their minds from Andrei's crying. Arseny even said something at the moment his wife was falling asleep:

"It's almost like our child drank the milk of a viper."

His poetic intuition could guess at something in the little man. The boy's angry look, his wrinkled and demanding face were signs of his future character. He would not smile or coo, like the new-borns usually do. Who knows what babies see in their first days on earth. Does their entire future life flash before them like in one's last moments? Or perhaps their "world perception program" is loading, they are orientating themselves in space. In any case, it seems that for Drilka, coming into the world was difficult and certainly not a happy experience

3.

"It turns out we have an interesting boy. I think that Andrei is destined to have the same poetic duality that runs in the family, where it seems like life is split into two dimensions, a real one and a poetic one. Arseny was either pensive and sullen, or jovial or indifferent and out of it. He either doesn't notice me at all, or bestows on me heaps of blooming bird cherry, that blows from the fence like a white cloud." So thought Maria, looking at her son's face, trying to guess the traits he took from his parents. It turned out that he was entirely his father's son. Here he had the black topknot, like a Dagestani, sticking up from the top of his head. But there was nothing of his mother in him…

We see a photo of Arseny and Maria, a beautiful couple but not at all alike! A quiet, gray-eyed round-faced Russian woman and the pale Caucasian prince with his oriental eyes and sharp eyebrows.

In 1934 Andrei's sister Marina was born, just as they had planned.

Arseny often visited Moscow as the breadwinner for a family that had grown larger. Maria understood this need, but nonetheless, thinking about the poetic circles of the capital, she was jealous of her husband and afraid of the temptations that would inevitably come up before someone so talented and prominent. And he was a hot-blooded man. But maybe there had been no Dagestani prince among his ancestors, as Arseny claimed there was. Perhaps he didn't know the truth? The secrets of blood, the most mysterious of secrets, the crossed destinies of men and women are unpredictable and often fleeting. It is possible that at the time of Lermontov's *Prisoner of the Caucasus*, a Caucasian or Tatar seed was secretly sown in his Polish and Russian family tree. Nonetheless, if we judge from appearances, then Arseny and Andrei without a doubt had southern blood. And also in their character — genial and unscrupulous, with a disposition toward laziness and giggling — there is no trace of the Russian mood. They had tight-strung wills, an uncompromising sense of honor, cocky impudence — and a harshness. Here is what Arseny Tarkovsky wrote after a fight over nothing:

If I were haughty like before,
I would have left you forever;
Everything that I couldn't do without,
Everything that wasn't worth the effort, —
And divide d my kingdom in two. I would say:

"You're going off with
100 promises, 100 celebrations, 100
Words. You can take it with you."

I'm left with a cold dawn,
100 late trams and 100
Raindrops on the tram tracks,
100 lanes, 100 streets and 100
Raindrops in pursuit.

What a sense of foreboding this is, frightening to imagine. Maria pined away, waiting for her husband to return from his latest trip to Moscow, unaware that a passionate affair had already been kindled between her husband and another woman. But was it necessary to think about that? She had children to raise. Little Marinochka, a sheer joy, eager to help everyone, to shelter every plant, every cat. She was marked with a sense of calm and the silky braids she took from her mother. She was a diligent and studious girl. Andrei, on the other hand, was difficult. He was unyielding, intractable and disobedient. One could not expect any kindness from this boy, who would only look back at you with his dark eyes.

"Mother, I'm leaving. I'm going to walk around outside."

He was very independent, read a great deal, wrote and drew some things, but also stayed away from home a lot. But he wasn't talkative and would give no accounts of his walks. His mother's hands could barely manage to smooth the pitch-dark curls on the back of his head, thick and almost like horsehair, before he would break away and run off to his own things. If it was like this already at such a young age, what would he be like when he grew up? She only hoped that his father would rein him in. They were of one kind and would find a common language.

And yet, what happiness it was to have a son and daughter. Arseny loved his children madly. Even if he fooled around on the side, he wasn't going anywhere away from his family. God forbid! She had no grounds to accuse him, he was not the kind of man who would lie to his wife.

In 1936 Arseny met Antonina Alexandrovna Bokhonova, the wife of a literary critic, scholar and friend of Mayakovsky and David Burliuk. Soon it became clear that this stately, lively woman, who knew how to put on a brilliant appearance, as well as her intellect, as if she was meant to be the companion of a famous poet, was not infatuation, but a love that could never be torn apart.

Arseny told his wife about this in the summer of 1937, with the two children holding on to her skirt.

"Antonina Alexandrovna and I have decided to live not far from here for the time being. So I will help you and I won't give up the children."

"You will be a guest at our house?" Maria tried to be ironic and to hold back her tears. Even now, as he betrayed her and the children, had become a stranger, he was still a part of her. This tough, remote face was the only one that she had loved and would ever love, until she reached the wrinkles of old age, gray hair and her last illnesses.

"I will visit you," Arseny emphasized, as he put some folded rubles under the knitted lace tablecloth. "This is for now, for your everyday expenses. I won't stay for dinner, forgive me. I must hurry."

"The children, at least say goodbye to the children!"

"I'm not dying. I'll come again soon," patting his children's cropped heads, he turned with the precise movement of a soldier and left. He was gone out the door and through the yard in a flash. The gate creaked, a branch of the old cherry tree swung… Was this the end? Choking a sob, she threw herself on the bed and bit the pillow so that she would not scream, would not cry out and disturb the children.

Once he had brought her heaps of bird cherry. No longer would someone bring Maria those fragrant bouquets. You couldn't expect such sweetness from Andrei.

Arseny divorced Maria Ivanovna and married Antonina Alexandrovna. At first they lived nearby. The children's father often came around to visit the old house and would certainly bring a present on one of their birthdays. For Andrei he bought a large album and watercolor paints, for Marina — notebooks, and for Maria — candies. But his visits always came as if in a hurry to get away without being seen by his former in-laws.

"It would be better if you didn't come at all," Andrei quietly warned his father, catching him at the gate. "If you do, mother cries the whole night. Marina too. I'm a man, I can manage without you."

He was a proud young man. He knew already that there was no point in loving the father that had left them. He felt only anger and wanted to fight. And still he wanted to hold on to him and not let him go, not let him go for any reason! The warm family hearth had turned out to be so fragile. There had been a home, and now it was all destroyed. He wept deep inside because one could bring nothing back. This is called "time", it only moves forward and never back. It's that simple, but one just can't resign oneself to it completely. One wants to leap back to yesterday somehow, into the past, when everyone was together, and stop time forever. His father stood on the path under the silver poplar, on a stone under which treasure was buried. It was a bright day. And he did not go anywhere. He did not leave their mother for another woman. And through the window, a dark-eyed boy stood looking at him.

Andrei tried with all strength to bring back that calm, warm day, the wind rustling the curtain and the grass outside the window, the old pitcher suddenly falling over and a trickle of white milk flowing out onto the floor. The stream slowed, then thickened along with subsiding wind, and now it spread ever so slowly over the wood floorboards… Stop! He narrowed his eyes, clenched his fists tightly. He opened his eyes to find the empty bench, the pitcher standing proudly, covered with gauze, a fly hitting itself on the glass and a clock ticking inexorably

Andrei grew up into a bright young man, a fidgety one who rushed about all day like mad. But he was not a simple guest in this world, an eavesdropper, a creator. He saw and noted everything. With the keen sense of a hound, he caught sounds and smells. It was as if he were a device that never stopped recording even fleeting impressions. Thus the world around him was imprinted in his memory forever, with all the slightest details.

He carefully and tenderly explored every corner of the yard, the boards of the fence, the trunks of the trees, every precious jewel in the immense earthly wealth in its enchanting variability. Showers, rains that would bring mushrooms, dew like little diamonds, shining in the first rays of sun, and wood chips, and fluff flying from a grayish thistle — all of this he greedily took in, absorbed, afraid to miss even the smallest part of it.

As Andrei wrote in his diary:

> I found the garden enchanting. It covered the space between the house and the three fences in a kingly fashion. One fence divided it from the street leading up to the whitewashed brick wall of the Church of the Epiphany on Simonovskaya Hill; the second divided it from the neighboring property; and the third fence, which had a gate on rope hinges, from our yard ... All three fences were *old* and therefore beautiful... The Japanese find a special charm in signs of age, exposing the essence of things. *Saba*, as they call the traces of the aging of things, is true rustiness, the charm of antiquity, the stamp of time...
>
> An artist feeds on his childhood and his own memories, the sense of immortality, his keen reflexes and simple happiness all his life. Childhood is the tree tops sparkling in the sun, it is one's mother wading through a meadow covered with dew and leaving dark traces behind her, like on the first snow...
>
> The brighter those memories, the greater one's creative potential.

Is it not here, in this powerful bond of all of his being with the living substance of God's creation, is one of the secrets of Tarkovsky's talent?

Chapter 2.
"I WAS REMARKABLY ATTRACTED TO THE STREETS"

I.

In 1939 it was time for Andrei to start going to school and his family returned to Moscow. They settled into their former rooms on the ground floor of a building on Shchipok Street (the ground floor was stone and the upper story was wood). Located in the Zamoskvorechye District, Shchipok was part of an area made up of a maze of alleyways. After the reforms of 1861, the street was dominated by buildings belonging to charitable institutions such as the Alexandrovskaya Hospital, the Solodovnikovskaya Hospice (now the Vishnevsky Institute of Surgery), and also mills and granaries. Until the beginning of the 20th century, mainly stone houses inhabited by the bourgeoisie, lower-class intellectuals and working people stood here. It is worth noting that none of the buildings on Shchipok Street are included in the city's register of historic places. Tarkovsky's house, which became a cult attraction after his death, was demolished, despite a great number of petitions to turn it into a museum for the great director. But these events are still far ahead of us.

At the time, under the old poplar tree, among the labyrinth of alleyways, stood a two-story house, inhabited by a large number of families and factory workers. Until they moved to Yuryevets, Maria Ivanovna's mother lived there with her daughter and second husband, and it was here than the divorced Maria came with her children.

Maria got a job as a proof-reader in the Pervaya Obraztsovaya Printing House. Andrei attended Moscow School No. 554 and took piano lessons at the local music school. He had to practice at his neighbors', because he didn't have his own piano.

Andrei was enchanted by music when other people played. But in order to learn for oneself how to extract this magical weave of harmonies out of a stubborn wooden instrument, one must perfect his technique: repeat the same thing again and again, train one's fingers. It could drive you out of your mind! Now if he just became a conductor, he could just wave and the whole orchestra would fill the air with a sea of magical sounds. All with a wave of your hand!

It would be great to work as a conductor. One can't dream of becoming a printer.

His mother took him to the cinema for the first time when he was seven years old. Earlier she had been afraid of harming the boy's mind with the impressions given by films.

In the Udarnik Cinema Theatre Dovzhenko's film *Shchors* was playing.

Andrei didn't remember the picture. The young lad, scarcely big enough to see over the back of the seat in front of him, remembered only the flickering of the screen and the black explosions among sunflowers with musical accompaniment. These explosions and sunflowers stuck with him forever. His opinion unchanged, Andrei would go on to consider Dovzhenko, with some qualification, a great director.

There were many books in the house. The boy read Andersen, Mark Twain and Cervantes. He loved *Robinson Crusoe, Gulliver's Travels*, the chivalric romances of Sir Walter Scott, Stevenson, the tales of the Brothers Grimm, and later, the prose works of Lermontov, Pushkin, Turgenev's *A Sportsman's Sketches*, the stories of Ambrose Bierce, Kipling and Alexandr Grin, Tolstoy's *Childhood* and *Boyhood*… He devoured books and mulled over his impressions with a great deal of seriousness.

Maria Ivanovna thoroughly developed her son's tastes and though she was without a husband, she raised an intelligent and gifted child. Allowing Andrei to read *War and Peace*, she patiently read sections along with him, explaining the characteristics and subtleties of Tolstoy's work, about the oak on the side of the road, about the moonlit night, about everything that her soul had absorbed. Her son took the baton and ran with it.

Maria Ivanovna saw the tense and gloomy brow, his dark and focused eyes as he tried to understand and register forever the abyss of Tolstoy's novel opening in front of him. She looked at Andrei and rejoiced: Arseny had a worthy son.

2.

The war destroyed this life almost as soon as it had begun.
In 1941 Maria Ivanovna, with the help of Arseny Alexandrovich, was able to evacuate with the children, again to the place they had lived earlier in childhood, the village of Zavrazhye. "These were hard times," Tarkovsky remembered. "I never saw enough of my father. Life was unusually difficult in every way. Still, I got a lot out of life. The best things I have in my life, I owe to my mother." Maria Ivanovna walked across the frozen river, dragged sacks of potatoes from distant villages, washed clothes in a hole cut into the ice, managing to cook for the whole family with what God had sent them, what she had traded for in the market or managed to stash away. All the while a taut string trembled in the childhood existence of the boy — a yearning for his father.

> As soon as we heard a man's familiar and unmistakable voice, Marina and I already ran toward the house. Something burst in my chest, I stumbled and almost fell and tears poured from my eyes. I saw his very thin face come closer and closer, his officer's uniform, his Sam Browne belt, his

arms embracing us. He drew us to himself and all three of us cried. We held each other as tightly as possible, I could only feel how my fingers went numb, so strongly did I grab his soldier's blouse.

"Are you back for good? Yes? For good?" muttered my sister, choking up, while I only held tightly to my father's shoulder and couldn't speak.

Suddenly my father looked back and straightened. My mother was standing several steps away from us. She looked at my father, and such suffering and happiness was written on her face that I looked away.

It was precisely then that the strongest attachment died in the little Andrei, it hid itself forever, the wounded love shrivelled away. He didn't want to be vulnerable any more, his heart wide open, rushing toward the deceptive temptation of loving and being loved. And without that, his secretive character was directed toward a defensive cruelty and distrust. The doors of his soul closed shut, only an elite could enter into it, and that was with difficulty and not for long. All the space within him would be occupied by his profession, which became a fetish to him, an idol.

Everyone felt the indelible stamp of the war, soldiers and civilians, the young and old alike. As Andrei wrote:

Anyone born after 1944 belongs to a totally different generation from the war generation, starving, afflicted early on with sorrow, united by the loss of our fathers, which came down on us like a calamity and caused us to be stunted in our twenties with twisted personalities. Our experience was as varied and pungent as the smell of ammonia. We soon felt the difference between suffering and joy and for all our lives would remember the nauseating feeling of emptiness where we had not long before placed all our hope.

This was an utterly exact and important confession for Tarkovsky: the bitterness of loss eclipsed the light of hope. Over the years his hope, stunted and sickly, would not get stronger but, on the contrary, would be plunged into the darkness of pessimism.

In the summer of 1943, his mother returned with her two children and his grandmother to their nest at First Shchipok Street number 26. The house resembled a barracks with its long corridor that divided it into two parts. The family had two rooms in a communal apartment with windows looking out onto the courtyard almost at ground level. In the kitchen, with a small window looking into the corridor, a light bulb was always on, floating in clouds of steam and smoke. On the gas stove there were bed linens boiling in zinc-coated boilers and pots and pans constantly hissed. They cooked in turns. Maria Ivanovna would come out here to smoke. With a cheap cigarette in her mouth, she managed to stir the laundry in the boiler, wash potatoes, clean the floor while hunched over, and additionally, wipe the soapsuds from the stove, burning her hands. The floors in this house were always cold, they practically lived in a semi-basement. The right side of the corridor housed a working men's dormitory. They occasionally made noise and the police would have to be called. There was nothing special about it, it was a life like anyone else. The important thing was to have a place of one's own that couldn't be taken away; that is already happiness.

In September Andrei returned to School 554 and after graduating went on to the Moscow 1905 Memorial Arts School. He could draw well and Maria Ivanovna decided he would grow up to become an artist.

It was then that disaster struck: Andryusha fell ill. He coughed and coughed, and it turned out that he had a lung abscess. In November they had to place him in the hospital for a long five months. For all this time Maria Ivanovna had to work double shifts in order to bring her son the expensive foods that were missing in the family's rations: butter, cranberry juice, sour cream. His father, upset to hear of his illness, came to visit him. Such visits were rare, however, because Arseny Tarkovsky had been injured and had great difficulty walking with his crutches. Andrei wanted to know more about how his father felt at war when he was so close to death, writing poems, went reconnoitring… And it was not easy for him later either. But Arseny Alexandrovich was marked by great modesty, especially with regard to himself personally. It was difficult to make him talk openly about his heroism. His son interpreted his father's restraint as mistrust, alienation, fear of misunderstanding.

Only once did his father read the verses he had written under fire. They were called *Bely dyen* (A Bright Day):

A stone lies by the jasmine.
Under the stone is a treasure.
Father stands on the path.
It's a bright, bright day.

The silver poplars are in bloom,
And the centifolia too,
Behind them rambling roses
And milky grass.

Never have I been
As happy as then.
Never have I been
As happy as then.

It's impossible to go back,
Nor can I express
How full of bliss
This garden was, like paradise.

Andrei burst into tears and buried his face in the pillow, because he had seen this "bright day" in his dreams a hundred times before. Now he understood that he was closer to his father than he had ever thought before. Indeed, he might have written such a poem himself.

When he lifted his head to tell his father that everything had remained in him exactly the same way, and he would certainly do something to bring that day back, there was nobody there.

Andrei was treated thoroughly and made progress. Fortunately the invention of antibiotics had taken the fatal sting out of this illness. With penicillin, a high-calorie diet and his youthful strength, he overcame an illness that until recently had killed young people mercilessly. He now thought often of his father, repeating the lines that were stuck in his head. Is it really true that then, right then, he had been particularly happy? In those years with his family, blissfully happy in the sun, absorbing the heat of the languorous garden?

Alas, he would have many victories and experience moments when he soared creatively, but happiness, so undisturbed, carefree, primitively childlike, no longer visited Tarkovsky.

"We, the children of the war," Andrei wrote in his diary, "soon felt the difference between suffering and joy and for all our lives would remember the nauseating feeling of emptiness where we had not long before placed all our hope."

3.

Andrei was released from hospital in the spring of 1948. Since he had missed a year due to the illness, Andrei entered the 9th grade in the same school. As soon as he turned 16 years old, he applied to join the Komsomol, the Communist youth league of the Soviet Union. He wanted to be a fighter at the "front lines of the builders of Communism". Realizing the seriousness of the moment he dressed in a white shirt and his grandfather's blue gabardine trousers, which his grandmother had adjusted for him, and appeared before the Komsomol district committee. He waited in the hallway, nervously biting his nails and recalling passages of Beethoven's *Eroica*. He heard the solemn beating of his heart and felt complete confusion: how could he translate these inspired sounds into words? How could he express how he felt now?

At last they called him in. As he entered through the long-awaited door, Andrei saw a long table covered with a red cloth and the Komsomol leaders seated in a row. Lilacs were blooming outside the low windows and the room was tinged with a green shade. He noticed a massive bust of Lenin on a stand in the corner, and behind it the scarlet banner of the USSR. Pride swelled in his heart: soon he too would wear a badge with such a banner and the letters VLKSM standing for the Komsomol.

"Now then," in the center of the row a man was sitting, bald, no longer young, in an old jacket with one sleeve empty and hanging limp, obviously a war veteran. He took Andrei's application from the pile in front of him. "Andrei Arsenyevich Tarkovsky, studying at school 554." His eyes fell on Andrei, who was standing in the center of the room. "What can you tell us about yourself?"

"I study. I like music, drawing, I read books. I want to be a builder of Communism."

"And what are you going to make of yourself? How will you build this Communism?"

"I want," Andrei hesitated. He knitted his brow and blurted out, "I want to be Beethoven. Ludwig van Beethoven."

"A composer, huh?" A hearty smile appeared on the chairman's face. "I'm afraid that for this country two musical figures like that would be a little too much already."

"He wasn't from our country, that composer," a woman seated to his left with a Pioneer necktie, a pioneer leader, explained to the chairman. "He was German."

"Then it's even more strange," the chairman chided Andrei. Andrei was deeply struck by the fact that this man had lost an arm in the war and, like his father, had become handicapped. He hastened to reassure him.

"No, of course I won't be like him. There can be no other exactly like him…" He looked up at the chairman with his fiery eyes, "But I have to try. I love his works. What would Communism be without great music?"

"Aha, that's where he wants to get to: a cushy job, all day long sitting at the piano until he wears his trousers out," a redhead broke in, who as Andrei remembered, often performed at school assemblies. "And what about breaking earth with a shovel on a construction site? How would you like that?"

"If it is necessary, if they send me to do it," Andrei's face reddened, embarrassed by his confession about Beethoven. He had thought he would amaze them, how could he have been so stupid!

"Hey, wait a minute, I know this guy." The disgusted voice belonged to Yakov Skvortsov, who was Andrei's neighbor. "You know what he wants? He just wants to climb the ranks of the Komsomol. He's a hipster! He hangs out with black market traders and dresses like an enemy of the people, in all those foreign clothes! He's just pretending to be ideologically correct."

The Komsomol heads whispered among themselves. "What do you say, Andrei, is Comrade Skvortsov right? Or is he just making that up?" the chairman questioned him with narrowed eyes.

"I'm not the enemy." Andrei brought his hand to his mouth and chewed his fingernails almost to the roots. He stopped in time and he clasped his hands behind his back. "But what he says is true. I have clothes that are not quite…"

"Not quite? Bah!" the freckled woman snapped angrily. "His appearance is fundamentally bourgeois and not appropriate for a member of the Komsomol. I saw him in the park with a gang of hipsters when we were patrolling. We chased them away, wanting to shave some of them. He's not one of us, this guy."

"Well, you see what people say about you. Yes, it looks like it's too early for you to join the Komsomol, Andrei," the war veteran said, shaking his head. "Let's put it to a vote, comrades. Who is in favor of Tarkovsky's application to join the All-Union Leninist Young Communist League? No one. Go home, lad, and think carefully about how you want to go on with your life, with the ideological youth or with punks…"

Thus Andrei didn't get to join the Komsomol. Later he did not dare enter the ranks of the Communist Party, which he would have liked to join not in order to advance his career, but as a sign of belonging to those who were building socialism in the USSR. He already knew that he was an outsider and that they would turn him down and torment him with mockery.

4.

The stars came together in a strange way over his common Moscow school. In one of his classes Andrei studied with Andrei Voznesensky, later a noted poet. Voznesensky was tasked with managing the school bulletin board and girls fell in love with him. Slightly stuttering, he would open school evenings with melodious poems. The blue-eyed Voznesensky made the acquaintance of that gloomy dark-haired guy from a literary family. It didn't turn into friendship because of Andrei's distant nature and their completely different interests.

Many years later, however, the famous poet would write a miniature portrait of his celebrated and untimely deceased classmate. His story is titled "White Sweater" (*Bely sviter*):

> While we were in group B of the 9th grade at school 554, a strange newcomer arrived: Tarkovsky, Andrei Arsenyevich. He was an absent-minded fellow. His hair, thick like horsehair, framed his pale cheeks. He had missed a year because of tuberculosis. He had a high-pitched voice, as if he were singing, and he drawled out vowels. He was capricious, not a good boy at all. I had seen him a couple of times before in the courtyard, we even played football once, but I only got to know him in school.
>
> We were closer to him than others in the class. He lived in a little wooden house, barely subsisting on his mother's salary as a proof-reader. We walked home from school the same way. All of the dirtiness and poetry of

our alleyways, the gloominess of an unchildlike childhood, the sorrows of the era of Stalin's cult of personality left a mark in his retinas, became the "Mirror" of the time, blurry and incomprehensible to the uninitiated. This is what made him the great filmmaker of the century.

…And so one day we were in the courtyard, hitting the same goal with a football. The goal was a concrete partition. There were puddles on the asphalt. Longing for the eternity that was passing by, an adult man, a criminal from the third block of the housing complex called Shka played with us. He had a gold tooth. He was a thief who had come out of prison.

Everybody was afraid of him and let him take their football. An unfamiliar pale boy stopped next to us. He was embarrassed with his net shopping bag with bread in it. I recognized him later as the strange new pupil joining our class. He was wearing a white sweater of thick, coarse knitting, probably homemade. "Stand in the goal," Shka told him in a friendly manner. His gold tooth flashed in his grin — he was looking forward to the amusement to come.

A white sweater is standing at the goal,
13-year-old Andrei.
Hit him, you hoodlum,
Hit him, you hoodlum,
white sweater
with your stolen football boot,
hit —

his intellectual face!

It's a one-goal game.
For he came dressed like a white crow
into the black grime of the street.

Hit the white sweater!
Missed shot!
Because he misses the shot, hit him!
Let Giulietta Masina wash it.
Give your sweater away
to an abstract-art museum.

Hit him, you child of the street,
for the mess you have at home,
because the light went out as soon as you were born,
because you know
your wide homeland
from the caresses of prison camps.

Hit him with a broom, kick him,
let's hit them together,
all those nerds with good and excellent grades,
hit the odd target.
You didn't smash through the goal,
you've smashed up a person,
because the roads in the country are bad,
because you were conceived in drunken sin,
because, waiting for the ball,
the goalkeeper, to spite you,
is facing you with his crotch out.

The duel with the great darkness is absurd.
But the white spot,
the smudge,
with his tired shoes
falls to his feet
taking all the dirt onto his chest.

Shka's sweaty face flashed in front of me with its intimidating gold tooth. The end was close.

> *The street has wiped its soles*
> *against the white sweater.*
> *"Andrei! We're fighting because of you!"*
> *You were cruel to us,*
> *you didn't want to conform,*
> *you didn't let us beat you up.*
>
> *You're going to kill him, you bastards!*
> *It's getting dark,*
> *And his legs and hands, once so white,*
> *are flying like a St. Andrew's cross.*

Yes, they were really going to kill him! I exchange glances with my pal. He understands me and, as if by accident, we knock the ball onto the traffic part of the lane, under the wheels of trucks. The ball gives up the ghost. It had got quite dark already.

> *As he was leaving,*
> *suppressing his cough,*
> *they all realised how ill he was.*
> *He walked,*
> *with his impeccable white back*
> *turned toward our darkness.*
> ...
> *Andrei, as you lie in that hurriedly dug, foreign grave*
> *in Paris you will recall that slush.*
> *You won't remember all the hooligans, the Shchipok lane.*
> *And maybe you'll suddenly fly back home?*
>
> *Forgive us if it's too late. Lie still, if it's too early.*

> *We don't know your worries.*
> *And in the meantime cinema screens flicker*
> *over the country,*
> *like your crucified*
> *little sweater.*

His poetic vision, over time and through Tarkovsky's tragic untimely death, made certain changes to the emotional construction of "White Sweater". Andrei's last terrible illness intensified the physical weakness of the stubborn boy that Voznesensky had emphasized, while his humble intellectuality expanded the theme of confronting the hooligans. The poet most probably did not suspect that the timid Tarkovsky was a friend of these hooligans, or perhaps he did not wish to spoil the poetic opposition between intellectuals and the mob with this detail.

Tarkovsky had a different attitude toward his childhood in the streets. As he wrote in a notebook:

I was spoiled and reckless. The street appealed to me with its attractive power, its freedom and the great opportunities to apply my true inclinations.

When I was at school, there was a time when I passionately played blackjack and a special game called *rasshibalochka*. Two people face each other, and each places a coin on the pavement or on a windowsill. You had to turn over your partner's coin by hitting it with your own. Then the money that the other person was holding in his hand passed to the winner. If the coin did not turn over, the loser paid the equivalent of the sum that his adversary was hiding in his hand.

I was lucky. I used to walk with change jingling in my pockets, weighing them down, and with rustling red 30-ruble notes. My mother kept money for keeping up our household in a walnut box, and sometimes I would quietly place a part of my winnings in it.

5.

Andrei considered himself a master of his craft and he greatly envied the semi-paralyzed old man who won every game. *Rasshibalochka* was one of the most common games for boys in those years, and it required mastery and invariable dedication. Here we find a confession that is clearly at odds with the familiar portrait of an unmercenary dreamer, of a Prince Myshkin who philosophizes in the language of cinema.

> I was remarkably attracted to the streets, with all of their "corrupting" influences (in the words of my mother). I was always drawn there by a zeal for loot, money. Dostoyevsky's Gambler and Raw Youth astounded me. It seems to me that I truly understood the Raw Youth when I wandered the streets with my pockets crammed with winnings. I also understood Dolgoruky's "idea" of becoming a Rothschild, and the motives which drew him and his zeal to games, to the accumulation of wealth.

This lad, growing up in poverty, liked to feel "rich", but he could never decide what to spend his winnings on. He was afraid to give everything to his mother lest she discover the source of his income. He just threw in a small amount and perhaps she didn't even notice it.

The situation changed when Andrei, now grown up, thought it exceptionally important to look stylish and original. This meant being what in Russian they called a *chuvak*.

"Look, all these thugs, these representatives of the 'gray masses', your friends, they don't have a clue that *chuvak* is an acronym, and it stands for *Chelovek, Uvazhayushchiy Amerikanskuyu Vysokuyu Kulturu* 'a person who admires American high culture'!" Andrei flicked Marina's nose. This diligent student with good graces had constant disagreements with her older brother about his friends from the street and his anti-Soviet pursuits. "Why do you suddenly admire Americans so much? Is there nobody to look up to in our country?

Look at the Komsomol, they aren't selling their country out for a pair of shoes."

"I'm not selling my country out. I won these shoes in an honest way. And I admire American jazz, which is their great popular culture."

"Your shoes too? You're wearing some awful kicks."

"I didn't buy them from black-marketers, by the way. They're made here, they are called 'semolina porridge' shoes. Look here," he raised his foot covered with a shoe with a very thick sole. "You take our mass-produced shoes and you glue a thick layer of plastic or rubber to it. I got myself cool kicks. Vladlen from a couple of houses over did it for me. His father works at a garage. He dragged off a whole tire from there. So, we cut out the soles. You like them?"

"Ugh, it scares people. Fitted blue trousers, a red shirt, a yellow jacket and shoulders. You look like a wrestler," Marina said as she put her textbooks and notebooks into her schoolbag. "You're like some kind of circus!"

"That's right, my dear sister," he straightened his tie with a herringbone pattern in the mirror. "The brighter the clothes, the better. By the way, I earn the dough myself!"

"Right, you've been loading boxcars," Maria gave a triumphant smile. "I know about your *rasshibalochka* tournaments!"

"I don't care if you know. And not all girls are such old-fashioned chicks like you. They like my outfit."

"The same kind of fools, bowing down to the Americans." She picked up her bag and proudly walked away, a good, upright and exemplary girl.

Andrei's concern for his appearance was a remarkable trait. A desire for beauty and harmony dictated his desire to have an appearance worthy of the attention and admiration of others, especially the opposite sex. In those years, hipsters set the tone by their behavior and clothing. They were considered anti-social elements, victims of the rotten ideology of the West. Completely unconcerned with the social roots of his aspirations, Andrei acquired the obligatory wardrobe: a stylish red corduroy jacket with stuffed shoulders, "semolina porridge" shoes and a checkered *kepka* hat. But even in the hipster outfit, he avoided gatherings, tried not to be too visible, to draw attention to himself. There was a clear tension between a feeling of self-worth and a fear of offending or being misunderstood. He acknowledges that he was "spoiled and reckless". He was indeed reckless all his life. Andrei understood his being spoiled according to his companions' thinking, who gave him plenty of punches and expressive vocabulary. He had a fierce temper and immediately got into fights, only slightly aware that his self-confidence, which had been hypertrophied from early on, could suffer from these fights. His hot blood would instantly be inflamed, and constant anticipation of dirty tricks determined his violent reactions to supposed (often without any basis) offense. From an early age he showed suspicion, mistrust, an exaggerated feeling of hostility and a constant readiness to defend himself. You could easily imagine him as a brave horseman of the Caucasus, clenching a dagger in his hand. One cannot find here the slightest bit of Russian humility and good-natured forgiveness, and not an ounce of self-irony. His innate sense of importance, of being off-limits to criticism, led him to take jokes seriously and to consider the slightest encroachment on his "honor" as an insult. "I was cunning and observant. Cunning gave root to my skills of observation and together with the inability to hide it, crystallized into some kind of awful and painful vulnerability."

Cunning was rather a quality that Andrei did not really have but wanted to. He wanted to exchange his naiveté for this cunning. His painful insecurity, his lack of understanding of how communication works in an informal group, was not something he imagined. He always felt different in any hostile environment, whether it was in the company of street kids, the Komsomol leaders, the Soviet filmmaking community or creative individuals abroad. This feeling was exaggerated, often to an unreasonable degree, due to his poor social orientation and burning ambition.

He was far from being an expert even in the etiquette of domestic life with family and loved ones around him. He was always on guard, suspecting his family members of critical and even hostile attitudes toward him. This feeling became the leading factor in his relationship with his father, and a source of tension between him and Marina and his mother. Beyond them, Tarkovsky had even more difficulties with his colleagues and lovers.

Tarkovsky's observational skills rest more in a refined perception of the smallest manifestations of the outside world, than in knowing how to relate to people. His insecurity, naiveté, hot temper, lack of self-irony and stubbornness were basic qualities that shaped his attitude toward his work, his colleagues and loved ones. All of this, which originated in the dusty alleyways of Shchipok Street, would become the cause of many fatal mistakes in his life.

"The street gave me balance in relation to the refined heritage I got from my parents. If I took from my father a part of his poetic spirit, then I took from my mother stubbornness, hardness and intolerance."

His remarkable character brought Maria Ivanovna's son constant controversy and endless conflict within himself and with society. As his sister Marina remembers, "Andrei was not the quiet, intelligent boy they usually beat up at school and in the street. Then again, he was intelligent — he could not escape it — and he read books, he went to music lessons until the war and he drew. But quiet? He was like a hurricane, jumping around, engaging in tomfoolery, yelling like Tarzan, climbing on the roof, voicing unexpected ideas, singing, skiing down steep hills and I don't know what else."

Andrei eventually abandoned his music lessons, citing the lack of an instrument at home. Of course, he was also tired of doing scales. He solved the conflict with them in a radical manner, announcing, "Ma, I've stopped going to music lessons. They are renovating and I have nowhere to practice," and then looked down under the watchful eyes of his mother. He heard a familiar sigh, thinking that his mother was resigned to the fact that her son would not be a musician. He was wrong: Maria Ivanovna made an agreement with Andrei's teacher that she tutor him individually, following the entire school curriculum. Natalya Alexeyevna, the music teacher, happily undertook to work with the dropout at home.

"You have a very capable son. He has perfect pitch and a genuine love of music!"

"Thank you, Natalya, for being so kind," his mother said as she held out a discreetly folded roll of bills.

"Don't even think about it! I won't take money from you. I know how hard-pressed you are and the boy is already very capable, he should go straight to the conservatory."

"Could he really get in?" Maria Ivanovna looked at the neat part in this pleasant woman's freshly permed hair, her lips painted like a little bow, at the turquoise flowers scattered on her flowing crêpe de Chine silk dress. This isn't some black-market trader or a woman with a sugar daddy, she thought. This is an ordinary colonel's wife, a teacher. That is how one ought to live, even down to her fingernails, short but well kept. Maria then said, "Andrei dreams of becoming a conductor. With a wave of his hand, a whole orchestra is at his command."

"A conductor has to know all the instruments. And in Andrei's case it was just a dream of a lazy person. He just needs to persevere. Try to push him!"

"I will push him. I will surely push him," Maria promised half-heartedly, because she always expected rudeness and solid resistance. If Andrei didn't want to do something, there was no way you could force him to do it.

6.

"He lacks perseverance. Or maybe a conscience? Ordinary human decency?" Maria looked out the window at her son's back as he went for "a walk". A red jacket with padded shoulders, close-fitting trousers and thick-soled clown shoes. Where had he got all of this from? Had he traded something for it? He was all dressed up and off he went out of the house — they're waiting for him, you see!

Oh, these dusty Moscow streets with their benches knocked over and scratched with knives, those wilted bushes and the walls painted with illiterate graffiti, hard for a proof-reader to bear, "Titewads will git whats coming". And of course they are short words, everyday ones, butchering the Russian language. This isn't the work of Andrei's hands, he doesn't make these kind of mistakes. And that obscene vocabulary... You can say many things about Andrei, but he doesn't use such words. But who knows what he's like when he's "with the gang". Maria Ivanova had guessed, he was running around with a red-headed kid named Khomychev who had served in juvenile detention for theft and now commanded a whole gang — clearly he was raising disciples. He belonged to a well-known family of black-market traders. The redhead's grandmother, who was called by the name of Khomoy, supplied the whole district with homemade liquor.

A couple of times Marina swore that she had smelled liquor on her brother. He, a cunning fellow, would come home late, slip into his corner and hide. Maria Ivanovna tried to determine what Andrei saw in such company.

"You don't understand," he snapped, beginning to bite his nails. "You are a victim of discipline, all your life you've walked on a tightrope, trembling before the authorities."

"There you go again! How many times must I tell you, only tramps bite their nails!" She slapped her son's hand in irritation, went to the kitchen and bitterly slammed the door. "So what now," she thought. "He's not going to be a musician or an artist but a thug? You've lost your son, Maria Ivanovna. Such are the fruits of growing up without a father."

Maria Ivanovna cried half the night. Where did he get it all from? After all, her integrity and perseverance were known to all of her co-workers in the printing works, and so were her honesty, diligence and high qualifications. Why weren't they passed down to him? Why didn't her son get any of that, was his mother meant only to cook soup and clean up after the children? And it was her own fault that she felt abandoned — it must mean that she's not so attractive if their father found himself another woman, and left her with two children! And those damn fingernails, he bit them to the roots! When he was an infant she had smeared them with mustard and covered them with bandages, but nothing would stop him from putting them into his mouth. She hoped it would go away with age, along with this neurotic absent-mindedness and the complete wilfulness in everything. "No, Maria, you can't manage with this son of yours."

Of course Andrei stopped going to his drawing classes too, although he was considered a capable pupil there as well. Yet again, "he wasn't patient enough". If only they accepted his paintings right away in the Tretyakov Gallery, but as it was, he could not stand sitting for hours, drawing a plaster ear placed on a chair covered with a wrinkled sheet. No matter how much his mother and grandmother pushed him, Andrei's education did not go well. His father probably advised him in his own, gentle way to be a good boy. Maybe it would have been better if he had whipped him?

Andrei Tarkovsky's report card, preserved in the VGIK archives, does not show any signs of diligence or interest in any of his subjects and clearly exhibits a lack of interest in the natural sciences and a passing knowledge in the humanities. Most probably, he had the knowledge, but it was deeper and more chaotic than the required curriculum.

After Andrei left school in 1951, he easily entered the Arabic department of the Moscow Institute of Oriental Studies. Surely his father's involvement in the poetry and philosophy of the East, the connection with its people, beckoned Tarkovsky into the spicy and sophisticated world of Arab culture. But here too he felt continually bored. Not everything was so easy with this intricate language, which required constant cramming. Andrei studied at the institute for one and a half years and, who knows, perhaps he would have graduated if it had not been for the concussion he sustained in his gym class, and certain circumstances which frightened his mother more than a concussion.

The institute did not dissuade Andrei from the bad influences of the streets. He often disappeared from home and made even more suspicious friends. He got pocket money somewhere. Expensive clothes appeared ever more often in his wardrobe and he said he had "traded for them". He stood in front of the mirror, washed his hair and put it back with a comb so that it would stick up over his forehead. He would say that he was copying Elvis Presley, an innovative American singer. After that he smelled for a kilometer of laundry soap, since Maria Ivanovna had hidden the sugar that he mixed with water to put on his hair. Marina hid her property from Drilka's raiding as well.

"Why did you take my glue?" asked the dark-eyed, pretty Marina with her hair arranged in a circle braid, frowning as she watched her brother's manipulations.

"Bug off, pipsqueak! Don't they call you a hoarder at school?" He held the drying construction with both his hands. "Just right!"

"Eesh, what a simpleton! I'm finishing school this year, by the way, with excellent marks! " Marina took her bottle of glue back. "I know, you're making a quiff like hipsters have. But it won't work, your hair is too coarse. You should use casein glue."

"Good advice, sis, but I'm not so crazy that I'd do that." Andrei answered only moving his lips, afraid to let go of his hair and move his head. "Casein glue holds so strongly that you'd have to shave it off later. You better teach your admirers, those ugly guys with half-box haircuts!"

"My admirers are real Komsomol members. They catch hipsters in the park and shave their hair off. And your beloved Elvis is also a hipster, not a Communist at all. A capitalist rock'n'roller, that's what he is! Watch out, Andrei, our boys will get their hands on you — they'll shave you and smear your trousers with tar! Then I'll have something to laugh at!"

"No, they won't," Andrei grinned, looking carefully at the stiffened construction on his head. He remained unsatisfied. It looked funny, the crest sticking up over his forehead and sticking to his hands. "You think you're so smart, you think you can scare me! I have plenty of friends myself. They'll defend me. Ah, damn it. Warm up some water for me, Marina. Warm up some water, I tell you! I think I need a different style."

He gave himself a buzz cut and told everyone that this was the latest fashion, even Elvis had already done it. He promised to get a photo from a foreign magazine.

He decided that he had to go against the flow. The hipsters at the height of fashion? To hell with them. The foreign close-fitted trousers could stay, though. And the orange jacket that he had bought in the market for the money that he had won in *rasshibalochka*; that would always be in style. At least the checkered *kepka* hat sat very well on his buzz cut. And the "semolina porridge" shoes that he got from a black market trader in exchange for an awesome tie with a palm tree, brought all the way from Africa by Voznesensky's uncle — that was it.

It became clear that it wasn't the institute with its Arabic writings that drew Andrei, but the crowd of hipsters and black market traders hanging out there. Maria Ivanovna, in consultation with her mother, took drastic measures.

This time she decided to put an end to her son's outings, and once and for all shield him from the corrupting influence of his bad company. Otherwise before you know it, he'd end up in prison together with his friends, the black market traders. It would be better than sitting in prison that he work in the open air with people with discipline.

She made herself comfortable with her proofreading work at the table opposite the entrance door — not even a mouse would get past her. The door quietly creaked open and the rascal sneaked past, hoping that no one would see him. He appeared and what a sight he was to see! He had a scratch across his entire cheek, a sleeve torn off, but his heavy shoes and close-fitting trousers looked fine. He hid his fear and took on a defiant look, as if he wanted to show that he didn't care about anything.

"Where have you been?" Maria asked her son point-blank.

He was unfazed. "They organized a session to test us at the institute. A real Arab came. Time is different for them so we stayed till late. Are you making something to eat?" He knew that the most important thing for a mother was feeding her son.

Maria Ivanovna brought potatoes on a sizzling skillet, then put a cutlet onto them from a pan. She sat opposite her son, staring at him.

He was similar to his father, but different. A hereditary tendency to lie and demonic eyebrows, the cheekbones of a Tatar, his thick, unruly hair. He was a handsome boy, slim, light, with fiery eyes. But now he had gotten completely out of hand, and before you knew it, the police would get him. He ate hungrily, not lifting his eyes. He had a fresh scratch and a bruise on his cheek, he had been fighting. And in the morning the jacket had been in one piece. Of course, "an Arab came"! She suppressed her wish to give the liar a whipping. On that very day she had found out that her son faced expulsion from the institute for his bad marks and absences. There was no point in grabbing the belt, you could sum it all up in just a few words: a child without a father.

"I'm happy you've chosen such an interesting profession. Traveling to the Orient, adventures, translating classical literature. You're already in your second year, if you keep up, you'll get your diploma in no time." She spoke in a monotone voice unable to pretend. He understood that his mother was preparing to give him a scolding and decided to speak bluntly.

"I'm out of the institute. I took my documents last month. And today I hung out at Khoma's place, the redhead. I owed him. So I have been winning back the money. Don't worry, ma, so what that your son did not turn out a respectable man or an orientalist."

"I understand. And we don't need an orientalist! We'll find you another career." Maria Ivanovna slowly put her proofs back in the envelope, tied the cord on it and rose from the table. She felt herself going pale, her lips turned to stone from a sudden surge of anger. This was anger at herself, a helpless hen who did not manage to take care of her son. Without Arseny, without the influence of a man at home. "Go to bed. I'll tell you tomorrow what I've decided."

The next day Andrei sat at home until the evening in total uncertainty. Marina had locked herself in her room and remained silent. Andrei heard his mother coming home. She slammed her satchel down on a chair. He heard his grandmother rushing out to meet her.

"Maria, you look awful. I'm making something to eat, cooking some soup. Shall I pour you a bowl?"

"Wait a minute," a stool creaked as his mother sat down. She put her head in her hands, as she always did when making a difficult decision.

"I've arranged for Andrei to go with a geological survey. They're going to the taiga to look for gold." She laughed bitterly and hysterically, then burst into tears.

Then, as her mother hugged her, she wheezed into her shoulder, "I'm tired, worn out. I could barely find the necessary people, barely persuade them."

"Are you serious, my daughter?" His grandmother was astonished. "Or is this just to scare him?"

"He'll leave in three days."

"Where? With whom? What kind of clothes does he need, what shoes? It's the taiga."

"He'll go in his high shoes."

"He needs boots."

"Where would I get boots?"

"He'll catch a cold"

"Let him."

"Since his lungs aren't well."

"Let him."

A sigh followed and then a long silence. Andrei went out of the house the usual way, through the back door. He believed at once in the taiga, and his mother's decision. It became clear to him that he had driven her to this. This was it.

7.

Andrei spent almost a year working as a prospector in a research expedition of the Academy of Science Institute for Non-Ferrous Metals and Gold in the distant Turukhansky District of the Krasnoyarsk Province. In reality he was a manual laborer, washing sand on the river Kureyka, carrying equipment from place to place. He did not shirk from his duties, covering hundreds of miles on foot through the taiga and compiling an album of drawings, which was later handed to the archives of the Institute for Non-Ferrous Metals and Gold. The expedition began in May, and in fact almost the entire cycle of nature from blooming to dying past before his hungry, observant eyes.

The dark-haired taciturn boy was tamed by a buxom working woman. She pitied him, and fed him, and washed his underwear. Andrei coughed, but he did not complain. He looked at everyone with suspicion, and sometimes he gazed at some stone or a dying tree and stayed in this reverie for a long time, as if delirious from some potion.

"Why are you so quiet now? You haven't fallen ill, have you?" Zinaida spooned him some barley porridge with tinned stewed meat. "Eat, it's getting cold. You will go counting crows in trees later."

"Then it will be late. You have to look at the trees at sunset. The leaves are transparent, like watercolors, and they shine. And they suddenly go dim, it means that the sun has gone down. And it's raining… Rain is a responsible phenomenon…"

Zinaida exchanged glances with a bearded geologist, he turned his finger at his temple to show that her friend was crazy.

"Draw something, make more drawings," Zina urged Andrei. "Make an artist of yourself." She admired her young friend's face. Maybe the guy was a little crazy, but he was intelligent, he had retold her almost everything by Tolstoy. And one could immediately see that he was not a simple lad, that there was a future in front of him.

A melancholy dwelt within him together with his admiration of the beauty of the taiga. This was the unbearable pain of being unable to capture it, to make time stand still, to hold on to this beauty somehow, preserve and pass it on to others. But how? Drawings, poems, but what would be even better, live pictures captured on film. In the dark hall people held their breath: explosions and sunflowers, only clumps of flying soil and the golden heads of sunflowers still reaching to the sun among the black death… It crashed right into one's soul. And he was no older than seven then. Now he was twenty, and he had a huge inventory in his memory — not from school, but from books, concerts at the conservatory, Arab philosophy, village life, Moscow alleyways, and now the taiga. What could he do with all of these things, if the contents of his memory burst and all that had been collected wanted to break out?

Chapter 3.
VGIK, "GIVE ME A CAMERA, AND I WILL TURN THE WORLD UPSIDE DOWN!"

I.

When he returned from the expedition in 1954, Tarkovsky gave his papers to the State Institute of Cinematography (often referred to by the abbreviation VGIK from its Russian name *Vserossiyskiy gosudarstvennny universitet kinematografii*). Why VGIK? He wasn't sure either. He could sense something in this new artistic medium, some hidden possibilities. A film camera, not a pencil. He would aim the camera and shoot, and there they would be, sunflowers and earth shaking from explosions … and the bright, bright day would return, start to breathe and sound forth again. It was like magic.

Among the crowd of students, a stern black-haired youth appeared, wearing an imported jacket, clearly bought from a second-hand shop, with a big book under his arm. He stayed aloof from the others as he walked out the door of the auditorium where the entrance exam was being held. He left at once, not pausing to share his experiences with the nervous crowd waiting outside. The boys were looking to see what the dark guy was carrying. It was *War and Peace*. Whoa, man, could it be a good luck charm?

The course was taught by Mikhail Ilych Romm, a cinema legend.

Later he told Andrei that when the admissions committee was deciding who to let in, they struck him and Vasily Shukshin off the list: Tarkovsky for his excessive intelligence and nervousness, and Vasily for his ignorance and backwardness. Romm however stood up for these young men, believing that the course should have brilliant and varied personalities.

When Romm gathered everyone accepted into the various departments, he looked at their faces and was struck by two in particular: a dark-haired young man with prominent cheekbones and deep in thought, and a simple fellow in a dark blue uniform with simple buttons. These were Andrei Tarkovsky and Vasily Shukshin. One was well-read, intelligent, but insolent. The other was at first glance simple-minded, but there was a bright and distinctive talent within him. He said that he had taught in a village, and he had been a pupil and a head teacher in the same school. He read intelligent books and, what's more, understood them. Romm was happy that he could take these young men under his wing.

Andrei took a closer look at the new students, especially the female ones, and immediately spotted something of interest: a coquettish girl with a sweet face reminiscent of his mother's, a graceful figure and a smiling mouth. She had an impish look in her eyes, however. All the while she was dancing some unknown steps in her white shoes. Though dressed of course in a provincial fashion, she had an impressive figure, being a busty blond with a ponytail. He stepped away from the pillar he stood by, his arms across his chest with an air of boredom like a Byronic hero, looking over the crowd of students who were shouting with joy.

He approached her with a short bow of his head, immediately giving her his old-fashioned gentleman treatment. In those days, shoes on a thick white sole were in fashion in the capital.

"Andrei Arsenyevich Tarkovsky. I'm a first-year student, studying under Romm."

"Irma Raush," she answered, holding out her slight hand. "Your future classmate and rival."

They walked down the steps into the small square.

"Do you live in the dormitory? Can I walk you home?" Andrei quickly found his bearings.

"Are we going the right way? You're from Moscow."

"You know from the way I talk?"

"From your shoes. You're a hipster."

"I'm a very creative and witty one. I'm going to Serpukhovskaya metro station and you to the town of Mossovet on the Yaroslavskoe highway. It's nearby."

"On the scale of Moscow it's nothing, but by our measure it's a whole other city. I still have to go down to the river and throw flowers into it. Look, Vasily Shukshin gave me some asters — he picked them from the flowerbed at some monument. He said that for luck I should throw them into the river and make a wish."

"Well, if Vasily told you this, there's no doubt. He knows all those village superstitions."

"He's a nice guy. And I really want to swim too!"

"Shukshin told you to do that too?"

"No," she laughed. "Because I'm so happy that I was accepted into VGIK. Just like this, wearing a dress. Let everyone laugh at me."

"No, you won't. The water is cold. But about those flowers, can I make a wish too?"

"I don't mind. There's so many of them." Irma buried her face in the bouquet. "Just make a really good wish."

"I'll make one within the bounds of socialism," Andrei agreed. "So our route is decided, to the river and to the city center. We'll walk through all of Moscow. Can you imagine how much we'll be able to talk?"

"This is how you'll walk a different girl home every day and question her," she laughed, balancing on a parapet broken by road works, swinging her white purse.

He walked alongside her, holding her by the elbow.

"You wouldn't want to break a leg at the beginning of the academic year."

"I don't intend to." She pulled her hair band off and shook her head, spilling a thick wave over her shoulders. "I'm not hiding anything about myself, but tell me something about you already. I'm very intrigued, I won't deny it. You resemble your father. I've seen his photo in the paper and read his poems. He probably has a lot of unpublished works?"

"My father has done translations his whole life. But he has also written things of his own. He dreams of putting out a collection. What do you dream of?"

They did not notice that they had reached the boulevard and were walking along the tram line.

"I dream of making a movie that makes the entire audience cry. Cry and laugh! They have to laugh. And I want to play a role in my own film, and then go to some international film festival in a white mantle! What do you think about my plans?"

"They're great. But it's me who is going to film you, I promise, and it'll win an international prize. Let's hear more about yourself."

"I came to Moscow from Kazan, but I was born in Saratov. My father is a Volga German. There were a lot of airplane factories in Kazan, and my father, an engineer, was transferred there before the war. That saved us. All of the ethnic Germans, families and children, were taken away from Saratov in a single night. My father couldn't find any of his relatives after the war. Later he was sent off to a camp too, but they didn't touch us. My mother was miraculously able to send him a package, and this saved him from starvation. But after the war, when he came back, their relationship didn't work out for some reason. My childhood was not a happy one. I longed to get out of the house as soon as I finished school."

"But why did you choose the department for directors? That's a man's job. You've got to learn to become an actress. You're so pretty."

Irma blushed. "It was only in high school that I changed from an ugly duckling into something decent, and all my girlfriends yelled at me, 'Go into the acting department! You've got to study to become an actress!' But I only wanted to be a director." She spun around, her staple fabric skirt swirling like a bell. "To Moscow, to Moscow! Just like Chekhov."

"Of course, Moscow. The most important things are happening here. And VGIK is the epicenter of the arts."

"So I hit the capital as soon as I got my school diploma, and right away I got into the directing department at VGIK! It was some kind of miracle. I had dreamed about it."

"I don't understand why I got in here," Andrei said. "An acquaintance suggested I do it, he even promised to pull strings for me. I thought those were just empty words. I got in because I know something about every kind of art and I'm full ambitious plans."

They walked up to the river. A class of first-graders — the boys in bow ties and the girls wearing nylon hair bows — sat right on the grass on the sloping bank, chattering loudly.

Irma suddenly burst into ringing laughter. "In their white aprons, they're so happy, those silly children." At once she became more serious. "Don't look at me like that. I'm not crazy, I'm just in a wonderfully festive mood today."

"Irma. That's a beautiful name and it suits you, it's something elegant, exotic. And you know, I'm also feeling good." He took her hand in his and gazed into her bright eyes. "I'm generally a gloomy sort of person. But here I am looking at you, and I'm happy!"

She burst into laughter. "We're a good couple!"

Andrei's thoughts turned elsewhere and he suddenly forgot his fascination with the "exotic" Irma. He stopped and looked her straight in the eye.

"And you know what the most important thing is?"

"What?" she asked, frightened by his serious tone.

"That we ended up under Romm!"

Then in his fifties, Mikhail Ilych Romm was already recognized as a master of cinema, a People's Artist of the USSR and five-time winner of the Stalin Prize. He had started off with the silent film *Boule de Suif*, and then he became interested in patriotic themes. The films *The Thirteen* (1935), *Lenin in October* (1937), *Lenin in 1918* (1939) and *Dream* (1941) brought the director well-deserved acclaim. The accolades came from Stalin's regime, but Romm, with all his heart as a "faithful communist" really venerated the leader of the proletariat, Lenin, whose work had been strongly distorted by his Georgian successor. The director's films about the leader of the proletariat were probably sincere, because they were moving, inspired and widely loved.

After Tarkovsky had graduated from VGIK, Romm would go on to film *Nine Days in One Year* (1961) and the documentary *Ordinary Fascism* (1965), vigorously releasing the creativity pent up within him in the spirit of this new era, warmed by the deceptive Khrushchev "thaw".

"Of course, we were extremely lucky," Andrei said and livened up. "Romm is a fantastic teacher. He is very ordered as far as theory is concerned. With any of his films — say what you want — you can see the hand of a professional at work. I have studied all his films. He gave detailed guidelines for how you should or shouldn't compose a shot."

"I remember clearly how at the entrance examinations you criticized his film *Murder on Dante Street*."

"But everybody then rose against this, this varnished fake. Is that what real cinema should be? It's nothing but a cheap commercial print." He became furious, cursing modern cinema and biting his fingernails. "Everywhere you look, all you see is pictures like from coloring books! Back then we tore apart not only his 'western gangsters', but also Isidor Annensky's *Anna 'Round the Neck*, and Mikhail Kalatozov's *True Friends*."

"Mikhail Ilych didn't show any offense. Everyone knows that he loves his students. He always protects them, even gives them money. Older students of his told me."

"They say that his students are like his own sons." Andrei involuntarily clenched his teeth — he didn't get on well with his father. Irma, poor girl, had also been abandoned. "Although fatherly sentiments are a difficult matter. Here's the river. I'll make a wish. Throw Shukshin's flowers in."

"I'll ask about your father later." Carefully stepping across the stones in her white shoes to the water, Irma bent down, holding on to Andrei's hand, and threw the asters into the river. Her blond, silken mane shot up. "There they go! Now everything I wished for will come true."

"Look now, you've promised," Andrei was frightfully serious.

2.

Andrei Tarkovsky's fate led him to cinema at a very good time. In 1956, after Nikita Khrushchev denounced Stalin's personality cult at the Twentieth Party Congress, a so-called "thaw" began. Under this springtime, life and cinema were renewed. Not long before, the directing department had not offered great opportunities. The annual production of films was meager and only venerable old directors could make films. When Tarkovsky entered VGIK, 45 films had appeared on screens that year, but in 1956 the number of films approached 70. In addition to the rapid growth in the number of films produced, the quality of them changed as well, as the war generation was now active. This created the phenomenon of the "VGIK School", filmmakers who were young but had lived through the war, and who sought to express their experiences in their work. In just two years, 1955 and 1956, young directors made about 50 films that boldly embodied new ideas, changed the means of expression and even the very idea of the hero.

In this short time, an entire constellation of young directors, writers, cinematographers and actors created films that have entered the canon of classic Soviet cinema. Among these were Vasily Ordynsky's *A Man is Born*, Mikhail Schweitzer's *Someone Else's Kin*, Stanislav Rostotsky's *Land and People*, Samson Samsonov's *The Cricket*, Eldar Ryazanov's *Carnival Night*, Grigoriy Chukray's *The Forty-First*, Alexander Alov and Vladimir Naumov's *Pavel Korchagin* and Marlen Khutsiev's *Spring on Zarechnaya Street*.

In 1957, films hit screens that shook audiences at home and abroad: *The House I Live In* by Yakov Segel and Lev Kulidzhanov, and the famous *The Cranes are Flying* by Mikhail Kalatozov with cinematography by Sergey Urusevsky.

Life at VGIK's directing department was in full swing. Everyone was considered a genius, and each knew how new films had to be made.

In his third year Andrei screened his coursework, shot together with his classmate Sasha Gordon. Biting his nails, tousling his hair, he sought to combine footage of an excavator digging up a land mine with Glenn Miller's saxophone melody *Stardust*.

Gordon nervously glanced at the clock, as time in the editing room was strictly allotted and another student had already looked into the room several times. Finally, that student came into the dark room and stood behind Andrei, looking at the screen.

"Hmm, a saxophone and a bulldozer," someone behind him said. "That's bold of you. But it looks weird."

"I know that!" Andrei turned off the projector.

"You needn't hurry, I'm not waiting for my turn. I'm only a first year student, I watch and learn. I'm also under Romm. My name is Andron, Andron Mikhalkov-Konchalovsky."

Andrei turned slightly to look behind him. "The background doesn't fit in at all. I try and try, and I keep getting garbage. But Glenn Miller is so cool. I won't give up on him, no matter what."

"He would turn in his grave if he saw what his music is being put to. Wait, don't get upset!" Andron put his hand in a conciliatory gesture on the shoulder of the dark-haired student, who was leaping up at him. "I'm not a total idiot, I understand everything. You need an effect of contrast. Maybe it should be less extreme?"

Andrei shook Andron's hand off his shoulder. "I don't need a mentor!" He took his roll of film. "The place is all yours."

They walked out of the editing room together. In the hallway, Andrei noticed that his "mentor" was wearing trousers of the most fashionable design and there was no doubt that his shirt, made of nylon which had only just come into fashion, was imported. This hip guy's gaze was pretty friendly, though, apparently because he appreciated the third year student's jacket, and his hair was boldly grown down to his shoulders (a phenomenon which the dean's office fiercely opposed).

"I'm crazy about Glenn Miller too. I can also see that you're trying to imitate Buñuel. Hey, don't you put on airs. I am too. I'm also crazy about Buñuel. And, in my opinion, the best films are Orson Welles's *Citizen Kane*, Renard's *Poil de carotte*, *The Grapes of Wrath*, *The Long Voyage Home…*"

"Exactly!" Andrei said, and took up on what Andron was saying. "And also *La Grande Illusion*, Chaplin's *City Lights* and *Modern Times…*"

"You forgot Eisenstein's *Ivan the Terrible* and Rossellini's *Paisà*! They're both in the top ten. Password accepted. Put it there!"

The two like-minded individuals shook hands.

Andron summed it up, "It seems to me that our task is to synthesize and develop the best there is within world cinema."

"And I even know what direction this 'best' should go in. Forgive me, I haven't introduced myself. I'm Andrei, Andrei Tarkovsky."

Thus they struck up a friendship, one that would later grow into a collaboration and eventually enmity and mutual misunderstanding. In the meantime, they often went to the Gosfilmofond archives in Belye Stolby and had heated debates over the films they saw there. These were films that had opened new possibilities for cinema and had become classics.

Naturally the films of Luis Buñuel, who counted Federico García, Rafael Alberti and Salvador Dalí among his close friends, could not have failed to attract attention from young filmmakers. If VGIK students were reminded of Buñuel, immediately an argument would flare up among them and a division made between the retrograde and the innovative. Between 1924 and 1927, Buñuel had been part of the Parisian avant-garde, where he shared in the aesthetic and social aims of the Surrealist painters, who had broken with bourgeois conventions of morality and art.

"This is a bourgeois abomination!" Vasily Shukshin protested after watching *Un Chien Andalou*.

"He's a genius, and you're a bonehead!" Tarkovsky came at the first-year student almost ready to strike him.

The Soviet people, whose ideas about cinema were based only on domestic productions and a rare few "foreign" films, could not even dream about such an approach to reality. Even if this approach were revealed to the students at VGIK, it was only within the "history of foreign cinema" which, according to the teaching of their elders, was full of shortcomings. For Tarkovsky and his new friend, who had subscribed to the avant-garde, exposure to the best of world cinema at Gosfilmofond opened whole new horizons.

Their discovery of the Japanese director Akira Kurosawa was a shock, inspiring them to search for new ways forward.

"This man is brilliant!" Andrei sighed. "He made *Rashomon* based on two stories by Akutagawa and in 1951 he won the Golden Lion at the Venice Film Festival."

"And he won the Silver Lion in 1954 for *Seven Samurai*." Andron was almost angry. "You think we can't do the same?"

"We'll make even better films. But Bergman, I can't believe his *Wild Strawberries*." He was either delighted or indignant with the film. "The boundaries between dreams and reality are blurred. There are no boundaries! You're plunged into a completely unknown environment where everything appears in different guises."

"It makes you question the world. And that clock without hands? What a loaded image, just try to decipher it!"

"I don't like to try to decipher something that isn't explained. It's precisely this fog of ambiguity that's most important." Andrei furrowed his eyebrows. "But still, Bresson is high class! He openly poses questions of morality and choice! And mind you, in his case there are no effects. No sets, no make-up, he doesn't even need professional actors. And those fascinating long, endless takes… What a bastard! As if he had ripped this all off of me."

"For me, Orson Welles is deeper. Just think, *Citizen Kane* was filmed in 1941! Our luminaries never dreamed of anything like this. What a balance between form and content! It's no wonder that he was immediately called a titan of world cinema. You can't recognize in it any predefined genre. The perspective constantly changes, which emphasizes the ambiguity of the main character, how he can't be reduced to any certain characteristics. How does he do that?"

Konchalovsky thoughtfully furrowed his brow. "What kind of magic did he do it with?"

"It's easy. He uses the magic of ambiguity, denying a primitive straightforward account. After all, what is he doing? Each time he offers us a completely different approach to the main character. He consequently makes it seem like Kane's character is deeper than we know at any given moment. The reality is broader and richer than what can fit into the frame."

"Yep, that is why it often happens that the creator of the film, I mean the director, is sometimes more interesting than the film itself."

3.

Andron and Andrei could spend hours discussing films, and their conversations revealed that they had a lot in common.

"Bresson, Buñuel, Bergman, Welles, Kurosawa, and maybe also Dovzhenko — they are absolutely brilliant! The rest is complete shit!" As always, Andrei made a categorical dismissal. "I'm an old hand. When I was a child, my mother suggested I first read *War and Peace*. Then for many years I couldn't stop reciting passages of it to myself. I appreciate the rich detail and subtlety of Tolstoy's prose. That's how *War and Peace* became my course in taste and artistic depth, and after that I can't read trash! I feel only disgust and contempt for that stuff."

"But even the elderly Tolstoy is far from ideal."

"In his book about Tolstoy and Dostoyevsky which I recently read, Merezhkovsky points out how characters try to philosophize, or philosophically evaluate the action, in the wrong places. That criticism is completely fair. But it doesn't stop me from loving Tolstoy for *War and Peace*. In that film even badly thought-out portions are made up for by talent and passion."

"Exactly, passion! But Visconti and Antonioni are cold as ice. No matter how clever they are at it, they don't move me."

The students at VGIK weren't aware that Fellini had already shot

La Strada and *Nights of Cabiria*, which would only reach the USSR five years later and would change the tastes of young cinephiles.

The future celebrities were having a bite in a cafeteria at sticky tables without chairs. In the corner some workers were quietly emptying their concealed bottles of vodka.

Andrei agreed, "Italian neorealism has run its course and is on the way out." He wiped his end of the table with the corner of a napkin. "Look," he said, moving closer to Andron. "We don't have to pretend that we're modest: only we know what should be done next. The main truth lies in the texture, it must look like everything is genuine: stone, sand, sweat, cracks in walls… And if someone is puking, he's puking for real!"

The men who were drinking vodka looked back at them. One of them, already unsteady on his legs, directed his steps toward the table of the two friends who were now almost shouting, but then, after he assessed what was on the table, he changed his mind and went back. He muttered to his companions, "It's a no go, guys. They're not getting hammered there, they're going crazy without booze. They must be those cinema guys from their institute."

"No makeup to hide the living texture of the skin," Andron continued to grow exciting and wasn't even trying to appeal to the common worker. "The costumes shouldn't be ironed, unwashed. They should be torn for real. And they shouldn't smell like a wardrobe."

"That's the awful thing about Hollywood! It's a theater of wax statues," Andrei was hurriedly stuffing sticky dumplings into his mouth. "A woman gets shot, but not a single hair falls out of her wig!"

"Did you notice how Alexandrov and his singing doll Orlova have tried to come closer to Hollywood aesthetics? No, everything, everything must be different!" Andron took away their dirty dishes and hurried to the exit. "Let's get out of this dive. No social realist could express this stench."

"What if we could add smells to the cinema…" Andron dreamed, tearing apart a sprig of lilac.

"Every single detail is visible there, every drop, every murmur!

And I noticed that quality images evoke smells from the memory of the viewer. They light a cigarette on the screen and you can smell it… Everything is submitted to the idea! That's what an *auteur* film means!"

The French term *auteur* had already appeared in Western film criticism. The term refers to the priority of a single author of the film, the creator, who has control of every aspect of the production, from the script to the final editing.

"There is no doubt about it," Tarkovsky said. "*Auteur* cinema, what else? We need a group of like-minded people, virtuosi, and the director manages the entire process, realizes his plan! This is going to be huge!"

"You know what…" Andron furrowed his brow. "What made us think that they would understand us?"

"Who, the audience? Oh yes, them. They'll understand us."

"And the authorities? They don't care for our kind of films. A writer can circulate his manuscript among readers secretly, *samizdat*. What can we do? Should we keep hitting our heads against the wall, or should we comply with the Party line?"

"You are completely wrong, my friend! We have to film whatever we think is necessary. And then, talent will always prevail."

"Well… And with what means is the 'talent' going to make the film? He will have to push the script through the authorities."

Andrei fell silent, remembering his father's unpublished poems and his sad "career". His understanding of the real situation in the USSR vied with his reluctance to face the truth. He loved his country and didn't want to know about its problems.

"Fine, let me have to fight with some gray-haired bureaucrat to make my films. I'm not against that. Just like every family has a black sheep, our country has some flaws. But you have to fight. An artist must fight for his point of view!"

"Let that scum in officialdom trample on him, crucify him!" Andron was often infuriated by Tarkovsky's complete apathy about society. He didn't want to know about censorship, about dissidence, and that was that.

"Let them crucify me," Andrei said stubbornly. "I won't give up."

"A life on the cross!" Andron grinned, offering his friend from the family stockpile a packet of Marlboro cigarettes that had been brought in.

"I've got my own."

Tarkovsky smoked Dukat cigarettes, imported cigarettes had not reached the black market yet. He wasn't doing so well financially either. He lost his street earnings, and it did not look like casinos would soon emerge in the Soviet Union. Though roulette was not *rasshibalochka* — even the possibility of winning some money was unlikely to attract Andrei. He didn't need any performance-enhancing drugs, cinema was much better than all those substitutes for thrills and victory!

They stood on the Sparrow Hills, and not only the city in the evening mist, but the whole world, lay at their feet. There were no barriers they couldn't overcome.

4.

Mikhail Romm, Tarkovsky's teacher and mentor, raised many Soviet directors. As he was a narrative and genre director, to a large extent he embodied the social realist cinema of the 1930s for his students. Many of his students rejected Romm's films and called to re-evaluate them. Tarkovsky, harsh in all his evaluations and rarely accepting of domestic cinema, gave Romm's films the harshest criticism. Nevertheless, this did not stop him from adoring his teacher.

"What is there to discuss? All this Leniniana is cheap garbage, it's shit," he said to Andron with a passion.

"Of course this isn't Bergman or Buñuel, but what fascinates me is that, with all his dedication to the truth, he doesn't suppress our own impulses! He tries to avoid crushing our creative personalities, no matter how wild they seem to him. And he does that so skilfully!"

"He's a unique guy. He's given money, got people out of trouble, done favors for them in their film studies, and defended the work of his students, even the ones who have denied the principles he stands for! He taught me very well how to put whatever I want onto film."

Tarkovsky studied at VGIK with great dedication, seriously and meticulously mastering the profession. He absorbed a greater range of studies than what the curriculum required. He read books on art and philosophy, learned about painting and listened to classical music. He had an excellent memory, a fine ear and a great craving for knowledge. It turned out that in addition to perfect pitch and an ability to draw, Andrei had an undeniable talent for acting. His portrayal of the old Prince Bolkonsky in the student play, without make-up, was remembered by many fellow students for the original and expressive interpretation he gave the role.

Tarkovsky's first achievement in his directing course was a short film titled *The Killers*. It was produced together with his classmates Alexander Gordon and Marika Beiku and is based on a story by Ernest Hemingway.

Hemingway had recently become popular among Soviet readers. This short story fascinated Tarkovsky and his colleagues with its bold restraint and its simplicity, under which a catastrophe is brewing quietly, without emotion. Two men walk into a bar in an American small town, wearing black suits and tight black coats. They are looking for a certain Swede whom they have been hired to kill. These criminals' leisurely conversation in the bar, their laziness in carrying out their task and the humility of the condemned man are depicted in Hemingway's concise and extremely expressive style, and this was to be expressed in the film too.

The doomed man knows what fate awaits him and he does not try to escape, "I'm tired of running away from them. Nothing can be done now." This huge man, a former boxer, only lies in his little room with his face turned toward the wall, meekly awaiting his death.

That role was played by Vasily Shukshin. He was not as muscular as the description of the part demanded, but he was very persuasive in the few lines that he was allotted. The most important thing was to maintain an air of suspense, and Tarkovsky had the camera move in a deliberate fashion, almost freezing on the meager details of the condemned man's refuge.

Tarkovsky played a patron of the bar, and the group aimed to depict the kind of American bar they had only seen in foreign films. Tarkovsky brought empty liquor bottles of the foreign brands which should line the shelves from home. He was utterly absorbed in having an "authentic atmosphere" in the scene. The film was a success and received great praise from Romm.

These studies fascinated Andrei, but they did not diminish his love for Irma. They were busy at the institute all day long, and when rehearsals ran late, Andrei waited for Irma. The two lovers walked the Moscow streets, talking endlessly.

"Andrei, I'm sure that you are secretly a Kazakh prince, or the descendant of a sultan." She touched his hair, brushed her fingers against his cheek as if to outline it. "Admit it already!"

"Fine, I admit it. Our family tree is complicated and many branches are woven into it. Choose whichever you like. I choose this lovely half-legend, where in a certain village of Tarki in Dagestan there lived the Tarkovsky princes, called the Shakhmali in the Avar language."

"They must be your ancestors!"

"Why not? On the other hand, my parents prefer to look to Polish roots. At the beginning of the 18th century, a minor aristocratic family named Tarkovsky lived in Volyn. Then my family turns up in the Zhytomyr province, and later in Elisavetgrad, which is now called Kirovograd. Let them have their way! Now it is you whom I'm interested in. Tell me something about the most interesting moment in your childhood, or when you were a teenager? Did anything wonderful happen?"

Irma giggled, "No, the Virgin Mary never appeared to me in the company of angels. And I never found buried treasure worth millions."

"Not like that! Something secret, something important?"

She thought for a bit and shrugged, "My childhood was sad. There wasn't anything wonderful."

"Wonderful things happened to me!" They sat in the empty yard of one of the houses in a lane in the Zamoskvorechye district, watching lights being switched on in the windows of the homes, most of which had the orange lampshades in style at the time. Andrei lifted his face toward the twilight sky, where the first stars had appeared. "Look, during the war, when I turned twelve years old and we went back to Yuryevets, the Simonovskaya church which I was baptized in had basically been turned into a regional museum. Only the basement had been left empty. It was a hot summer, you could see the trunks of the linden trees shimmering against the whitewashed walls of the church in the background. I was with a friend who was a year older than me, he made me jealous of his bravery and his frenzied cynicism. We lay for a long time in the grass and, squinting because of the sun, we watched a low window not far from ground level, black next to the bright white walls with fear and greed. The idea of a burglary had been worked out to the smallest details. I can only remember one thing for certain: I had to crawl through the window after my enterprising friend. He was the leader of this operation and slipped first into the cool darkness of the church basement, and I followed behind him. For a long time we wandered in the echoing basement, through its hushed, mysterious nooks and crannies. My heart was beating from fear and self-pity, as I had set out on an evil path."

"In a pile of trash dumped in a corner of that huge vaulted room, we found a bronze image of the church. It was just a fancy stamped thing. We wrapped it in a cloth and were about to go back out when we heard shuffling footsteps. The footsteps were getting closer. We hid behind a heap of books. In the side door, the hunched figure of an old man appeared, wearing a faded padded jacket. He walked past us and slammed the bolts of the front door shut. I can't remember how we got out of that basement. I remember that my teeth were chattering from fear. We didn't know what to do with our find, and thinking that it was an object with supernatural powers that might have the utmost impact on our fates, we buried it behind a barn under a tree. I was scared. For a long time after that, I was expecting terrible consequences for this horrible crime before the mysteries of the unknown."

"Is your family devout?"

"Well, my grandfather and my grandmother of course, but in secret. My mother crosses herself, unthinkingly I suppose, and is afraid that someone might see her do it. My grandmother had me baptized, and the fact that I had stolen from the same church wouldn't stop bothering me."

"You were right when you talked about the mysteries of the unknown. I also have this feeling like there's some all-knowing director who I have to play a role for, that is, live my life for in a pure way, without making mistakes or breaking the rules of truth and morality. Your theft was the act of a child, a great trifle. The Creator cannot punish someone who doesn't know what he's doing."

"But this affair still worries me, even frightens me. Sometimes I think that I will go back to Yuryevets and dig up the buried treasure. For some reason it seems like, at that moment, I will be happy."

"Okay, then! The first thing you'll do after graduation is find that relic and bring it back to me. Promise me that."

"We'll go to Yuryevets together, after all, you will be my wife," said Andrei seriously, as if it were a matter of course.

Irma stood up and took a step back, looking with shock at the man in the red jacket with padded shoulders, at his pale, almost severe face and his eyes shining in the twilight.

"That's a cute joke, but I don't think it's funny."

"I'm not joking at all. I will marry you, and now we are finally going to kiss."

The multi-colored leaves of autumn were glistening under the streetlights. Moving shadows lay on the ground at their feet like a living carpet. Night fell mysteriously and invitingly on a bench behind the streetlights and some bushes with round, white, crackling berries. They stood in an embrace, holding each other tightly, having brought their hot lips together, which they found so delightful that it made them dizzy.

The sky had gotten dark, and someone put on Shulzhenko singing her song "The Blue Headscarf" on a gramophone at the windowsill.

"Now we are officially bride and groom. I wished upon your asters when they were floating down the stream, 'I will marry Irma Raush.' It came true!"

"Oh my," she sat down on the bench. "Andrei, I have to think this over. You see, everything is just starting for us, our work, living on our own. So many possibilities are open to us, and suddenly we have to make a home and I should turn into a matron."

"Just give it to me straight: you don't like me."

"I really like you, Andrei. But I haven't thought about marriage at all."

"But you've realized that it would happen?"

"Sometime in the future. And then, I don't know your family, your parents."

"So we'll have to meet them."

Soon after that, Irma was drinking tea with rye and honey crackers that Andrei's grandmother had baked. The women sat talking behind a round table covered with a lace tablecloth, growing fonder of each other.

Moscow was an exciting place in the 1960s. Although the Iron Curtain had opened only slightly, through this small gap fresh developments poured in from around the world. Budding directors stood for hours to get into an exhibition of paintings from Dresden or a Picasso display. They fought to get into Paul Scofield's *Hamlet* and watched from the balcony, standing room only, the stagings of the Berliner Ensemble and the plays of Jean Villard.

They went to the conservatory regularly. Irma was struck as she looked askance at Andrei's pale profile while he was completely caught up in Beethoven's Seventh Symphony.

On the way back she said, "You were like someone sleepwalking, caught up in a lethargic sleep."

"First of all, sleepwalking and lethargy are two different things. But I really love Beethoven's Seventh, especially the second movement. That's the place where…" He hummed the main theme with impeccable accuracy.

Irma was saddened. "I still have so much to learn. And you, you're so special," she broke off what she was saying with a long kiss. "Will you come to my dorm? I have the room to myself today, Olga's away on an assignment."

5.

Of course, he was special. He was extremely sensitive, with refined attitudes, allowing him to pick up on the smallest impulses coming from the outside world.

One day, late at night, Andrei was walking Irma home. They walked on the pavement along a row of maple trees which had not yet lost their crimson leaves. "The autumn painted the maples with some kind of magical colors…" Humming Bulat Okudzhava's songs (which were becoming popular in those days) as they went along, Irma hopped on one leg across the cracks in the asphalt.

The shadows of the tree branches waved in the wind under the light of the street lamps, penetrating the leaves. Shadows loomed before them and, like a carousel, passed under their feet before reappearing in front of them.

Andrei stopped like someone entranced and said, "You know, I will film all of this! These steps, these shadows. It's all possible. It will happen, it will! Give me a camera and I will turn the world upside down!"

Andrei continued meeting with Irma, although it soon became clear that they weren't at all right for one another. Irma did not understand, how she, a simple girl from the country, managed to attract this dandy from the capital, who could not imagine life without going to the conservatory and wearing fashionable shoes with thick white rubber soles. He would become a remarkable director, one of renown, but as a human being he was complicated. He was severe, gloomy, easily offended and always insisting on the rightness of his own opinions.

Even in an ice-cream shop, Andrei obliged her to eat the same chocolate flavor that he liked.

"Isn't it good?" He licked his spoon.

"Of course it's good, but I've been looking forward to tutti frutti ice cream since this morning," Irma pushed her empty bowl away. "You don't understand that the problem isn't the ice cream. We have completely different tastes in everything. You're amazed at how that scene of the girl being raped and killed was shot in *The Virgin Spring*, and I liked the chorus of dwarfs in *Snow White*. Of course, I'm just using the dwarfs as an example! I am not into gloom and despair. With the films I make, I want to leave a light, joyful impression on people. Just think about how hard life is for many people. I could bring light into their lives!"

"Their lives are aimless and trivial because they want them to be that way. They won't take a single step toward their own spiritual growth. I have faith that film is not mere entertainment. Film is the most powerful and the greatest medium for touching the deepest, most secret places of the soul, the mind and who knows what else is important within us."

"A lot. You just have to know how to reach those secret places. Your father knows how to touch the deepest parts of oneself."

She lowered her face and slowly recited:

> *And this I dreamed, and this I dream,*
> *And this I will dream again sometime,*
> *And everything will repeat, everything re-embodied,*
> *You will dream everything that I saw in the dream.*
>
> *There, to one side from us, to one side from the world*
> *Wave after wave breaks on the shore,*
> *And on each wave is a star, and a person, and a bird,*
> *And dreams, and reality and death — wave after wave.*
>
> *No need for the date: I was, and am and will be,*
> *Life is a miracle of miracles, and on my knees*

Alone like an orphan, I dedicate myself to wonder,
Alone, among mirrors, fenced in by reflections
Of cities and seas, iridescent in the haze.
And a mother in tears takes a child on her lap.

"It's great!" She wiped away the tears that had welled in her eyes. "Everything is so true that it makes you cry. How does he do it? How can you express this in film?"

"I'm convinced that a camera is capable of everything. Of course it's easier for a poet, a painter, or even a composer, because he alone has control over his own ideas and how to realize them. But a director? That's even more difficult than being a conductor or the manager of a chemical plant. These verses of my father are like film! But how can I transfer that tangled ball of deep thoughts and feelings which get under your skin alongside the words to the screen?"

"And they leave a mark on everything you'll go on to think after that, everything you do and feel. Even if you don't realize it." Irma's eyes lit up with revelation, "They have become part of me, and a part of you. We are related through the blood of poetry."

"What you're saying is beautiful," he paid the bill and got up. "Shall we go?"

"Let's go out into the sun. Please, you promised to tell me about your father."

Andrei shrugged, "Fine, if you're really interested," They turned into the first lane. "Well, you know how he left us. He shouldn't have left mama like the devil commanded him to. Arseny Alexandrovich's luck hasn't been kind to him afterward. He was in Moscow when the war broke out. In August he saw me, my mother and my sister off during the evacuation to Yuryevets in the Ivanovo Oblast. His second wife and their daughter went to Chistopol, where the members of the Writers' Union and their families were evacuated. He stayed in Moscow and went through military training along with other Moscow writers, but the medical board rejected him with the decision that he was 'not suited for active-duty mobilization'.

He longed to serve his country, as he put it. Patriotism runs in our family."

"Of course Arseny Alexandrovich had taken part in the poetry meetings that the Writers' Union had organized for Moscow residents, but the thought that bloody battles were being fought in the field wouldn't leave him alone. In September 1941, my father found out about Marina Tsvetaeva's tragic death and wrote some elegiac poems. You see, they had met not long before Moscow was besieged. Marina was in love with him with some final bitterness of farewell... She couldn't live without falling in love."

"I understand her very well. Without love, there's just emptiness. Life can't exist in emptiness."

"It's just that if there's a little too much of this love, then..." Andrei gave her a sullen look "It's very painful."

"That's true." Irma thought for a moment. "To love and suffer is the only way out."

"I'd rather suffer for other reasons, creative ones, for example. Anyway, going back to my father, on October 16, 1941, the day Moscow was evacuated, he went together with his elderly mother under fire to his wife in Chistopol. There, in the rear lines, writers were stationed with their families. The intellectual wealth of the country was kept there. For the two months that Comrade Tarkovsky stayed in Chistopol, he sent some eleven letters to the Writers' Union Presidium. He asked to be sent to the front! In December 1941, this patriot finally got called to Moscow, and from the capital he was mobilized in the active-duty army. In January 1942, my father was given the assignment of military journalist. He was a war correspondent for the army newspaper *Boyevaya Trevoga* (The Alarm of War) for a whole year. Every other day he would go to the front to gather information and he took part in battles. He was awarded the Order of the Red Star for that."

"You're talking in a slightly ironic fashion. You shouldn't do that. Your father is a great person."

"As a writer he's one of the best living, that's true," Andrei said firmly. "But as a person... He could be a better person. But that's part of the tricky subject that you call 'love'. Fine, I'll tell you some more. Tarkovsky's poems were printed in the pages of *Boyevaya Trevoga*, praising the feats of the soldiers and officers. He made fun of Hitler's soldiers with doggerels and fables. Then he could make good use of his experience in the newspaper *Gudok* (Hooter). Soldiers would tear out his poems and carry them in their breast pockets along with their documents and photos of loved ones — that's the greatest reward a poet could get. And what is amazing is that in the atmosphere of the fighting, doing his everyday work for the newspaper, he didn't stop writing poems for himself and for future readers. In my opinion, these are the poetic masterpieces like 'Bright Day' and 'Night Rain'..."

"I remember 'Night Rain'," Irma walked up to a linden tree and began reciting:

> *There were drops of rain,*
> *Flying from the light into the shadows.*
> *By chance we met*
> *The first time on a rainy day.*
>
> *Only rainbows in the mist*
> *Around the pale streetlight*
> *Told you in advance*
> *Of how close my love was,*
>
> *About how the summer had passed,*
> *That life was uneasy and bright,*
> *And you hadn't lived but a short time,*
> *Such a short time you had lived upon the earth.*
>
> *Like tears, the raindrops*
> *Glistened on your face.*
> *I still don't know what kind of*
> *Madness we are living through.*

I hear your distant voice,
We are unable to help each other,
And the rain was knocking on the roof all night,
And then was pounding all night.

Andrei sighed, "Can you imagine, I think I envy my father. If only someone could recite my poems in such an inspired way. And every time I'm amazed that he was able to love so much."

"Was able to?"

"And continues to love. Only not my mother. Okay, look, all the horrible things were yet to come, poor father…"

"At the end of September 1943, he was granted a short period of leave in recognition of his heroism in battle. On October 3, Marina's birthday, he visited Peredelkino, where we were temporarily housed. What a day that was! I think the three of us, my mother and her two children, felt the same thing: why isn't this person, whom we so warmly love, not ours? My mother could not take her eyes off of his emaciated, tortured, beloved face. She was surely thinking, 'There he is, a real man, a soldier, a hero.' How we all wanted to cling to his tunic, girdled with a Sam Browne belt and say that all was forgiven and now we would be together forever. Alas, this was just a moment of illusory happiness, as my father had to hurry to get back to the front. In December 1943, he was wounded in the leg by a shell. In the terrible conditions of the field hospital his leg developed gas gangrene, the worst form of gangrene. The field surgeons cut off sections of his leg five times, as he didn't want to lose his knee, which he would need to walk on a prosthetic leg. He suffered hellish pain and barely survived. His wife Antonina Alexandrovna managed to get a pass to the front lines. Fadeyev and Shklovsky helped her. She brought my wounded father to Moscow. Here, at the Institute of Surgery, the finest surgeon Vishnevsky carried out already the sixth amputation on my father's leg! He survived, but he walked out of the hospital on crutches. He looked… He was very proud, but he held onto his wife and was afraid to fall down."

"It was hard for him to get used to his disability. Of course, his second wife helped him and friends came. My mother visited him, along with me and Marina."

"So Arseny Alexandrovich's life turned out okay in the end?"

"Oh, no! My father and Antonina Alexandrovna separated. Who would have thought? It was such a love — she had saved him from death — and suddenly she left him. I don't know exactly what happened between them. Life became meaningless for my father. Only willpower and poetry kept him on the edge of despair. There was also his secretary Tatyana Ozerskaya. I think that with Ozerskaya he was lucky. She is also a translator and managed to get my father away on a visit to the Caucasian Republics, to see the poets whose work he was to translate. Marina went with him, and Ozerskaya's son too. Not long after, my father divorced Bokhonova and officially married Ozerskaya. And again work, work. He went on tours for artists, participated in national literary reviews, met with poets and writers, undertook serious training in astronomy…"

"And not a single collection? Rented rooms? Your father is obviously not a careerist. He didn't know how to make something out of all he had done."

"A day came when he finally got his own place, though. I remember that day like it was yesterday. I think that the third year at the institute had just started. Yes, it was in September 1957…"

In September 1957, Andrei put on his grandfather's old suit that his grandmother had altered for him, put his hair back with a wet comb, and headed over to his father's "new digs": Arseny Tarkovsky had finally been given a room in the cooperative writers' apartment block near the Aeroport metro station.

Andrei returned home quickly and sat down to read. The women had gathered in the room and silently looked around at each other.

"Well, how is it there?" His mother could no longer bear the silence.

"It's fine, but it hasn't been furnished yet… Those cutlets smell good."

"What, they didn't feed you?" asked his grandmother, aghast.

"I said I wasn't hungry."

"Right, you were in someone else's house," Maria Ivanovna said curtly.

"She's a good woman, this Ozerskaya," Andrei defended his father's new wife. "She takes good care of my father. She's quiet, educated and she loves him. You can plainly see that."

Maria Ivanovna's shoulders shook. She covered her face with her apron and collapsed onto a chair. After she had cried enough, in a completely girlish, sorrowful voice she lamented, "But for God's sake, tell me, if Bokhonova left him already, why did he have to take up with this woman with a child? What about us? What have we done wrong?"

Marina muttered in a gloomy tone, "Tatyana saved his life. After Bokhonova left him, he carried that poison within him and intended to put an end to the pain. But she stopped him."

"God, didn't I stop him? Didn't we have those years of youth together and didn't I bring up his children?"

"Ma, that's just how it happened," Andrei put his arm around his mother's trembling shoulders. "This is what he left behind for you." He took a sheet torn from a notebook from his breast pocket, on which the words of "Bright Day" were written and which he always carried with him.

"Left behind for me?" his mother asked, looking closely at the crumpled sheet of paper.

"It's your handwriting that's scrawled on there." After she had read it, she folded the piece of paper, clasped it to her breast and left the room without a word. She went into the kitchen to smoke, re-read it and cried.

6.

Not long after that, Andrei took Irma to Golitsyno, where Arseny Alexandrovich rented a small dacha. Irma could sense in Andrei some kind of solemnity, he even recited sonnets by Shakespeare, but all the way there she acted foolishly to annoy him.

"Do you remember the O. Henry story about the two gold-seekers in Alaska who were trapped in a snowdrift?" she asked. "They had only two books: Shakespeare's sonnets and a book of useful tips for housewives. While they waited for others to dig them out, they read their books until they fell apart, one Shakespeare and the other the useful tips."

"I know, I know! I wasn't born yesterday. Man doesn't live on Shakespeare alone. Should I tell you how to clean suede with an onion? I've scrubbed my jacket a hundred times."

"When the two men had been freed from the snow and developed feelings for a girl, one constantly read her sonnets, while the other entertained her with various tips on keeping a home."

"Of course the silly girl chose the second one. But I've got an intellectual girl, I entertain you with sonnets!" He looked her over in a scrutinizing fashion. "Be more careful about how you behave with my father."

"What, do I look like an idiot for you to warn me like that?"

Irma looked away and did not talk to Andrei until the green door of the low house opened, behind which the familiar face of the war correspondent Arseny Tarkovsky appeared: his protruding cheekbones covered with taut dark skin, and his intent eyes under the furrowed brow.

"Come in, don't be shy."

He was alone in the room, surrounded by scattered books and gramophone records. A large telescope stood on a tripod by the window, watching the heavens. Music had been playing and Arseny Alexandrovich took the record off.

"This is Irma Raush, future director. This is my father, Arseny Alexandrovich."

"Nice to meet you," she said shyly, curtsying and offering her hand.

The poet's hand was strong and dry. "Please sit down, Irma." He looked around and took a bowl with biscuits down from the shelf. "I don't even have anything to offer you. Will you have tea? Oh, I completely forgot, Tatyana has made jam. Now I finally have an occasion to share it with someone."

"Don't go to any trouble, please," Irma said. "I've been eating raspberries growing along the road from the station."

"How are things at home?" Arseny asked his son, deftly turning around on his crutch in the cramped room to reach the cupboard.

"Will you allow me to manage for you?" Irma said, taking the tea set out of its box. Absorbed in her own thoughts, she did not listen to the conversation between father and son.

Irma immediately thought that the two were not alike on the outside, but one could not fail to recognize that they were father and son. Perhaps they had a common way of thinking, an inner rigidity, wisdom, reservedness. Andrei became clearer to her, and she even thought that in a few years he too would be such a man: calm, wise, with strikingly kind eyes and sharp wrinkles at his cheekbones. And the look in his eyes — sometimes attentive, at other times absent-minded, as if he were simultaneously with you and somewhere far away, as if he had just dropped in to visit from eternity.

Over tea, she ventured to say, trying to avoid being embarrassed before the poet she loved, "I really love your poems. I've learned many of them by heart. You know, whole little *samizdat* collections are passed from hand to hand. You've left a very great legacy."

"Legacy! That's a good word for an obituary. But even at my advanced age I haven't managed to get a collection. There's a funny story about that. Ah, forget about it."

"Tell it to me please, Arseny Alexandrovich. After all, I'm drinking tea with my favorite poet. What would tea be without a funny story?"

"In 1945, I was preparing to publish a book of poems that had been approved at a meeting of the poetry section of the Writers' Union. The manuscript was signed off by the publisher for printing and it had reached the galley stage. And just then (you don't remember of course) there was a purge of writers."

"A decree was issued at the highest level," Andrei explained, "that was titled "On the Journals *Zvezda* (Star) and *Leningrad*". When they cracked down on Akhmatova and Zoshchenko, they smothered other writers too."

"Particularly me," Arseny said. "The government required more ideology, but in my book there was not a single poem in praise of the "Leader", and only one which mentioned the name of Lenin. Of course printing of the book was halted."

"But then they came crawling to you!"

"That wouldn't interest Irma. Better to eat your blackberry jam."

"Irma is a future director," Andrei insisted. "She should be familiar with the history of the nation and its best poets." He pressed his cigarette butt into the ashtray and went to open the window. "The raspberry-canes are right under the window! How wonderful."

"Okay, Irma, listen to this anecdote. During the preparations for the celebration of Stalin's seventieth birthday in 1949, members of the Central Committee assigned me as one of the best Soviet translators to translate some of the poems Stalin, or Dzhugashvili as he was then known, had written while he was young."

Irma smiled, "What great trust they had in you."

"It was do or die," said Andrei as he placed berries picked from a bush onto a saucer.

"That's not the point! I suffered terribly. I received word-for-word translations and it was all immature drivel about flowers and streams. But he wrote them, the murderer! That our generalissimo was a monster I already knew well. My wife and I thought about it: this lyric poetry and the Stalin Prize wouldn't bother us at all. We were living, I should say, in poverty. We didn't have any money left over, and then the collection would surely be published. 'But the shame?' I asked. 'I couldn't wash this shame off me for the rest of my life.' So I couldn't decide anything, it was the sheer hell of temptation."

Irma cringed. "After all, it was dangerous to deny Stalin something."

"Everything was resolved satisfactorily. The leader didn't approve of publishing his poems, and the word-for-word translations about flowers and streams were demanded back. In the summer of 1950 I went to Azerbaijan, to Mardakyany and Altı Agaç with my daughter Marina, Tatyana Ozerskaya and her son Alyosha Studenetsky."

"I remember that Marina was very happy," Andrei grumbled.

When they were heading back on the local train, Andrei stared intently out of the window at the passing landscape. Finally, without turning his head, he said, "We don't see each other very often. My father thinks that I have some secret resentment against him, and since he feels this way, he's angry at me for some reason. He probably didn't want to have a son like this. Not in these shoes. He wanted a serious orientalist with glasses and translated poems."

"You have a lot more in common than meets the eye. Something I can't put my finger on."

Only later did Irma understand that the father's poetry and the son's films were linked. They have the ability to awaken in people the best of what they had only darkly guessed at and had been blindly searching for all their lives.

7.

After Andrei and Irma finished the third year of their studies, when everyone had to move on to various studios for practical training, they understood that there was no way they could be apart. They got married without saying a word to anyone. Irma's mother, who found out after the fact, almost suffered a stroke. Maria Ivanovna reacted to her son's act stoically; she had already become accustomed to his antics. Nevertheless, bitterness stung in her heart: why did they do it that way and not in a civilized manner? Did she have anything against Irma? Didn't she want them to be happy? She didn't show it, but the offense stung her heart.

Irma admitted to Arseny Alexandrovich that she had decided to marry Andrei after she had met him. He laughed heartily at this and told his friends about it. Irma developed warm feelings for her father-in-law, which survived even after she and Andrei divorced. Arseny Alexandrovich and Irma both loved stories, and they gave each other books with humorous inscriptions.

The newlyweds had to rent lodgings, and they arrived at their new apartment with two suitcases and books. Their suddenly moving to a new house thankfully did not resemble the establishment of a family life, but was more like an adventure. Doing it this way was easier for Irma, because she was afraid of being sucked in by everyday life. A husband by her side and she, as the lady of the house, accepting friends over! She never ceased to be in a vivacious mood and people came to gather at the Tarkovsky home, which was lively, interesting and jovial. Everyone was young and pugnacious, like puppies: Vladimir Vysotsky, Gennady Shpalikov, Andron Mikhalkov-Konchalovsky, Vasily Shukshin and other young people from VGIK were always ready to "chatter about art" over boiled potatoes, sprats in tomato sauce and vodka.

"*The Woman in the Dunes* is a real masterpiece!"

"It's a masterpiece. But *Wild Strawberries* is a hundred miles ahead of it!"

"Guys, what are you talking about? *Seven Samurai*, that is the highest class. It doesn't eliminate Bergman, though."

The voice of Vladimir Vysotsky interrupted their argument, "Where are you today? Not on Bolshoy Karetny!" Everybody took up their favorite songs: the "choir hour" began.

Tarkovsky sang along only half-heartedly or not at all. This was not his kind of music. He did not like such a disorderly hubbub, goofy jokes. He only became impassioned in his toasts after he had drank sufficiently; it was as if he then took off his armor of severity and aloofness. But more often he had a gloomy look on his face, and then he met Irma's watchful gaze, full of adoration and something else — maybe it was pity or concern?

"You're impossibly childish and uptight!" Irma said. "These days you can't be such a Chekhovian 'man in a suitcase'." By morning everybody had left and she was taking away the dishes after the feast. "Andrei, dear, you must be more relaxed. You must stay friendly with people who are attracted to you, otherwise you'll end up lonely. Your only friends are Andron and Vasya. They're wonderful guys! But there are much more interesting people around! Take Vladimir Vysotsky, for example."

"He sings well and writes funny songs," Andrei obediently agreed. "It's just that I don't need anyone else. I've got you, my wife. You are so beautiful." He pulled a pin from Irma's ponytail, scattering her long blond hair. "I think that when I was born, my mother's hair was just like this. Make a braid!"

"Tomorrow," she said, taking off her apron. "Now it's time to sleep."

8.

The collaboration between Tarkovsky and Andron Mikhalkov-Konchalovsky continued. They were trying hard to break through to the cinema they dreamed of.

In 1959, Tarkovsky wrote the screenplay *Antarctica, Distant Land* with Andron and Oleg Osetinsky excerpts from which were published in *Moskovsky Komsomolets*. Tarkovsky offered the screenplay for production to Lenfilm, but it was turned down. In April of the following year, Andrei and Andron worked enthusiastically on the screenplay for the film *The Steamroller and the Violin*. The screenplay was accepted by Mosfilm's recently founded Yunost (Youth) unit and Tarkovsky was granted permission to submit *The Streamroller and the Violin* as his thesis for graduation. He offered the young cinematographer Vadim Yusov, with whom he had already become acquainted, the chance to film this short. Yusov was somewhat surprised by this student's ambition and agreed.

The simple, heart-warming story is about the friendship between a boy learning to play the violin and a stream-roller operator. The film's concept and imagery clearly bears the imprint of the films of the French director Albert Lamorisse who Tarkovsky and Konchalovsky loved. That director's 1956 short film *The Red Balloon* won the Palme d'Or at the Cannes Film Festival and an Oscar.

An admiration of Lamorisse is also noticeable in Konchalovsky's graduation thesis *The Boy and the Dove*. As Konchalovsky said, "Why did Lamorisse have such an impact on us? He once again shattered our understanding of cinema. The films *Crin-Blanc*, *The Red Balloon*, *Le Voyage en ballon*, brought a new twist to sound cinema. There is no dialogue in these films, the story develops beyond words, but sound nonetheless plays a very important role. It was like pure cinema, complex in form, and also attractive to us because it did not require stars, or even actors. A few types of characters were enough for him. He featured mute or even inanimate characters (a horse, a fish, a balloon or a boy), and that meant that the real author is the director, that he impregnates the surrounding world with his attitudes, makes it anthropomorphic, makes it his own."

In Andrei Tarkovsky's film there are also certain fixed types of characters: a boy, a worker, some bullies. Nonetheless, Moscow becomes the main character, old and renewed; the bright steamrollers in cramped yards, a child's violin, pleasant summer rain, red apples piled behind a shop window.

The running time of the film is less than 50 minutes. Over that short length, a story plays out which starts on a sunny September day in the yard of an old house in Moscow, where a seven year-old boy, who diligently attends a music school with his violin, lives. The "musician", as the local bullies call him, crosses the yard each day under their derision and mockery. One day the kind operator of a red steamroller, compacting the fresh asphalt over potholes in the courtyard, stands up for the violinist. He not only chases the bullies away but also allows the boy to operate the steamroller. Holding his breath in delight, the boy tries to control the huge machine. Thus begins a brief friendship between the two.

The boy's new friend calls him as he returns from the music school and invites the boy to go on his lunch break with him. The story focuses mainly on their walk and the fleeting events are turned into real adventures. A river of life floods the capital, and everyone is caught up in its rapid flow. The "musician" stands up for a child who has been attacked and gets back his ball which has been taken away in a fight with an aggressive bully. In a merry rain shower the two friends lose and then find each other. In the glistening downpour a new episode begins: a crowd looks on as an old house is demolished: a heavy iron wrecking ball smashes the thick brick walls again and again. In the film this episode has an optimistic tone, as a new Moscow will grow and flourish in place of the dilapidated past. A scent of September apples blows from a short sketch: the boy stops at a shop window with mirrors, behind which a saleswoman hands a bundle of red apples to a girl with bows in her hair. The apples get scattered, and their multiplied reflection dances in the sheen of sunshine among the reflections on the wet street, a trolleybus, and some houses. The reflection whirls, glittering with colors, like in a kaleidoscope.

The conflict that arises between the two friends is small but symbolic: the boy angrily throws the bread that he had bought for their common breakfast onto the ground. This act outrages the worker, who explains to the "musician" the price of bread. As a show of contrition, the boy plays his violin under the echoing arch of the courtyard. After being tormented by school exercises with a metronome, the young pupil for the first time plays freely and joyously, heeding his inner voice. The worker listens to his new friend's playing with baited breath. Now he looks with respect at the callous from the violin on the little "musician's" chin. The last shot of the film is gaily picturesque: the boy in his red shirt runs on the wide, freshly-paved street toward the shining red steamroller.

This graduation thesis of Tarkovsky, so different from his later work, already shows some signature touches. The collaboration of Tarkovsky and Yusov distinguishes itself with its richness of color, the expressiveness of every detail. From the opening shot of the entrance to an old Moscow building, decorated by a stained-glass window, to the noisy gateway or a parquet corridor in the a music school, everything here bears the stamp of authenticity, an awareness of life in the capital. The brightness and the rich meanings behind the distinct episodes give the whole story a polyphonic tone.

With 46 minutes of screen time, Tarkovsky manages to say a lot: about friendship, labor, the beauty of the world and human kindness, the charm of old things dating from Moscow's past and the wave of renovation coming to its yards and lanes. The optimistic vivacity of the short's mood, the expressive construction of a shot, rich in color — all this does not seem characteristic of Tarkovsky to those familiar with his subsequent works. Rather, it looks like a borrowing from some different aesthetic. Never again would he allow himself to entertain the audience with these light, colorful games, to adopt such a vulgar concept as the joy of being. From this first reel only a few techniques would remain, which Tarkovsky would use with extreme caution and at crucial moments. The light and the color of the main characters of this lively short film would stand in sharp contrast to the tragic tone of the gloomy black-and-white.

In 1960, Andrei Tarkovsky graduated from the directing department at VGIK with honors. His graduation thesis *The Steamroller and the Violin* brought the novice director first prize in 1961 at a New York festival of student films.

It was a fine beginning, but Tarkovsky and his co-author Konchalovsky were already working on a new screenplay. In the meantime, Tarkovsky also managed to act in the films *Zastava Iliycha** and *Sergei Lazo*. In the latter, he played a White Army villain who shoots the hero. The director of *Sergei Lazo* was Alexander Gordon, who would later marry his sister Marina. Tarkovsky persuaded Gordon to shoot the climactic scene, where the hero is dragged by his feet through the mud to the firebox of a steam engine where he will be burned. An unexpected effect was thus achieved.

"My film is doomed," Alexander Gordon said as he returned from the meeting of an oversight committee.

Marina was shocked. "What's wrong? Everything is within the right ideology."

"It seems like everything is, but not everything! I am afraid that they are going to axe the picture," Gordon laughed nervously, looking at Andrei.

"Because of me?" Andrei guessed.

---

* This was eventually released under the title *I Am Twenty*

"You, our great genius, constructed the shot so that Lazo was dragged by his feet, and it showed his smashed face going through all the muddy puddles at length and in detail. Plus, mind you, it is accompanied by a Wagner opera soundtrack."

"So what? In my opinion it's a beautiful overture to his horrible death in the furnace."

"The censor thought differently. He told me, 'Why does our hero have to be dragged by his feet for so long, and with his face in the mud? Does this bear any resemblance to the traditional climax of a film about the revolution? It's a mockery, a lack of professionalism!' In addition, the arts council judged that 'Tarkovsky portrayed the White Army soldier so naturally that he reveals in himself the essence of a White Army soldier.'"

"That's nonsense. I've never sympathized with the White Army. Don't be so gloomy, Alexander, your film will be released. And I'm apparently going to frighten the censors with my 'hostile nature' for a long time. That's interesting, what is with my face?" He looked into a mirror hanging on the wall. "I've got a completely Soviet appearance."

"Especially in your trafficker get-up or the White Army uniform," Marina reproached him.

"Don't judge by appearances. All right, I'm not Shukshin-like enough. But in turn I have a lot inside me. Although Vasily has that too." He suddenly became angry. "Anyway, did they go completely crazy there?"

Alexander smiled, and Marina, always very serious, looked at her brother worriedly. She knew how easily anger could break out over his handsome face, how greatly Andrei could antagonize people. Already rumors were circulating in VGIK: "He's talented, but unyielding and arrogant". He had a long road ahead of him.

Chapter 4.
IVAN'S CHILDHOOD, MAKE WAY!

I.

At Mosfilm, the young director Eduard Abalov undertook a film titled *Ivan*, based on the eponymous novel by Vladimir Bogomolov. Coming up with a script proved difficult. Bogomolov himself and his experienced co-writer Mikhail Papava (a well-known journalist and writer for the screen in those years, writing scripts for such films as *Akademik Ivan Pavlov* and *The Great Warrior Skanderbeg*) could not find a single approach. The film was not especially pioneering. It is a completely commonplace story, already realized many times before in different variations, of a little "son of the regiment". In the chaos of war, Lieutenant Galtsev finds the orphan Ivan and brings him into the battalion. The boy becomes a fearless scout and is killed while carrying out his mission. After the war, Galtsev meets a soldier on a train with his pretty pregnant wife. The young officer, who seems familiar to Galtsev, turns out to be Ivan, who has miraculously escaped death.

The happy ending reflected the style of the time — a young hero, taken under the protection of the Soviet army, could not be killed by the Germans. "God bless peace!" Galtsev pronounces at the end of the film.

In November 1960, members of the artistic council at Mosfilm viewed the film and were despondent.

Boris Barnet was outraged. "Inside the boy there should be irrepressible hatred for war. Apart from his cunning and charm, we should constantly see his all-consuming wish for revenge. And he can't be smeared with make-up! He came out of the dirt. The others too — everyone's so clean, shaven, with make-up and fleshy lips."

Other members of the board noted the lack of any great tragedy, "This isn't a war, this is a day at the park!", "There's no rockets, just joking around!" They especially did not like the protagonist, "He's a boy kept like a pet, plump and well-fed."

Production was suspended. Abalov's expenses were written off. They consulted Romm, who could be entrusted with finishing what had already been started. Romm recommended Tarkovsky.

A couple of days later, when he had read the story, Tarkovsky came to Mikhail Ilych. He immediately noticed an excited impatience in Tarkovsky's usually gloomy face. "I'll take on this film," Tarkovsky said from the doorway.

"Well, Andrei, very little money has been allocated for the film now, and there's only a short time to complete it. Do you think you could re-shoot the film under such conditions?"

"I'll shoot the film all over again from scratch."

"With so little money?"

"I have a new solution," Tarkovsky said, squinting. He paused, having seen Romm raise an eyebrow, and he explained, "Ivan has dreams."

"Dreams, uh-huh, and what does he dream about?" Romm knew that one would not get an ordinary response from this guy.

"He dreams about the life he was deprived of, a normal childhood. You understand, in his dreams there should be the normal, peaceful childhood of a village boy. But in real life there's the terrible senselessness of a child being forced to fight."

"I understand. You will play on the contrast between the two worlds. What about the boy?"

"All the actors will be different."

"Don't forget, you've got little time to do this."

"But the main thing is that I've made an artistic decision. It will determine everything. I already know how the characters should look and what I am going to shoot."

Tarkovsky also knew who he was going to work with. He formed a new crew: Andron Konchalovsky, Vadim Yusov and the composer Vyacheslav Ovchinnikov. Most importantly, he found an impressive child, Nikolai Burlyayev, who Konchalovsky had already filmed in his short film *The Boy and the Dove*. Film production started afresh.

On a summer day in 1961, Valentina Malyavina, a charming girl came to audition for Tarkovsky. She could not take her eyes off the back of this elegant young man, who was thoughtfully gazing out the window at the roof of the opposite house.

"What kind of dreams do you have?" he asked straightaway, without turning around or greeting her.

"Different kinds. I often fly in my dreams."

"Me too!" He turned toward her and interest awoke in his gloomy face. "And when you fly, do you see the ground or what?"

"Both the ground and a lot of sky. And everything around me is so beautiful. I feel happy!"

The director grunted, satisfied, and wrote something on a piece of paper lying on the table.

A meeting of the arts council considered the idea of a new crew. Andrei looked like an entirely respectable artistic personality in his elegant light-gray suit in a checker pattern, a neatly knotted tie and his hair cut short. With his emphasized elegance, his cool and his meticulous precision, he covered his weaknesses by preventing any disparagement on the part of the committee. The luminaries of filmmaking considered the young candidate, who would save the ruined material for the film, with curiosity.

"Andrei Arsenyevich, would you please justify your artistic solution," the chairman suggested.

The young director cleared his throat and blurted out, "The material that Abalov shot is no good. We will do everything over again from scratch."

Those who knew Tarkovsky have remarked that he clearly did not have a gift for oratory, and not for diplomacy or restraint either. He spoke with difficulty, in complicated sentences, and with little interest. He often did not notice that he was stepping on someone's toes. Clearly neither an orator nor a diplomat, Tarkovsky's language was film.

"I am absolutely convinced that the anti-war theme will move viewers, if we make the final scene in the form of an interrupted dream. We want to start with a scene like this: a boy is running and catching up with his childhood. It will be done one way or another, but we can see the need for dreams and the idea of the finale — a photograph of the tortured and murdered boy. After that comes a rupture and then, the first dream will continue, the one that was at the beginning of the film. The idea is that this should repeat, that is, his childhood is again and again destroyed." Having finished his quite incomprehensible speech, he sat down to hear the discussion.

He left with Andron. They darted around the corner, sat on a board left over from the renovation of a building wing and lit their cigarettes.

"High five!" Andron said, stretching out his palm. Andrei slapped it with all his strength. "We did it! The bigwigs have approved the main plot of the film. You know, if even they got it, this is going to be huge!"

"Alexandrov summed it up when he said bluntly, 'In these circumstances and with these people, a very good picture could come out of this.' It turns out that he still thinks something about the profession."

"This is an example of something that you personally cannot accept does not always have to be wrong."

"I am the *auteur*, the measure of all things. My film director's *self* is the epicenter of its own world. And that's how it's always going to be," Andrei stated intently, without the slightest humor.

"Come on, don't get angry like that," Andron frowned. "I'm not trying to get into an argument with you. Right now I'm only thinking about our film. Mind you, mister auteur, you ought to do everything faster and cheaper than usual, so that you can settle the debt in a way and justify the trust that has been placed in you."

"What's important is that we ought to do it better." Andrei could not wait to begin scouting for locations.

"There you are!" A worried Irma appeared from around the corner. "I've been looking everywhere for you. I've planned everything. Let's run to the shop, meet up with the guys and head to our place. I've made vinaigrette salad according to your mother's recipe, a whole bucket of it, so we can celebrate." She glanced at Valentina Malyavina, who had modestly sat down next to her. She noticed the way Andrei and Andron glanced at her and her woman's intuition told her that something was going on.

"You're going to play the mother, Irma. It's a minor role, but an extremely complex one. Look, you didn't invite a lot of people over, did you? It's still too early to celebrate, too early…"

Vadim Yusov, who was around the same age as Andrei and had already filmed *The Steamroller and the Violin* with him, noted that Andrei Tarkovsky had qualities which were rather unfavorable for working in cinema. He was disinclined to communication with a large amount of people. He desperately sought friendship, but found it difficult to engage with people. He was extremely trusting and defenceless at the same time, even helpless in terms of discernment and tactfulness. However, he was demanding enough and uncompromising in pursuing his artistic goals. Angry outbursts, which sometimes came to blows, and rude and deprecatory language toward his colleagues diminished the crew's creative spirits. But Andrei was forgiven everything. His talent, imagination, and the immediacy and precision of his brilliant solutions won him surprise and even admiration, overpowering the offense he caused.

Andrei paid a great deal of attention to his appearance when he was on set. Clothing meant a lot to him, but he had very few opportunities indeed to buy new clothes. He had to limit his concerns about his dress to carefully selecting his shirts and shoes. He loved to experiment, for example putting a band over his unruly hair. By this he foresaw the bandanna, so popular in the field in wars to come. Vadim Yusov, with his keen cameraman's eye, noticed that no matter what Tarkovsky was wearing on set, there was a sense of being well-groomed and a careful attention to his appearance even in the way the ragged padded jacket hung on his short-statured, thin frame.

2.

They decided to film on the banks of the Dnieper, where the plot of the story had taken place. The only other location was a grove of white birch trees near Moscow. They rejected the use of sets, feeling that the film should be shot only in natural settings. They built a first-aid post from birch trunks themselves, while a ruined church and abandoned villages were found in the vicinity. The only thing left for them was to find props for the scenes of army life in the trenches.

While Vadim Yusov was scouting the area, he noticed a black, decaying forest. It turned out that some enterprising people at a collective farm had flooded the zone, intending to make a lake, but the water had run off into the forest. For years an impassable swamp stood there full of black mud and mosquitoes. It smelled of dead animals and rot.

"It's great, just what we need," Tarkovsky said as he walked to the edge of the swamp and looked over this dead wilderness. "Here everything is deep, scary and realistic. This isn't a place for a romantic adventure."

Yusov approved. "The location is expressive. The scarier the surroundings, the more heroism is required of the boy," he said as he walked back to the bus waiting for them at the road.

"He's not a hero." Andrei straightened his foppish plaid cap. Even in overalls and boots he still managed to look elegant. "The boy shouldn't seem valorous and glorious. He is the sadness of the regiment. He is an avenger, twisted by the nightmare of war, who no longer fears death or pain." He kicked a rock from under a wheel of the bus. "Just think,

Ivan is from my generation! I was the same age when the war began. I'm living *his* life. I'm living a life where this could have happened to me too. Let's go."

Bogomolov's story, written from the point of view of the young lieutenant, consists of several encounters with Ivan, a 12 year-old intelligence operative who has lost everyone close to him. Tarkovsky's film, on the other hand, is shot from the point of view of Ivan, who has often been identified with Tarkovsky himself. That is, Andrei himself could have walked this road if he had encountered similar circumstances. In filming Ivan, Tarkovsky made a film about himself, proceeding step by step along the path of a young boy caught up in the war. He captures on film the images originating from the boy's maimed conscience, plunged into hallucinations, like an escape from the nightmare that haunts him. This could have happened to Andrei himself, he felt this with his whole being. This is the source of the incredible poignancy of the image of Ivan. Tarkovsky's ability to stop time and reverse it gave the film its main idea of comparing and contrasting two different layers: war and peace. The reality of war and the memory of peace exist in a single dimension of time.

The film begins with the serenity of a sunny village day, recreated with such palpable, almost hypnotic power that the viewer cannot help but submit to the atmosphere on the screen, enter into it.

A small blond boy chases a butterfly and hears a cuckoo under a hot midday sun in the intoxicating air of a forest in bloom. He starts running and suddenly Ivan is weightless and flying through the air. He sees the trunks of trees, clouds, a forest clearing, his own shadow over the surface of a meadow and his mother waving up at him. The camera floats above the foliage toward a peaceful river that sparkles in the sun. There is a shaded forest place, a wood-lined well and his mother. The sweet, tender woman stands with a full bucket and says "Drink, my son!" The boy, dressed in shorts, rejoicing in this great and beautiful world, crouches toward the container of life-giving water.

Then there is the dead, silent forest, black water, covered with duckweed. The boy walks knee-deep in this evil wilderness. This is no longer the fair-haired little boy running through the sunny forest after a butterfly. This is a scout, secretly wading across a black swamp, mistrustful, reserved.

There is a swampy marsh with black trunks that stick out of the foul water. Cold and death lurk here. Two dead Russian soldiers with nooses around their necks and a board on which is written "Welcome!" lay in the bushes along the river bank.

The war enters the film through images of a mangled, mutilated world. The dim sun barely breaks through the dead skeleton of a windmill, some kind of charred machine, the skeleton of an airplane marked with a swastika looms out of a field, the roads are torn up and full of mud. Death reigns here: the mutilated trees are blackened, the murdered soldiers with ropes around their necks again and again come into the shot. The lapping mud of this early, lifeless spring (which was to become a symbol of decaying Russia, going mad from blood and chaos in Tarkovsky's next film *Andrei Rublev*) sets the tone.

The boy's consciousness is painfully divided, the daytime happiness of his dreams and his night-time horror exist at opposite poles that sometimes converge and cross. Ivan's soul proves to be a repository of a black and a white pole, harmony and disharmony.

The happy dreams break into the subconscious of the child who has barely dozed off, with a hot midday and the kind face of his mother who is waiting for him at the well. Again there is a rupture and the mother falls face first into the ground. The world is swept into the invading chaos: moaning, weeping, sobbing, and someone else's voice talking gibberish.

These two planes constantly shift and create a sense of horror, an irreversible catastrophe. A stable set of elements exist in the film that repeat from one episode to the next, like in a symphony where the main theme and changing harmonies exist side by side, are interwoven, contrast, oppose or reinforce each other.

There are two different lives, two different boys. The boy that Ivan was, and the new boy passed through the meat grinder of war, are not at all alike. On the screen the face of the 12 year-old scout is emaciated, covered in blackened skin, the aged face of a much older person. There is the alertness of a lurking wolf in his eyes and an awareness of his own necessity. This is how the 12-year-old Tarkovsky himself could have felt — the director drew those images from his own soul.

"I am Bondarev," Ivan says to a soldier who has detained him, demanding to speak to his superior. He is aware of his strength that lies in his lack of fear of death, his lack of fear of killing and being killed.

His tattered rags barely cover his flayed body, he is hungry and exhausted. The important information that Ivan has gathered, however, gives him a sense of power and importance. The screen had never before seen before such a "son of the regiment", shivering from cold and tormented.

The war in post-war films was primarily about defending one's motherland, and the heroism of these defenders of the motherland results from the extent of their patriotism. Tarkovsky's film is not about this, however. His film is a shout against the inhumanity and unnaturalness of war in general; any war, yesterday, today or tomorrow, both for the aggressors and the defenders. As long as people on this planet kill each other, Ivan, a product of the war, is the most terrible phenomenon: a personality that cannot be restored, man as the result of a deadly machine. The war will end, walls for new houses will be raised and the wounds of the earth will heal, but the young men who have passed through Afghanistan, Chechnya, Iran, Palestine or any other "armed conflict" in the "hotspots" on this planet, who have been soldiers and bear within their living flesh these twisted, mutilated souls, will never be the same again. Those psychological casualties poisoned with hatred are a special kind of creature. Nobody will ever make them feel love, pity or compassion or simply enjoy a summer day like before.

War broke Ivan while he was still a child. The indelible horror of *what he has seen* dooms him to isolation. They try in vain to send him away to the Suvorov Military School, but Ivan can think of nothing but vengeance. The movement of the film constantly walks on the edge of death — the boy's soul is killed again and again, again his murdered mother falls into the grass. Violence against the spiritual world of human beings happens many times, just in different shades. The shift from harmony to dissonance, from joy to pain, is a process that Tarkovsky is able to insert into the viewer's perception, making him an accomplice in his plan.

"Ivan has been forged by the violence he has internalized. The Nazis killed him when they killed his mother and massacred the inhabitants of his village. Yet, he lives. But at the same time, in this inevitable moment, he sees his future crossed out. He cannot break the link between war and death; in order to live, he is now in need of this cruel world. By his wartime actions he frees himself from fear, but then he again becomes overwhelmed by sorrow. The little victim of war knows what is expected of him: fighting, blood, revenge. Love is for him an everlasting dead end." These were the words of Jean-Paul Sartre, who considered this one of the most powerful films he had seen in recent years. He denied any disputes about Tarkovsky's strategies: expressionism, symbolism or metaphors? He was one of the first to understand that everything is more complex than a set of techniques. Tarkovsky was working with his own soul, the soul of a seer, not making it up, but already aware of it, because he himself could have been Ivan.

We are talking here only about the type of narration, the very essence of the film. "The war kills those who fight in it, even if they survive. In war all of the soldiers are mad: this child, a monster, is an objective witness to their madness, because he is the maddest of them," writes Sartre, a great explorer of the human soul.

Thus the war theme about a heroic boy, a little avenger, develops into a universal symbol of the human catastrophe everywhere. The film has only brief scenes of fighting or attacks, but the ruined birch trees from which the medical post was built strike at one's heart. In combination with the tragic, forbidden love of the nurse Masha and Lt. Kholin, the image of desecrated nature, like an image of failed love, is painful. The feelings of the young people have barely emerged before they are interrupted, just like the voice of Fyodor Shalyapin, which comes from a vinyl record that is taken off the gramophone, is cut off. These two people have no future — a tragic ending consisting in the death of one of the lovers is not forced on the audience. These two characters simply break off their emerging feelings, as if terminating the life of an unborn child.

In a diary kept during the filming, Malyavina wrote, "Today there was fog. Andrei took me by the hand and led me to the Swan Pond. He left me on the shore and walked away. He put his thumbs and forefingers together to make a camera shot and began moving slowly toward me, looking through the mother-of-pearl fog at the sleeping swans, at the pond, at me. He came right up to me… 'It's like in a dream, a beautiful dream,' and he kissed me. I took the genius, not the man into my heart. I loved him with a very special love, especially as I was married at the time to the actor Alexander Zbruyev."

The whole crew was aware of Tarkovsky's affair with Valentina Malyavina. Irma did not make a scene in front of her husband but only asked, "Is it serious? What's going on between you two? Is it time for me to look for my own place?"

"Nonsense! You, an intelligent and refined woman, are telling me such a silly thing. That's so boorish! You know yourself that in order to film an actress, the director must establish a close relationship with her. One's family is sacred."

"So, this is your rule. It is so and ever will be?" she sighed heavily, imagining the long series of her husband's future dallyings in store.

"Yes, that's how it's going to be if I am going to make films," he threw his cigarette down and crushed it with the heel of his boot. "Falling in love changes the whole creative energy! And it's necessary, it's simply necessary to feel a little bit dizzy. Both for me and for her."

"Well, if it's like some way of enhancing your creative performance, and if I'm no good for this purpose any more…" Irma thrust her chin up, and bit her tongue. "Basically I'll try to understand you and feel that our family is more important than the kisses of every new girl that comes along. I love you, Andrei." She buried her head in his shoulder. "Do you really need me?"

He stepped back with a stern face. "Irma, I beg you, don't start any more fights during the shoot." His face suddenly reddened with anger. "You can see that I'm making a film! I'm living inside of it, and I won't allow anyone to disturb me," He threw the thermos full of coffee that he had made for Irma onto the floor. She then burst into tears: she hadn't had a single cup of it…

3.

The film canvas is full of small details that reinforce the opposition of the main themes. Some fleeting details are intended to engage the viewer, awaken his empathy, and others are woven into the story. The blown-up village cemetery with the ancient cross looming over it, a crazy old man who lives with a chicken in a "house" of which only the stove remains — there is continually pain that does not leave the viewer indifferent.

In the trench, located in the basement of a ruined church that serves as battalion headquarters, no one pays attention to the words scribbled on the stone wall. This wall falls several times into the shot in passing: "There are eight of us. We are all no older than nineteen. They are taking us to be executed… avenge us…" This twisted stone wall torments Ivan. At night, obsessed with revenge, he sneaks into the basement. The light he carries illuminates someone's coat on the wall. In his hand he carries a knife. In a broken voice, choking on the hatred, he threatens the coat: "I will put you on trial! I will have my revenge on you… I…" Then he cries from his helplessness. The dream and hallucination, like a vicious circle, has no end. In it his mother will always fall dead and the white light will turn black.

Retribution comes to pass, however. The silent trench is flooded by the jubilant noise of May 1945 at the Reichstag. The bodies of Joseph Goebbels's six children lie on a sheet spread over the pavement, poisoned by their own mother, curly haired girls with their faces turned away. The frightening documentary footage, inserted into the narrative, prepares for the turbulent ending. The dossiers of the arrested are scattered next to the dead bodies of the children, in the dust of archives in a bombed office. A record is open to a page with a photo of the martyred Ivan with the note "executed". There is a pause for a second. Had Tarkovsky conducted an orchestra, like he had dreamed of as a child, he would certainly have held this moment of silence before bursting into the powerful finale.

A truck speeds through the woods, the rear full of freshly picked choice apples. The joyful, dark-eyed girl from Ivan's dreams sits among the apples. There is a quiet sparkling river and horses on the riverbank calmly drink from it. The truck lets out a torrent of apples straight onto the white sand, and a horse munches on the juicy pulp with pleasure. It takes a bite of one apple, then of another one. Heavy rain, a life-giving rain, falls on the peaceful earth.

His mother brushes her wet hair from her forehead and leaves with the bucket. The children are playing hide-and-seek. A fair-haired, smiling Ivan holds an apple in his hand. This is the last vision of his short life, the last return to the world he had left behind. He laughs merrily, trying to catch up with the girl running over the sand. There is a downpour of rain on the apples and the surface of the river. The fair-haired boy holds out the beautiful apple to the dark-haired girl. But why is the sky so gloomy, and why does a charred black tree rise from the sand right at the water's edge?

4.

Tarkovsky shot *Ivan's Childhood* over four months with a budget of 24 thousand rubles. Soon after, the first screening was held at Mosfilm for members of the Union of Cinematographers. As an excited Mikhail Ilych Romm left the cinema, he said, "My friends, today you have seen something extraordinary. There has never been anything like it on our screens, but believe me, this is a great talent."

After the screen had gone dark, no one in the cinema dared to breathe. Only after some time had passed came a roar of applause.

"Andrei, it seems you've made a great film. I sat there with my mouth wide open at your inventions!" said Andron, who had played one of the main roles in the film. He took his friend by the hand, "And I am a great actor too! I've reserved us a table at the Hotel National, we'll celebrate."

"So I didn't borrow that purple dress from Lidia in vain!" Irma glanced at Valentina Malyavina, dressed in black. "And I beg you, imagine me as a wife and a future director, not just a mother-to-be," she said, patting her swelling belly.

Ivan's Childhood was placed in Category 1, which meant a distribution of over 1600 copies and a wide release. The film appeared on screens in June and, furthermore, was presented at the Venice Film Festival and won its highest prize, the Golden Lion.

Tarkovsky went on stage with his dark-eyed starlet Valentina Malyavina to receive the prize under the shining lights of the Palazzo del Cinema on the island of Lido. This moment would remain fresh in his memory as a symbol of a well-deserved reward for his work.

At home they celebrated more. Irma, already with a pronounced belly, made the guests feel welcome.

Weighing the award, a winged lion, in the palm of his hand, Andrei stated, with a victorious glitter in his pitch-black eyes: "This will be enough for gold teeth for everyone at Mosfilm!"

"What do you think, is this animal solid gold?" asked a curious Vadim Yusov after the crowd around them had left. "We'll find out now. Give me a screwdriver, Andrei."

After unscrewing the sculpture from its pedestal, they were disappointed to find that the Golden Lion was iron covered with a thin layer of gold.

"What a farce," Vadim would comment about this episode, meaning either the young prize-winners' naive search for gold or the fake gold on the prize.

"Little Arseny and I are happy with it nonetheless," Irma said, patting her belly.

Konchalovsky, astonished, asked, "So it's clear already, you're expecting a boy?"

"There's no doubt about it, we'll have an Arseny Andreyevich," Irma said with a smile.

"Well, there you go, my friends and comrades. And someone said that we wouldn't be understood! That they would stop us. They understood, they understood well enough! The entire international film world was shocked. Make way for the newcomer!" Andrei exaggeratedly made himself comfortable on an old sofa, a gift from someone. Irma sat by his side. Mikhalkov-Konchalovsky leaned his elbows on the table that had not yet been cleared, gently caressed the Golden Lion and yawned.

"For the newcomers," Irma corrected him. "Who knows what you would have done without Andron, Vadim Yusov, and of course little Nikolai Burlyayev."

"You shouldn't forget the others, either. For example, Valentina Malyavina, in my opinion, did very well. And your humble servant is not among the least either," Andron reared up and thumped himself on the chest. "Anyway, it's time for me to go beddy-bye. You've exhausted us, you genius."

"You know what I think, we'll make a new smash, a film that everyone will…"

"They'll be stunned," Irma hurried to finish his thought. "I'm warning you for the hundredth time, Arseny should hear only cultured speech. Though he is still here inside me, he remembers every single word."

"Let him remember them then: we'll make another film, a film about everything! About the past, present and future. I feel it deep inside me, as if I've already made it and then forgot about it. But now it's coming through." Andrei closed his eyes, gazing into his imagination. "There will be snow, wet snow, and men on horseback, Tatars. Men will fight in the mud, and there will be a golden dome and horses, and also an iconostasis. One made bright, washed with rain…"

"I know!" Andron said dreamily. "Ancient times, but everything is the same like always here. And shot in black and white."

"It will be the most important film of our lives," Andrei said. He put his arm around his wife and murmured to her belly, "You'll see, Arseny."

Following his win at the Venice Film Festival, Tarkovsky won the award for Best Director at the San Sebastian International Film Festival. In September 1962, the Minister of Culture Yekaterina Furtseva congratulated the studio on its big victory.

The press was buzzing about the award-winning young Soviet director. It seemed like a new powerful source of energy had burst open, and the critics tried to figure out what it was made of. A wide variety of ways of referring to Tarkovsky's style arose: "poetic", "metaphorical", "symbolic" and other descriptions in the complicated language of cinema.

Andrei insistently rejected all these pigeonholes: "This is simply observing things, an image of life in film. I do not make anything up. I make a film as simply as a Japanese person writes a haiku."

Tarkovsky didn't try to be cunning, he did not pose. In the cinematic language he created, there is little of the rational, and even less of the artistically constructed. Spontaneously, using a stream of images coming from depths unknown to him, the depths of his own being, he created a very special, complex and multi-layered world. He could not even clearly articulate what he wanted to achieve. He felt the result he needed with a kind of sixth sense, one that cannot be easily translated into the language of film scholars. "Here it should be raining! Wet apples on the sand. The soft lips of a horse," he stated emphatically and categorically. But why? In what dark corners of Andrei's memory had the image of apples washed by rain become lodged? Did he dream of it, was it molded out of the whole of other impressions? The secret of his gift is unknown. For him a film was not a deliberate work of art, something built up from sophisticated constructions, but a reflection of a reality open to him alone, the reality he sensed within himself, like another possible fate for Andrei Tarkovsky, tragically embodied in the film. Because of this, the river, the apples, the forest, the mother and the well are so palpably beautiful, and the horror of the loss of a world destroyed by war is so palpably sharp. Everything is very simple.

But this light-hearted simplicity, which is in fact the highest degree of complexity, already had Tarkovsky's unique stamp, something that belonged only to him and could not entirely be deciphered.

Tarkovsky's triumph with *Ivan's Childhood* followed from his success with *The Steamroller and the Violin* and promised more tangible victories in the future. Tarkovsky had no doubt that each new work of his would be crowned with awards at the most prestigious festivals.

In 1962 Irma bore the 30 year-old director a son, fair-haired like in the film and tranquil. They named him Arseny after his grandfather. Mosfilm gave the young parents-to-be their own flat. In the autumn of the same year, Tarkovsky and Konchalovsky, in collaboration, had already prepared the first draft of a screenplay titled *The Passion according to Andrei.*

"This will be huge!" Andron assured him, weighing the heavy stack of pages in his palm.

"I'm afraid to saying anything," Andrei squinted sneakily. "But I have the feeling that we'll break through!"

Alas, at this point the optimistic development of Tarkovsky's creative life was interrupted. The tragic path of a creator, undesirable to his home country, had begun; a path of struggle and defeat. Even on the set of *Ivan's Childhood*, Andrei had said to Yusov with a prophetic sadness: "Now filming is finished, you will all leave, but I will remain with the picture, be responsible for it, and accept all the suffering for it." Everyone had laughed.

Something completely unbelievable at a first glance happened. It was not in spite of the awards bestowed on the film, but rather because of them, that the "young and upcoming" winner at international festivals came under suspicion of his superiors in the Soviet filmmaking industry. What had made them perk up so much abroad? What hidden meaning, hostile to socialist ideology, did foreigners find in this confused film, full of vague hints? The officials naturally sensed that this was a foreign development, a film incompatible with the traditional format of patriotic–heroic themes. It was clear (especially to those in power) that the farther away they could stay from the film the better — and from those young, desperate "innovators", able to surprise one with who knows what, especially in the eyes of the West which was watching eagerly. Thus *Ivan's Childhood* was treated with caution.

Showings of this film, which the distributors labeled "for children/young adults", were limited to matinées. Extra copies of the huge run were destroyed. In spite of these strategies to keep the film away from audiences, crowds thronged cinemas thirsting for it. The foreign press would not stop mentioning the name of this director, and so the Soviet film officials harassed him all the more. Such a reception was an extremely unpleasant outcome for the officials who had found the film "incomprehensible". Who would answer for this foppish, obstinate guy and for the vague "subtexts" and "metaphors" in his film?

No one could have imagined that Tarkovsky would soon start production on the "film of films" and what would be a real headache for the apparatchiks at Goskino and at Mosfilm.

PART II. Making films is a moral activity

*"For me making films is a moral activity
and not a professional one. I have to
preserve the perspective that art is
something extremely serious and a
duty, and not something pigeonholed
into notions like, let's say, theme, genre,
and form."*

Andrei Tarkovsky

Chapter 5.
ANDREI RUBLEV, THE FILM OF FILMS

I.

Dmitri Likhachev urged audiences and, most importantly, Soviet film administrators to approach Tarkovsky's films carefully, as they represented a new and extremely important phenomenon.

"When encountering Tarkovsky, we must get used to his language, to his way of speaking. One must train oneself to be perceptive, to decipher the separate components of work even at an early stage.". Those are some big demands! Launching courses for "training viewers" to decipher the delirious visions of the "avant-garde"? Soviet film administrators cringed like they had a toothache. However, the real pain was yet to come.

Advance publicity for the film *The Passion according to Andrei* did not raise suspicions. It seems that Konchalovsky was its main author: all the emphases were placed correctly, with an understanding of the situation in Russian cinema.

"Our aim is to seek out and discover the sources of the Russian people's invincible creative energy and the belief that we, the authors, have in its power, in that long-ago era. The film should reflect authentic, natural images seen and heard in real life," Tarkovsky and Konchalovsky said in defence of the script that the two had written in collaboration. "In making a film about 15th-century Russia, we don't want to follow the path of the tradition of painting, as it would result in stylization. One of the goals of our work is to recreate the real world of the 15th century, to make the audience believe in it and not think it's something exotic out of a museum, to reach the truth of perceiving it directly. For us the hero of the film in a spiritual sense is Boriska. The film is intended to show how, out of that dark-age, a frantic energy awakens in Boriska and enlightens Rublev."

Tarkovsky had hardly entered VGIK when he felt that his main adversaries would be his inevitable intermediaries: the camera and the screen. A composer, painter or writer does not need intermediaries to transfer what he has thought up, but a filmmaker requires a whole team of like-minded people who have mastered certain technologies. Even then, the ideal that arises in one's imagination is unattainable. The camera and the screen, how can one make them unnoticeable? Through his career, Tarkovsky would fight for naturalistic images and eradicate artifice, the slightest bit of forgery, lies, the tangible effort of building another world. As if from a flame, Tarkovsky shies away from any form of rational constructions: metaphors, symbols. He strives for a complete illusion, putting the viewer into another dimension beyond the limits of the screen, into an image born out of his will. Ingmar Bergman, a major "dream-catcher" on the screen, acknowledges that "Tarkovsky is the only one who managed to find the keys to the door of the room where dreams are hidden."

In December 1963, the literary screenplay *The Passion According to Andrei* was accepted and published by the journal *Iskusstvo Kino* (Film Art). Historians and film critics argued about whether the fantasy involved in the film's reconstruction of Russian history was acceptable or not. After all, very little information about the historical Andrei Rublev has come down to us.

"This is not a cheap popular print," Andrei explained. "Our film is about how a people's longing for brotherhood in a time of savage infighting and the Tatar yoke gave birth to Rublev's masterpiece icon of the Holy Trinity."

The declaration of the authors' screenplay was completely in line with the prevailing ideology. Only for people who knew the history of Russia did legitimate questions come to mind. Why did this "brotherhood arising from the longing of the people" not prevent Ivan III from crushing the free city of Novgorod? And the masterpiece Trinity did not stop Shemyaka from taking hold of Vasily II, who was then praying in the Troitsko-Sergievsky monastery, and blinding him, after which the great prince remained in the Russian synod under the name of Vasily the Blind.

The writers of the screenplay deftly parried the attacks and talked about the spirit of history, the soul of the people, the great power of art and the other ideologically correct prerequisites for their film. Tarkovsky however did not intend to make a film about "the people's longing for brotherhood"; the Russophile sentiment in historical films had run its course, and he was not at all inclined to such idyllic attitudes, especially when it came to cinema.

Interestingly enough, at the same time a huge advertising campaign started for Bondarchuk's film adaptation of *War and Peace*. Shooting a four-part epic adapted from one of the fundamental works of Russian literature was a huge event. The whole country awaited this film, and the press constantly featured detailed reports from the set and interviews with the director, cast and crew.

Tarkovsky never aimed to make a screen adaptation of Tolstoy's novel; Bondarchuk's exemplary work, even if it was of high quality and meticulous, did not attract him. *Hoffmanniana* or some independent story based on Dostoyevsky was more his territory, he strove all his life to realize such visions. Nonetheless, he was tortured by envy of Bondarchuk's film. Regardless of how great that screen adaptation would be, he intended to shoot something completely different: his own story of the history of Russia, poignant and tragic, far from a stylized depiction, though extremely realistic in its manner of execution and well grounded.

This picture, epic in scope, required enormous financial resources. The first rough estimate determined that the first scene alone, the Battle of Kulikovo, would use up almost a third of the funds allocated for the film.

"If you agree to get rid of this scene from the script, we will start production," Goskino categorically demanded of Tarkovsky.

"So the whole film hinges on the battle!" Tarkovsky's team were downcast after he had told them about his talks with the studio heads.

Andron whistled. "But how then are we going to show the strength of the Russian soul, which they themselves required from us in the first place?"

They considered the matter for a while and ultimately decided to go along with Goskino — the situation was hopeless.

"We'll get rid of the battle," Tarkovsky reported to the administrator, who was looking past him indifferently. "But I must warn you, the film will lose most of its patriotic spirit."

"But you can emphasize this point in other ways."

"Other, cheaper ways? With a painted backdrop on a set?" Andrei said sarcastically, cringing.

"Yes, with a backdrop. I think that Eisenstein's experience with his great film *Ivan the Terrible* would benefit your film."

"It is exactly this historical costume drama that we want to get rid of in cinema. *Ivan the Terrible* and *Alexander Nevsky*, that's opera, theater! Cardboard and papier-mâché. Everything looks kitschy. This costume museum approach to historical films is unacceptable."

"You're being too blunt, comrade Tarkovsky. What about fairy tales? You can't deny that *The Tale of Tsar Saltan*, which is proving very successful in cinemas, is a great film."

"Ugh, it's not even worth talking about that film. It's stupid, cheap theater, tasteless!" Andrei became furious. "That film is so monstrous that younger generations should be banned from watching it. But it could have been made so much better!"

"I hope you don't consider Bondarchuk's historical costume drama approach to Tolstoy's great novel as mistaken."

"It is a meticulous adaptation of a bestseller in world literature, a special genre. I suppose that in this case it is appropriate. But making such film depictions is not my thing."

The official, who had already decided that Tarkovsky was not going to give up his Battle of Kulikovo so easily, loosened his necktie and changed to a soothing tone, "You don't need to make those kind of depictions! It's not necessary. Produce a tale using all your imagination, along the lines of your historical chronicle." One could hear the insistence in the voice of the official sitting behind the desk, whose temper was rising. "But no battle!"

"No battle," Andrei responded through clenched teeth.

"We have a deal," the official told him and slid a sheet of paper to Andrei across the desk. "Sign the commitment, Andrei Arsenyevich, saying 'We'll stay within a million rubles and have gotten rid of the Battle of Kulikovo.'"

After taking the heroic historical scene out of the film with a single stroke of his pen, Andrei left the office.

Film production started. The first expedition set off to Vladimir and Suzdal, where, in the surrounding villages, the crew built sets with the money allocated to them. They searched for architectural monuments related to the 14th through the 16th centuries. They decided to film on the Nerl River and in Pskov, Izborsk and Pechory, on the outskirts of which they found abandoned villages and burnt-out churches.

The scriptwriters carefully studied the historical sources. Tarkovsky was ecstatic when he found that very little information was available on the life of Rublev, and it was full of mysteries and uncertainties, leaving space for his imagination to roam free: he could make a historical chronicle according to his own rules. It would not be a historical chronicle of course, but a chronicle of his own impressions and insights about the "true story" of that long-ago era — a "true story" in that there would be no doubt about its authenticity. Even the facts that they managed to find in historical documents turned out to be only bits of trivia in the epic canvas of the film. The rather neat script, built out of scenes connected by the plot, was transformed into a chaotic series of sketches, ordered according to rules known only to Tarkovsky for creating the "reality" of the 15th century. Tarkovsky based his approach on a denial of the historical method, kitsch, psychology, paintings, legends and everything that his intuitive insight did not reject. Doing away with commonplaces, everything that could be recognized as historical and museum-like — was a rule that Tarkovsky imposed on himself. This particularly resulted in the film crew's care about the authenticity of every shot, its ugliness, the unsightly naturalism of the texture, which had no connection to "art".

In addition, certain indispensable rules are at work in the structure of the film: there are no plot twists, no logical actions. We find unintelligibility, allusions difficult to clarify, a visually enticing (or repulsive) rhythm in the shots. The film has a multiplicity of interpretations, a multi-layeredness which the director himself did not undertake to interpret. He never sought to remake Beethoven or achievements in poetry, but he wanted to find a way of setting down some deep process awakened in his soul under the influence of poetry or music.

In those days, obtaining good art books with reproductions of paintings was difficult, but Andrei owned excellent foreign editions. These were not gathering dust on the shelves but lay open: Dürer, Bosch, Breugel. Yusov recalls how they would play guessing games, leaving only a small fragment of a painting uncovered, based on which one would have to identify the painter. Tarkovsky's imagination was fired by motifs from paintings, like the music of Beethoven which was constantly playing in his home. In this state — bursting with feelings that could not be expressed in words and a drive to splash this accumulated potential onto the screen — he started shooting.

First of all, he took the connecting plot thread out of the script material, letting the story fall apart into disparate fragments that have a more subtle connection to each other in their visuals, pacing or colors (a contrasting alternation or merging of black and white in all their different shades).

Instead of the Battle of Kulikovo, the prologue of the film was changed to *The Flight*. In the first shot after the opening credits, viewers see the white stone wall of a cathedral and in front of it a shapeless monstrosity sewn from leather and sheepskin. A fire is burning under the leather bag bound with ropes. Around it the place is bustling with people: someone is hurriedly rowing a boat, another runs into the cathedral, which stands on a riverbank, and from the window at the top he looks out over boats on the river with men and women sitting in them. The people crowd around the fire and tear at the ropes holding the bag. The embers of the dying fire, the excited faces and the river — all this, shown with brief panoramic shots that constantly and sharply change their format and are edited in a cut-up pace, endows the action with a breathless, almost frantic rhythm. The strangeness of what is happening is emphasized by the muffled staccato cries, heavy breathing, grunting and groaning.

Finally they cut through the rope, and the meaning of all this fuss becomes clear: the bag made out of skins and the man strapped to it begin to rise! The crowd emits a single cry: "A-h-h!" and on the screen everything changes: there's a wide panoramic shot from above on the heads in the crowd, the river and the people in boats.

The camera soars and the audience flies along with the man, feeling the butterflies in his stomach, the exhilaration of flying. He overtakes a running herd, flies over a river, over a city from centuries ago, over lakes. One hears laughter, the man chuckling, his enthusiastic cry, "I'm flying! Arkhip, I'm flying! Hey! E-e-e!"

Then suddenly there is a rapid downward spiral. The frightened face of this aeronaut is shown in close-up. One hears him moan, "Arkhipushka-a-a...". The water gets closer and after it the ground is rising up toward the man. There is a thump and a freeze-frame; the motion has finished. He's dead, the end.

The freeze-frame is followed by an unexpected scene: a horse lying on a riverbank is filmed in an accelerated mode and then slowly lies down, rolls on his back and again lies down. Right after this we see the fallen bag, from which the air is escaping. Thus, with a whistling sound, the broken man's life departs from him.

The joy of living, represented by the frolicking horse, and its end are closely related, nearly inseparable. Death is terrible, but it is the only payback for the daring flight, for that brief display of courage in front of everyone.

Already from the prologue the film departs from the script. Something has happened here, a significant scene that determines the main principle of the film's construction: so real that it could be naturalistic, a cruel depiction of earthly existence, as well as the poetically free flight of the spirit. As in *Ivan's Childhood*, two poles are defined, which attract a series of different scenes and episodes.

From this moment it is almost as if the film finds its own laws of development. It grows like a living organism, obeying mysterious forces. It branches out, buds, shoots out leaves, blooms and bears fruit.

The secret of these laws of growth were inside of Andrei Tarkovsky. Discarding the script, he shot a different film as if by instinct. He not only made the meaning of the canvas unrecognizable, but he changed even the very texture of the cinematic language, just like cutting up a skillfully woven carpet and putting the pieces back together again into a whole, following different rules to create a mysterious decoration. He undid the symmetry, the rhythm of the pattern, the original concept for the entire piece. He did not worry about the seams, the joints, the tears. On the contrary, he strove to distort the regularities, wash it of intelligibility, annihilating even the beauty that arises by chance. In all of this Tarkovsky transgresses the prescriptions set down for Soviet filmmakers: in the film's naturalism, in its denial of an "artistic construction of the plot" and a straight-layered interpretation of the storyline.

Such scenes of cruelty — torture, fighting, death, massacres of people and animals — had never before been seen on Russian screens. And what about the openness and erotic intensity of the scene *The Night of Ivan Kupala*? Naked figures run through the forest toward the dark water, joining together and making love. The predawn mist hides the details of the scene from the eyes of the audience, and from Rublev who is shocked by the ancient ritual. But this enhances the feeling of the free liberation of the body, the primitive union with nature. It is during this night that the monk Rublev commits a sin of the flesh.

Tarkovsky's imagination is working red-hot, as if he has tapped into some unknown source. He shot and shot in a fury of improvisation, exceeding the film stock and budget allocated to him. Ideas came one after the other, and the hope of editing the film in a way to bring everything together — and there were many ways of doing so.

2.

In Vladimir, the entire cast and crew stayed in a hotel. Andron Konchalovsky often came to the film shoot and frowned more and more. "You messed up our script, old friend."

Late at night, after filming, they sat at different tables in the hotel restaurant. The lights had been turned off, the orchestra had long since left. Auntie Klava put the chairs on the tables and the tablecloths up, and then mopped the floors. She carefully avoided a table at the wall with the sign "Administration", where two filmmakers were smoking and deep in conversation. Hot food was brought to them, soup and goulash.

This was the care of Larisa Pavlovna, an assistant director. She got on everyone's case. "Don't you understand," she urged the hotel administration, "these two Soviet film geniuses have to discuss some creative issues!" She made salads herself and refused to sit with the two authors of the script. She knew that they were having a complicated discussion. She herself set Andrei to this conversation.

"You see, old man, you're gone astray. I saw it, I saw it…" Andron stubbed out a cigarette and filled their glasses.

"You didn't like it?"

"Well, how should I say that," he lifted his glass. "To success!"

"To success." Tarkovsky chuckled. "So, you think it won't turn out well?"

"Let's be calm about this. Our script is no good at all, it's plain as day."

"Without the Battle of Kulikovo it doesn't sound the way it should any more. And anyway, it's useless to slip notes to a composer, another kind of music is playing in his head! I'm not able to shoot according to the script. My imagination, my own ideas are taking over."

"That's it," Andron raised his fork with a pickled mushroom speared on it. "That's it, your own ideas. And tell me for God's sake, Andrei, what kind of ideas do you have? Only save me that bullshit about the great Russian spirit. You're doing something different instead."

"I can't spout slogans. Everything is much more complicated than that — about the spirit, and about the greatness of Russia. It wasn't only the Tatars who spilled blood. Our ancestors tormented themselves with internal conflicts. The rulers couldn't divide the power among themselves. There was discord everywhere. Chaos, filth and darkness."

"But there's Rublev and his Trinity! It's unclear whether he brought light to darkness or he was sick of the backwardness and the general sense of neglect!"

"I'm afraid of there being just one meaning to it, of explaining everything. Everything is more complicated if you dig deep down."

"And what's there, deep down?"

"The spirit, Andron, the spirit! The spirit is more important than material things. The spirit is the core of everything."

"And the soul? Has the soul been done away with after all? I've already heard you gave the actors that spiel. Pardon me for saying it, but you can exhaust any actor with these speeches of yours."

"I'm not explaining things clearly? And what can I say exactly?" Andrei pushed his plate aside. "This is *my* vision, you understand, my feelings coming from inside of me."

"The resources of your mind are not analytical but intuitive. You yourself don't know, where you get those images from and what for. It's hard for you to explain the problem to a scriptwriter or an actor. The script gets in your way. You don't even need actors, you don't need their emotions! You don't need the life inside of them. All of your characters are just Tarkovsky. What's important to you is not a human personality and the world. Your world is again the reflection of the indistinct face of the genius at work."

Andrei grew pale, the color draining from his sharply defined features. "You, you're just jealous! Yes, yes, you're jealous."

Andron laughed defiantly. "What am I jealous of? I wasn't going to make a film like that. We're not clashing, you and me, Andrei, we're not competing. I'm going in a different direction. For me art is a communication of love, and love is by definition emotional, heartfelt. You can keep your obscure verses," he stood up to emphasize his last sentence, "take a cow: it moos, but who the hell knows what it's mooing about."

"So it seems that I express myself to the audience in an unintelligible noise?!" Andrei sprung up, clenching his fists. For a moment the two friends were locked in a fiery glance. "I never want to see you again, never, you hear me? I'll kill you, you bastard!" Holding his anger, Andrei rushed through the door and almost knocked it down with his shoulder.

They tried once more to have a normal conversation under the snow-white walls of the church.

Andrei, his cap pulled down, tortured Anatoly Solonitsyn with coaching. "Your job, Anatoly, is to be silent and watch, watch and be silent." Andrei went back to Andron. "I'm fighting with everyone to get rid of their emotions, but they still try to add pathos to their acting, no matter if it's with their eyes or with their knees!"

"You have great actors. Their emotions should move audiences," Andron said with smoldering resentment.

"But I don't want to move them! I want people to sit and find healing for their spiritual deformities. But emotions and sentimentality are hostile to spirituality!"

"Look at where this has got you to, aspiring to the title of a prophet battling against human qualities!" Andron could not resist making the charge. "You exclude any possibility of empathy on the part of the audience! You destroy any continuity of emotion, rhythm, music, meaning. You play charades to guess at, and there's no clues! No viewer is going to break through to your precious meaning and stay to the end of this multi-layered masterwork!"

"Andron," Tarkovsky straightened the saddle on a horse moving past them, "you are jealous. I see nothing but jealousy in your patronizing advice. The cast and crew are working like mad and no one doubts that we are making a brilliant film."

"Well, God help you," Andron said, then turned and walked away. He had decided not to show up again until the end of filming. It had become apparent that their paths had split and it was unlikely that they would find a common language.

Andrei was buzzing with a constant tension. He was irritable enough already, as if balancing on the edge of a springboard, but the feeling of a swimmer before his dive in Andrei's case extended for months. Every day he was at the start line, every day was decisive.

Already in the first scene it was apparent how complex the film was going to be. The whole cast and crew felt that they were participating in the creation of something huge and utterly new.

Irma Raush plays Durochka, a character present throughout who reveals the most vivid and painful moments of the film. Irma proved a fine actress, but something clawed at her soul. Andrei was bursting with ideas and energy, he was bold, daring, unpredictable, wonderful, irritable. He was a ball of lightning, a powerful charge of some unknown energy… And the reason was? Alas, the reason was clear. Where had that tiresome bulging-eyed pest of a woman come from?

Mosfilm served as the pimp that foisted that lethal weapon onto their hated Tarkovsky under the cover of an assistant. Larisa Kizilova bore the name of her first husband, with whom she had a five year-old daughter. Larisa was a woman from a simple family. Looks were Tarkovsky's complete ideal. In photographs she bears a striking resemblance to Irma Raush, as well as toward the most important woman in Tarkovsky's life: his mother. The credulous Andrei, of course, could not discern in the fire of his love that predatory nature which Larisa hid behind her straightforward flattery, her cunning tactics, her capability for any kind of tricks. Such was her way of conquering the respected director Tarkovsky.

"Andrei Arsenyevich, are you getting the crowd on Calvary ready?" Kizilova inquired as if devoted to her work, although she did not even think to undertake any effort aimed at helping the film shoot.

It was enough that she had blue eyes with eyelashes heavy from mascara, a tight mohair hat under which she hid her fair hair, not luxurious enough to leave it hang free. And, most importantly, it was enough what happened between them during nights in Andrei's room. The formal way of addressing each other would forever remain in their relationship, along with the magical effect of their sexual relationship.

A large blue-eyed blond with a country woman's build and a hot Russian temperament fond of drinking and carousing, Larisa loved celebrations and knew how to arrange them. Her goal was to ultimately conquer Tarkovsky and isolate him from his wife and friends, who had some influence on him and could serve as reminders about his life in the past. Her methods were simple: the bed, where she was highly experienced, and flattering speeches that extolled Andrei's genius during the obligatory toasts around the table and in everyday conversations with members of the cast and crew.

Larisa immediately took a commanding role in the Vladimir hotel where the cast and crew were staying. She acted like a typical general's wife in terms of her great influence on her subordinates. She could find her way in or out everywhere and was able to organize little "parties". She would lie through her teeth, and she kept undesirables away from Andrei. Extolling the genius behind Tarkovsky's every step with great zeal, she filled the cast and crew with a sense of belonging to something great and an awareness of its importance.

She shared a hotel room with Olga Surkova, an intern who had arrived from Moscow and was also the daughter of a famous critic who headed the Script-Editing Collegium of the Cinematographic Committee (at the Council of Ministers of the USSR) at the time. Olga became Andrei's trusted friend and collaborator. She wrote a book after his death in which she tells of her close relationship with Tarkovsky over many years, of her devotion to the maestro and the disappointment that befell her.

On the set of *Andrei Rublev*, Larisa drew Olga to herself and made this trusted young lady an ally in her struggle to have Tarkovsky.

Larisa Pavlovna gave Olga part of her own work in organizing meetings and the maestro's meals on the set, serving him sandwiches that she had prepared herself. In this time she managed to run off to the marketplace and buy groceries. Afterwards, she cooked delicious soups and plump cutlets on the stove that she had smuggled into her room. The hotel administration, bribed by Larisa, turned a blind eye to the illicit feasts and allowed her to make special conditions for Andrei. When the whole cast and crew had to go to the hotel restaurant after filming in the cold February air, Andrei, Anatoly Solonitsyn and Olga Surkova headed for a hotel room where a rich meal prepared by Larisa awaited them. Larisa was a master at organizing feasts and maintaining a jovial atmosphere. With raised spirits they ate, drank and talked almost until morning. They offered marvelous toasts and recited poems. It was routine for Larisa to offer heartfelt comments about her happiness at working with such a great director as Tarkovsky. Andrei, inspired by alcohol and the company of a woman he was in love with, would without fail recite poems by his father and quite often Pasternak's *Svidaniye* (Rendezvous), putting his feelings about Larisa into each word:

> *The road is buried in snow,*
> *The roofs bend from their burden.*
> *I go to stretch my legs:*
> *You stand behind the door.*
>
> *…*
>
> *The trees and fences*
> *Seem far off in the fog,*
> *Alone in the falling snow*
> *You stand at the corner.*
>
> *…*
>
> *As if there were under my ribs*
> *Tipped with antimony,*
> *There grooved a nib*
> *Scratching you into my heart.*

Helpless in his life and business affairs, he believed that he had found in Larisa a selfless Russian woman, an aide and protector. Irma, on the other hand, as he heard from Larisa on a daily basis, did not love her husband and was characterized by all manner of female weaknesses that insulted his purity and virtue. The verdict was indisputable: he would have to send Irma and his little son Arseny far away.

When Irma came to the film shoot, Larisa brought her dinner from the room in the restaurant. Having let her thin blondish hair loose, which she had previously put up, laughing loudly and feeling herself the queen of the ball, Larisa went out to the restaurant surrounded by a retinue of men from the crew. Andrei sat there with his wife. All of the restaurant staff knew Larisa and greeted her when she appeared. The orchestra began to play, and she went onto the dance floor, always in the center of the circle of people enthusiastically clapping.

They repeatedly played Larisa Pavlovna's favorite hit song "The storm has brought earth and sky together..."

She told everyone that she had been a prima donna at the Bolshoi Theater School and had competed with Plisetskaya, but a heart disease had forced her to abandon ballet. She lied readily and with great inspiration: her father was an admiral, while her mother was a fashion designer. It never even occurred to her that she was too heavyset to be a ballerina.

Andrei sat at the table with his wife and literally lost his mind watching this dancing queen. Inflamed with jealousy and having had too much to drink, he once crushed a glass in his fist so hard that he got glass splinters in his palm. He was also said to have started tearing off the restaurant wallpaper in one of these rages.

It was, in fact, clear that Tarkovsky's feelings for Larisa were so strong that he could not work. It was enough for Kizilova to leave to Moscow to arrange something, and then the producer Tamara Ogorodnikova would search for her and ask her to come back immediately as Andrei Arsenyevich was unwell.

Another whim of this man in love frightened the entire crew. Once, when he saw some horses grazing, he boldly mounted a black stallion. He was immediately thrown off, but his foot was stuck in the stirrup and the horse dragged him across the field. His head repeatedly struck the ground. The horse reared up and Andrei pulled his leg away, but he walked with a limp for a long time afterwards, as the horse's hooves had struck a muscle, and his head did not feel well after hitting the stones. Who knows, maybe his fate had sent that black horse to sow the seed of illness in the body of a healthy man? We cannot know the secret course of fate that weaves its invisible webs.

3.

Tarkovsky's high-strung nature, ringing from tension, was passed on to everyone else.

Work on the film proved intoxicating; it was clear that Tarkovsky was making an unusual film, that every shot secured their future success. Doing their utmost, everyone expected a triumph, because in their eyes they were giving birth to a miracle. Tarkovsky was obsessed by the idea of confirming the success of his first film by ensuring an undeniable victory with the follow-up. That meant that he had to work with a vengeance.

Tarkovsky often had to travel to Moscow and show the footage he had shot to his superiors at the studio. Few of them could understand the general idea of the film. Their shock at what they saw clearly exceeded their enthusiasm for it. Most of all, the administrators were troubled by his exceeding the running time and the budget. The film could not be split even into a two-part feature. Tarkovsky began being reproached by Goskino and the studio.

"The material you've shot does not even fall into a two-part format," the head of the production department looked at the director severely. "Clearly, you have lost your way, you destroyed your conception, got bogged down in countless irrelevant details. I'm not an art historian but an accountant, but I'm speaking now in the name of the film staff familiar with the material. All of my comrades who have seen your footage deem it necessary that you make significant cuts."

In the office of another supervisor, who oversaw ideology in film productions, he did not meet with amazement either and the same demands were repeated.

"Let's not talk now about artistic mistakes. Whether it is a good film or not will be seen after the final editing. But right now it's obvious that you need to take scissors to your material."

"I will shorten it as I can if I feel this is necessary for the film," Tarkovsky said curtly, unable to even maintain an illusion of compromise.

"Andrei Arsenyevich, my dear fellow, doesn't it seem to you that the leisurely pace you take threatens not only the audience's appreciation, but also the film itself? This tedium and slow pace is not the best quality for a spectator and dynamic form of art. And you must understand, every minute and every centimeter of film stock costs money! I hope your co-author on the script Andron Konchalovsky has already talked to you about this."

"The pacing will stay the same. I'll make this film in my own way," Andrei accepted the remarks about tedium and excessive length without comment. "I just don't understand why Goskino has steadily refused to pay for the last stage of work on the film, sound and editing, when huge sums go to films that are far less important. You give a green light to the heavily subsidized undertakings of Bondarchuk and others who are making these giant films that don't have much of an audience."

"I hope I don't have to explain to you what a government order means? And a screen adaptation of a perennial Russian classic? Of course we give a wide road for a film of great ideological importance."

"But the cultural and spiritual content of the film is less important for you?"

"Forgive me, comrade Tarkovsky, but since we're already on this subject, Bondarchuk's film is awaited by the international community and the entire Soviet people. Everyone, big and small! You are a director of films for an elite, working for a small following of intellectuals. Aren't you spending too much money on satisfying a bunch of snobs?"

"I work for the people!" Tarkovsky sincerely believed in what he said. "Who am I if not one of the people? And why, if I am part of them, can I not be the people's voice?"

"We'll see about that if the film is released in cinemas."

Tarkovsky's submissive position is surprising. Such a conversation among equals could have easily led to blows. He was impertinent toward the authorities, without going beyond the bounds of decency. These were obvious manifestations of Tarkovsky's social immaturity. He always shied away from ideology and, genuinely uninterested in social mechanisms, he avoided involvement in any "faction". A policy of non-interference in societal affairs seemed to ensure greater creative freedom. Most importantly, he really treated every kind of dissident action or underhanded rebuke with a certain disgust. Later Tarkovsky would strongly reject the invitation to participate in the exhibition "Underground Art behind the Iron Curtain" organized in Venice. At every press conference, even at difficult points in his life, he would avoid making negative comments about his country.

He did have a good grasp of the ideological situation, he did not understand at all the backstage games of film-making, the intrigues, he was afraid to get involved in dirty political affairs. He truly loved Russia with its culture and history. In Tarkovsky's pointed detachment from social life, there may have been an element of fear inherited along with the great Russian cultural tradition: the fear of the intelligentsia who died during the time of the revolution, and the fear of the Stalinist era, which his parents had lived through and which was evoked with such penetrating insight in a scene in his film *The Mirror*.

His passion for the "best among women" proved energizing. Andrei increasingly felt currents of genius within himself. On the set he was seething with energy, biting his fingernails and leaving the actors exasperated with requirements that changed spontaneously — here he needed snow, or rain, or fire, or a torture scene, or a pagan succumbing to the flesh. He had control over every detail, but he sought the right tone for every scene.

The Golgotha scene is one of the most memorable in the film. The Russian Jesus is nothing like the canonical one. He drags his cross behind him through a village, feeling faint. There are no raging mobs around him demanding, "Crucify him!", but instead a bunch of beggars in rags, as if they are doomed to follow the condemned man.

Rublev's vision of Christ is crucified alone on a snow-covered hill near the white walls of a monastery. He makes the final steps in a peasant's linen shirt with ease, going over the mushy wet snow as if he were walking on water. Behind him trudge Mary Magdalene and his Mother in poor, soaked robes and threadbare shoes made of bast. How kind the expression on this Christ's face is after he slips on the slope and with thirst brings a chunk of snow to his lips. Pressing himself close to the snow, he gives everyone who will remain on this earth a long, final glance, loving and suffering, knowing in advance all the vanity of all the people's efforts to follow him. Only a toothless light-haired little girl smiles at him in the last minutes.

When Anatoly Solonitsyn, a hitherto unknown actor from the provinces, got the chance to play Rublev in Tarkovsky's film, he was in a continual fever, whether of uncertainty or hope. He idolized Tarkovsky and was tortured by his own feelings of inadequacy. He was ready to wallow in water and mud in piercing rain, and also to give the right sound to the role, choking himself to the limits in order to evoke the weak and broken voice of Rublev, who finally speaks again after a two-year vow of silence. He tried to live according to this vow in real life, eating almost nothing at all and hardly speaking. A book-lover, he went through all the second-hand shops in Vladimir, wandering around the city stooped over, unshaven, smelling of cigarette smoke, with a feverish look in his deep-set eyes, hiding his balding head under the collar of his old coat.

The part of Rublev, which was written in the script as a logical development along psychological lines, underwent changes during production which destroyed and demolished the character. After seeing the film, many critics felt that the way Solonitsyn played the role seemed weak, but the actor was only doing what the director wanted.

Tarkovsky's Rublev does not have any heroic qualities like dedication or courage, and he does not show any eagerness to be a monk — he crosses himself only a single time in the whole film. In the vast panorama of Russia, ignorant and sinful, flesh of its flesh, his unassuming appearance reflects the general background of ignorance and material and spiritual poverty.

Everything is mixed up in filth and blood here. In a completely unpretentious and ascetic fashion, Tarkovsky shows how people have become accustomed to this routine and sense of hopelessness. Fighting, violence, cruelty and life in impassable filth are the lot of this land which has lost its spiritual core or never had one to begin with.

The pagan festival constitutes the contrast here. The same people become one with the awakening nature. Such a view of the material world, barbarian in its core, changes Rublev's attitude toward carnal sin as well. Only one sin weighs on his mind, the killing of a soldier who wanted to rape Durochka.

In the film good becomes evil, love and compassion become sin, but sin becomes spiritual elevation. Rublev's vow of silence is a way of turning away from sin, but at the same time it is an escape from life, the mortification of his gift.

The scene with the bell, viewed as the main symbol of the film, arose spontaneously out of Tarkovsky's imagination. He felt the need for a powerful jolt that could shatter the painful atmosphere of hopelessness. The adolescent Boriska (played by Nikolai Burlyayev, the now grown-up protagonist from *Ivan's Childhood*) molds a bell, working on a whim and white-hot inspiration, not knowing the secrets of this craft. The low and imposing sound of the bell, resounding in the tense silence of the crowd's eager expectation, is a breakthrough to some higher truth that wrests Rublev out of his silence. He feels the need to return to painting icons, work which he had tried to stifle with his sacred vow.

After he hears the great sound of the bell, it is as if it overcomes his most recent sin, he opens his mouth and calls on Boriska to come to Troitsa, so that they can work wonders for the people in the name of the Holy Spirit.

Harmony is born out of the general discord. Tarkovsky somehow manages to combine the incompatible: the material and grossly sensual with the highly spiritual and divine. The contradictory impulses and catastrophe that make up the film give birth to light, in the final frames, when sheets of rain run down Rublev's icons to the sound of thunder, the world turns into color. In the roar of this welcome storm, the downpour of color and the harmony of the figures in the Trinity give a sense of solemnity, of grandeur. In order to give birth to this wonder that blinds us, it was first necessary for the man to trod in filth for a long time. The viewer takes not only a happy ending from the film, he or she also takes from it this light that has arisen from a world of darkness, as well as an awareness of its the accidental nature, like the ray of a star, of the blinding miracle.

Another scene also remains in one's memory, however. In a destroyed and desecrated church Rublev says, "Russia, dearest Russia, she bears everything, she will bear everything. How long will it continue, Theophanes?" The ghost of Theophanes answers, "I don't know. Forever. Probably forever."

Rublev's argument with Theophanes the Greek forms the intellectual leitmotif of the film: are the people in darkness or not? What is their path to the light, and is there one at all? Regardless of the victory with the cast bell and Rublev's rise, the film, constructed from darkness and arising from the depths of history, leaves one with a sense of distress. The blood, the torture, the suffering and the spiritual numbness highlight the rare flashes of illumination. The soul of the people does not prevail against the darkness.

This is not because of the Tatar yoke, and not because of the infighting among princes that drowns Russia in blood and folly. The tragedy of Russia is inside of it, a punishment consisting of being godforsaken, an overwhelming ancestral curse. The horror of life is explicit and everywhere, but beauty comes only in flashes, unable to save this world.

It is this meaning which Tarkovsky places into the roles of Irma and Solonitsyn. In this chaotic world it is better to be Durochka. The mute Durochka is in fact the most radiant thing in the film. The actress depicts not her madness, but her rejection of the intellect, her resignation and her uselessness. (For this role Irma, the only one of the actors in the film, would go on to receive an international award, the Étoile de Cristal.) Solonitsyn portrays a broken spirit, a man in a state of inner catastrophe. His role gives the film its tone. Artistic creativity forces its way out of the depths of Rublev's spirit by a ray of the epiphany. His enlightenment, however, is bound to be only a single flash, just like the other manifestations of spiritual power in this land.

Beyond the intentions of Tarkovsky, who did not intend to pass sentence on the "soul of the nation", and only looked with the prophetic ability of his genius into the abyss of history, the basic meaning of the film is a terrible one: chaos and submission are Russia's lot, this godforsaken people's way is difficult and hopeless.

Almost half a century has passed since the making of this film, but this length of time, and the decades and centuries before them, only confirm the general idea emerging from the fabric of this film. The past and the present of this nation proceeds as a series of tragic events, no matter how much we hope for the arising of a "national idea" that could turn the people back from this path of cruelty, filth and ignorance. Often looking at the reality of yesterday and today and reflect on the future, we have to admit that Berdyaev had it right when he wrote in his 1918 essay "The Fate of Russia", "Russia is the most lawless country, the most anarchic. The Russian people are the most apolitical people. Russia is a country of abject servility, a country that lacks awareness of the rights of the individual and does not defend the dignity of the individual, a country of inert conservatism, a country of hard lives and heavy flesh." These words of Berdyaev articulate the feeling that the film evokes. And no matter what depths Tarkovsky would think about, the film became prophetic: Russia has not been given aspirations toward wellbeing of the flesh or spiritual accomplishment. The forces of discord, the lack of a system or a clear reason to live have triumphed — it is like the ravings of a drunkard. But here an antithesis arises, the Trinity which casts a gleam of light onto the profound darkness. Is this a hope given to the world from above? It is a hope that leaves open the question of whether Russia is godforsaken?

The saddest thoughts come to mind for audiences of *Andrei Rublev* today. The era in which the film was made still besotted with hopes for "eradicating the old order of things", for the triumph of a "bright future". That is what Soviet cinema was for, the most humane in the world which acted like a large-scale, a hypnotic illusion that could build utopias to soothe the people lost in the chaos of false ideals.

However, a purely pessimistic interpretation of *Andrei Rublev* is just one of the most clearly manifested possibilities in the present situation. There have been a multitude of interpretations depending on the viewer's cultural baggage and his own feelings.

Much later, only when Tarkovsky himself was no longer with us but it had become possible in Russia to write about his films, there have been professional critics who have finally received the right to show interest in his work and propose different interpretations of his films. The ambiguity of *Andrei Rublev* has allowed a wide range of interpretations. Is this a godforsaken people or are they a God-bearing one? One can find a basis for both claims in the film, as well as ascribe to it ideas of "Slavophilia" or "Slavophobia". *Andrei Rublev* fits within several conceptual frameworks that could provide an adequate reading: the Western culture of the German Romantics, a set of attributes of an alchemist and European mystic, an encyclopedic dictionary. Many critics, knowing of Tarkovsky's passion for the East and Zen Buddhism, found distinct traces of these philosophies in the film. As it turned out, Tarkovsky had not been unaware of Egyptian mythology and Taoism. Certainly no one doubts that Andrei Tarkovsky's language of film had absorbed the poetry of Arseny Tarkovsky, the impact of medieval iconography, music and the fine arts.

The search for hidden meanings in Tarkovsky's films — after *Andrei Rublev,* he made five more films with his characteristic style featuring a cryptic subtext — continues. It seems that the whole world has embraced this deep, comprehensive look at the film that refers to its higher meaning, to a transcendent God. This means that Tarkovsky succeeded in reaching his goals, to get people to look into the misty depths of the universe and the human spirit — and once they've looked into these, to ponder them.

4.

When *Andrei Rublev* was finished and the first version shown to the studio heads, they demanded Tarkovsky make 26 cuts.

The director, who had expected a triumph, was stunned. His neurosis was inflamed by constant outbursts of anger and irritability. It was hard to get close to Tarkovsky when he was in this thundering rage. Only with effort could Larisa keep Andrei from clashing with the authorities, refusing to let him out of the house.

His co-author on the apparently unnecessary script, Konchalovsky, tried to calm him down. They met on neutral ground, in the park of the Exhibition of Achievements of the National Economy.

"My god, this is where we need to film the city of the future," Andron said, looking at the outdoor pavilions with exaggerated amazement like a visitor to the capital. "By the way, in Alexandrov's film *The Shining Path* the ending, which crowns the weaver's career, was shot here. Dunayevsky's score was brilliant, remember? 'Greetings, land of heroes, land of explorers, land of scientists!' Orlova sings, flying down the road in a black sedan, about all these wonders."

"In my opinion, this fake Potemkin village has nothing to do with art. Want to have a smoke?" Andrei had noticed a secluded bench under an arbor covered with roses.

"Let's just pop into the Zolotoi Kolos restaurant after we talk. If we've got some work done, can't we eat something decent?"

"Just send the bill to Mosfilm and say that it is money spent on 'fixing Tarkovsky'. They've drawn up a list of 26 areas for shortening the film. Did they hire you to persuade me to do it?"

Andron sat down on the bench and put one leg on the other. "I'm not bothered by the mentally unstable. You've been traumatized, you're got a right to strike out."

"Twenty-six!"

"Just like the 26 Baku Commissars. They gave you this number deliberately."

"You're acting like a provincial master of ceremonies."

"Where have you seen them? But to give you a clue about the aforementioned character, I'll tell you a story. Armenian Radio asks, 'What's the difference between a problem and a catastrophe? The answer is, the flowerpot falls from Academy member Arapetian's balcony with his favorite flowers in it and breaks, that is a problem, but it's not a catastrophe. If our dear, beloved government goes on an airplane, and the airplane crashes, that's a catastrophe, but it's not a problem!'"

In fact, one could be sentenced to prison for such a joke.

"I don't like these attacks on the government and all the other 'pearls' of Armenian Radio," Andrei said, without the slightest hint of a smile. "I think we were talking about my film,"

"About the cuts, this is a problem, but it's not a catastrophe! Old friend, you can see for yourself that making cuts to the film would be good for it. God, how I slashed the length of my own *The Story of Asya Klyachina*! It was a bloody task, but I still think it was the best thing I've ever done."

"Of course you slashed it, it was shelved."

"I saved it! And trust me, the cuts didn't make it worse. Now I know, if you want to achieve a greater effect, you should certainly cut the running time!"

"No way! I'm doing it in a different way. In order to strengthen the effect, I slow the rhythm. My ideal is Andy Warhol's *Sleep*," a challenge could be heard in Andrei's sarcastic declarations. Andron tried not to succumb to his provocation. He wanted to convince his friend.

"Ah, yes, the famous piece by the eccentric genius. For the whole course of the film, someone is sleeping and the camera follows this process."

"That's it. But the only time he rolls over, we perceive it like the climax of the film."

"Isn't there very little meaning in such a protracted joke? And to be honest, there are places in *Andrei Rublev* which you could cut entirely without compromising what you are trying to express. Forgive me, but those long shots and some of the dialogue seem disappointingly pretentious to me."

Andrei stiffened. He had already swallowed his anger at Andron's initial provocations and tried to get by without a fight. It was a normal conversation between these friends.

"I tried with all my might to make it simpler. Only the basic unvarnished truth remained!" He bit his nails, holding back his growing resentment.

"Simpler? You don't even realize how seriously you relate to yourself and everything you do. That lack of irony and self-deprecation is a dangerous symptom."

"Yes, my films are not comedies. They already asked me at Goskino, 'Why is everything so gloomy with you?' I told them, 'If you want to laugh, go see a comedy.'"

"You've got a brilliant knack for setting officials against themselves, but they decide the fate of the film, and you kick the ball into your own goal!"

"The audience is on my side. These right here!" He pointed at some girls walking by.

"You remembered the audience? Ha, you seem to have spit on every way of drawing an audience."

"A man should learn to work on himself. To delve into the meaning placed into the film." Andrei repeated his credo in the strict tone of a schoolmaster.

"Think about what happens: you dig so deep and are so afraid of something so base as being easily understood that you only obscure the meaning. Your picture is a tiresome search for something that can't be expressed in words and is as unintelligible as a cow's mooing."

"I've heard you draw comparisons to a cow before."

"You'll hear them from others too. Look, my dear friend, first you took from the script its backbone of clear meaning. Everything began to drift, lost its outlines, and once deprived of intelligibility, it became something indistinct. This is how it ended up, the unintelligible mooing of a cow who knows something of colossal importance."

"I understand what you're getting at with this. But concreteness, clarity of meaning — all of those are secondary products of the spirit. They are deceptive. One ought to draw from the bottom of the source, somewhere that isn't blurred by emotions."

"Everything will remain untapped if you don't manage to draw the viewer into your game. Pushkin, who was not prone to compromising his art, said, 'The people, like children, have to be entertained. Laughter, pity and terror are the three chords of our imagination that make for dramatic enchantment.'"

"Can we sit down with you guys? We'll eat ice cream and listen to you talk about Pushkin!" A vivacious girl in a colorful bell skirt and plastic clip-on earrings, who bore a strong resemblance to Valentina Malyavina, pushed her friend forward. Both of the girls were enjoying popsicles.

"Aren't you an actress?" Andron put on a deliberate amazement. "I've seen you and your friend somewhere before. At Mosfilm! Look, my friend is a noted director. He can put you in his next comedy."

"Andron, stop mocking me. This is a serious conversation." Tarkovsky got up and walked along the path hung with roses, wearing a fashionable jacket and Polish jeans. Andron, who was also wearing jeans, but original American ones with a Super Lee label, walked behind him, slightly shuffling his imported moccasins.

"Oh, Galka," they heard the girl squeal behind them. "Look at how stylish these guys are!" They assumed a dignified air, but Andrei was not put out by the beauties.

"You keep coming down hard on me! You either drag in Armenian

Radio or Pushkin. Look, I don't care what an audience thinks of a given scene. It's enough that I know how it affects me personally," he exaggeratedly tapped himself on the chest.

"In that case, Andrei, it is suicide! And don't thump your chest so expressively. The fuzz will get you for it. We've come to a cultured place, a place of recreation for the 'people' you so love."

"Stop clowning around! It would be suicide to cut those twenty-six scenes."

"Just get rid of the parts that you don't like yourself. Then, the requirement is technically met. If they don't buzz off, you can fight for whatever remains in the film."

Andrei, who was seething with barely suppressed anger, suddenly burst out in mephistophelian laughter. "All right, I understood correctly that Goskino has sent you to persuade me to make cuts to the film. Traitor! Yes, yes you are. You want to ruin my picture." Andrei set upon Andron with raised fists.

"I'd love to give you a good thrashing right now," Andron said as he quickly walked away down the alley, away from the temptation to smack this budding messiah right in his ugly little mustache. "Farewell, genius."

Konchalovsky would go on to write in his memoirs, "He was often an unpleasant man, angry and harsh. From behind all that, a strong conviction showed through, that everything ought to be done just the way he was doing it."

5.

Scandal hung over *Andrei Rublev* from the start, a sign that Tarkovsky had indeed done something extraordinary. Some were choked with envy, some were truly indignant, and for some the new film aesthetic was simply over their head. Many others, considering themselves followers of the avant-garde, were simply ashamed to talk about the boredom and annoyance they had experienced during those long hours in front of the screen. To criticize Tarkovsky in "progressive" circles was equal to admitting one's own lack of taste, backwardness. For some reason hardly anyone committed a slip of the tongue and let themselves acknowledge the phenomenon as a remarkable one, but not appealing to them personally: "That's great, but it's not to my taste." In order to discern the quality in this rejected work of art, one had to be an expert.

There were few such people among the apparatchiks overseeing films, and they did not have a commanding role. A few of them might have been among the audience as well.

In August 1966, when editing was finished, Andrei started on a long road of struggle and defeat. Of the twenty-six cuts demanded of him, Tarkovsky made eighteen, and the film benefited from them. He refused to cut the film further and thus damage its meaning.

In the beginning, Andrei thought that the complications that arose from *Andrei Rublev* were the meddling of some stupid, despotic officials or the result of backstage intrigue by the venerable old directors who did not like him. However, the atmosphere was becoming heated and came to involve the authorities at higher and higher levels.

Alexei Romanov, the Minister for Films, initially looked favorably at *Andrei Rublev*, but after the first screening of the picture for the studio bosses, reproach rained down on his friends and crew. Some accused the director of Slavophilia, while others on the contrary accused him of Russophobia. The tabloids published articles about horrible things that had happened on the set of *Andrei Rublev*. Even before the screening, gossip spread that during filming, Tarkovsky had almost deliberately burned down the Dormition Cathedral in Vladimir, had set fire to cows and had broken the legs of horses. The producer, Tamara Ogorodnikova, completely dedicated to the film and its director, explained to all authorities that the cow was covered in an asbestos coat, that the horse had been taken from a slaughterhouse and was in any case doomed, that under the roof of the church feathers and rags had accidentally caught fire from the smoke set up by pyrotechnicians. Nonetheless, the situation grew tense. Romanov's support began to waver, as he did not know which position to take.

The first screening took place at Moscow's Dom Kino cinema. It was shown three times and the future of the film depended on its performance here. However, these screenings were only a prelude to his disgrace, the conspiracy of press silence about the film.

The first public showing of *Andrei Rublev* for film professionals was held in the main hall at Mosfilm. This day, which Tarkovsky had awaited for so long, dashed his expectations. His cherished dreams of triumph turned to disaster. The lights went out in the hall filled with his friends, colleagues and studio staff. The opening of the film went by in a tense silence, but as the various scenes were shown, which had already been labeled "cruel" and "naturalistic", there was a roar of righteous indignation, at times descending into booing. A loud shout from one of Mosfilm managers sounded like a verdict: "This isn't art, it's sadism!"

The film ended and the gloomy audience headed for the doors. Tarkovsky, pale and tense, stood alone at the exit from the hall. He remained alone as the people walking by avoided his glance and tried to go around him. Konchalovsky also left without hiding his disappointment in the film.

Only Olga Surkova and her mother came to shake Tarkovsky's hand and thank him for the film. It was clear that *Andrei Rublev* was going to be shelved.

Yevgeny Surkov, a critic sympathetic to Tarkovsky and at the time the head of the Script-Editing Collegium of the Cinematographic Committee, tried to save the film and showed it to members of the Central Committee. Leading directors attended this screening, including Leonid Ilyichev, Filip Yermash and Georgi Kunitsyn. They discussed the film offhand and sent a transcript of the meeting to the Central Committee.

During the discussion, many directors expressed their excitement and someone called Tarkovsky the "new Eisenstein". Unfortunately, Mikhail Romm stayed at his dacha and did not attend, not out of fear of displeasing the authorities, but because he was among those who genuinely did not like *Andrei Rublev*. Tarkovsky was offended by his teacher and never forgave him this "betrayal".

He also did not forgive Andron's arrogance. They met soon after the screening like two men at a duel, ready to fight to the death. In a yard along one of the Mosfilm streets, a caretaker was sweeping bright-yellow ash-tree leaves with a rustle, and a girl was riding a tricycle while her mother sat knitting and keeping an eye on her.

"You've betrayed me. After the showing at Mosfilm you pointedly turned away, and everyone saw it. Do you want to curry favor with the higher-ups?"

"Knock it off. You yourself know that that's not it. I can announce even on the radio that you messed up the script! There's nothing left of it, just tatters, and it is all shot at a snail's pace!"

"Tell me the truth, you're afraid to defend me in front of that herd rising against me!"

"That's not fair!" Andron sat down on a bench. "Why should you vent your anger at me? I always tried to impress upon you that such a plodding pace is suicide for a director. You only end up with an empty room."

"I know that you need action, sentimentality, entertainment value. Your aim is to seduce the audience. How vulgar it is, just like your fringe leather jacket."

"Goodbye," Andron said and stood up. "I'm not going to have this kind of conversation. Besides, there's nothing to talk about." He left without saying goodbye and shaking Tarkovsky's hand.

"Hey!" Andrei shouted at Andron's back draped with a stylish jacket. "You know that we've never had anything in common besides a love of expensive and fashionable clothes. Just remember that!"

From that day on, they tried to avoid one another.

Andrei Rublev was shelved. All of Tarkovsky's petitions to make another film were denied. He found himself practically without a job and lived with Irma and his son in poverty. The rare visitors to his home, a small apartment in front of the Kursky railway station, were shocked by how poor this director was, when his name was known throughout the country and abroad. A playpen stood in the center of the room, full of books. In one corner there was a cot, and in another a table with a kitchen stool. The wall was covered in a zigzag of broken plaster. "They've been looking for wiring installed in there," Andrei explained. Some withered flowers stood in jars. That was his entire decor, the dwelling of an outcast persecuted by the government, a dissident pariah.

In his experiences with society and politics, Tarkovsky never raised a storm and never sought to tangle with anyone. He did not take part in any protests and did not sign any letters. He was afraid of ruining his reputation as someone dedicated to his country. He avoided Western journalists who posed provocative questions, and avoided making any statement that could be ambiguous in a political sense. The ways of Yuri Lyubimov, who turned every premiere into a scandal for the state, were not his style.

He demonstrated his loyalty, but the authorities did not appreciate his actions or even understand them. Being truly afraid of the uncanny power of his films and the unpredictability of the scandalous film director, they tried to cut off his oxygen supply. He wanted in fact to be treated kindly by the authorities, to be successful and bask in honors and praise. He wanted to have all the signs of success a "prominent figure of Soviet art" could have: a country house, a car, trips to film festivals, travel permits. The state of an outcast who invited the fear and contempt of those in power, was a noble state indeed, but not favorable for a happy life and creative energies. Even the Master, the protagonist of Mikhail Bulgakov's famous novel, who was a man of the highest spirituality and who had glorified the last journey of the poor Yeshua, dreamed about fame, decent clothes, dinners at Griboyedov's house, about "literati shaking hands with him in awe".

As Mayakovsky proclaimed, "I want to be understood by my country!" Tarkovsky also wanted to be understood and welcomed in the circle of the elect. It is unlikely that any artist who couldn't overcome being misunderstood, wanted to "pass through their native land to one side like a shower of slanting rain."

It happened, however, that without Tarkovsky's knowledge, *Andrei Rublev* crossed the Russian border and took the West by storm. As a result, its creator gained a reputation, perfectly reasonable in those years, of a "slippery figure".

6.

In the winter of 1966 in the screening room of Soyuzeksportfilm, *Andrei Rublev* was shown to Sergio Gambarov, the president of a West Berlin film distribution company, and Alex Moskovich, co-owner of a French distribution company and representative of Soyuzeksportfilm, which sold films to France, Switzerland, Spain, Portugal, and local collaborators. All of these professionals knew that Tarkovsky had shot something interesting and scandalous, but they were shocked by what they saw.

They were fascinated by the epic scope of the film, even without clarification of its uncertain idea. There were obvious signs that this would be a film of the highest rank: its new approach to a historical theme, its harsh realism, its innovative language, and the establishment of an oppressive atmosphere with a stunning breakthrough to the light in the brilliantly constructed ending.

Alex Moskovich broke the silence, "We're dealing with a potential winner of the Grand Prix at Cannes." Only Viktor Roshchin, a consultant for the Western European division of Soyuzeksportfilm who knew what kind of reputation the film had at the highest levels, looked at everyone with surprise. Indeed, Vladimir Baskakov, who had the last word in the policy of the USSR State Committee for Cinematography, had advised everyone not to say a word about the film to foreigners. The apparatchiks who ignored this "advice" and defended the film, suffered for it and were declared anathema.

However, these foreigners decided to fight for the film through Paris with the help of Cannes Film Festival director Robert Favre Le Bret, influential cultural figures, French Minister for Cultural Affairs André Malraux and others. Tarkovsky was known abroad, as his first film had been a sensation. Furthermore, everyone knew that in Soviet film history, talent often reached screens through recognition in the

West. Kalatozov's *The Cranes are Flying*, Chukhrai's *Ballad of a Soldier*, Iosseliani's *Falling Leaves*, Parajanov's *Shadows of Forgotten Ancestors* and Konchalovsky's *The First Teacher* were unveiled domestically only after they had won recognition at European film festivals.

In March, Favre Le Bret came to Moscow to choose films for the festival. The State Committee for Cinematography refused to show *Andrei Rublev* to him, claiming that the film was not ready yet. Favre Le Bret managed to see some raw footage and was stunned by the film. However, his negotiations with the Soviets about nominating the film for competition proved fruitless. They sent Sergei Yutkevich's *Lenin in Poland* instead.

"This regime doesn't have long to live. It's stupid," said Alex Moskovich about the Soviet underhandedness with showing *Andrei Rublev*.

The next year the French decided to renew their fight for the film. At the end of March 1969 a miracle happened: the leadership of Soyuzeksportfilm approved the sale of the picture to France.

Favre Le Bret still wanted *Andrei Rublev* to compete at Cannes, but then, like in a bad thriller, special representatives came from Moscow with Alexei Romanov, then President of Goskino, as their head. The Soviet embassy in France gave a dinner in honor of their guests, where the Soviet comrades told the French minister André Malraux that, unfortunately, the film had already been sold to the French company DIS, and thus the Soviets had lost the rights to show the film at the festival.

Upon hearing the announcement Malraux, a man of high European bearing, remarked with a smile, "Well then, ladies and gentlemen, we will ask DIS to show the film at the festival out of competition. You wanted to use the sale of the film to avoid presenting it within the competition program. We will play our game at a higher level. We'll arrange some special out-of-competition screenings at the Palais des Festivals. They will create some buzz around the premieres."

Before the opening of the festival, the Soviet leadership undertook various efforts to disrupt the showing, but the French stuck to their plan. Sent by Moscow to present the film, the Deputy President of the

USSR State Committee for Cinematography, the famous documentary filmmaker Anatoly Dmitrievich Golovnya, left the festival after he learned of the plot against Tarkovsky. He said, "I am a Russian and I must share the tragic fate of art in my country." He understood that he had been sent to the festival as a scapegoat.

The French carefully prepared for the screening of the film. Posters of a burning icon, illustrated booklets and pamphlets about the makers of *Andrei Rublev* were released. These fueled interest in the already infamous film.

On the first day that *Andrei Rublev* was shown, a large crowd gathered on the festival grounds. The morning saw the arrival of representatives of the European press and accredited journalists from the United States, South America, Scandinavia, Japan and also the "socialist camp".

It became necessary to add two more showings on the Sunday of the festival. After the final shots of an iconostasis and stallions cantering on a green field, shouts of applause rose up in many languages. Some of the audience members openly wept.

The same thing happened during the following showings. The triumph of the Soviet director was mentioned in newspapers around the world. Only the media in the USSR remained silent, in spite of the presence of correspondents from *Pravda*, *Izvestiya* and *Literaturnaya Gazeta* at the festival.

The president of Soyuzeksportfilm found himself besieged by distributors wanting to buy the film. He managed to negotiate the sale of *Andrei Rublev* to the owner of a leading Western European film company for an enormous sum. Alex Moskovich and Leonid Brenes drew up a contract.

The buzz surrounding the film lasted until the end of the festival. Sadly, this went on without the filmmaker and his cast and crew, who had remained in Moscow, but Alex Moskovich telephoned Tarkovsky to tell him of his success. At the end of the festival, the out-of-competition film was awarded the FIPRESCI Prize of the International Federation of Film Critics.

At the end of the summer, copies of the film were sent out to larger French cinemas. *Andrei Rublev* sold out for an entire year. The highest praise of the film appeared in the media. Tarkovsky was called the successor of Eisenstein and Dovzhenko.

In the USSR there was still a conspiracy of silence. Not a single positive review could break through the wall of censorship. Only thanks to the heroic efforts of individual critics and publishers could one manage to get around the obstacles in place and get a real appraisal of the film into print.

The Soviet leadership's insistent denial of *Andrei Rublev* is fully understandable. Yes, there are no openly anti-Soviet statements in the film, but everyone understood that it presents their motherland's history in a less than positive light, with no patriotic tone to it. Tarkovsky's fellow filmmakers, feeling left out, enthusiastically supported the authorities. It was clear to them that Tarkovsky had broken through to the international filmmaking avant-garde and ranked with Fellini, Bergman and Bresson. Out of envy, Tarkovsky's peers supported the war against him.

It eventually became known that Demichev had decided to sell the film to other countries and had given appropriate guidance to Romanov in the presence of Kulidzhanov. The apparatchiks, however, could not allow this ideologically ambiguous film to leave the country. Chief Ideologue Mikhail Suslov spoke very negatively about *Andrei Rublev*. He banned the domestic release of the film and cancelled the decision to sell the film to other countries. Soyuzeksportfilm had to terminate their contract and pay millions of rubles in penalties. As a result, Alex Moskovich refused to work with the Soviet Union ever again, and Tarkovsky's hopes at winning the gold at a festival were dashed.

7.

Tarkovsky was encouraged by foreign filmmakers' interest in *Andrei Rublev*, but the opposition at the Mosfilm screenings and the hounding in the press had dealt him a heavy blow. After yearning to see his film on screens and to evoke an amazed response from viewers, he now understood that he was not making films for himself and a few friends alone, but for a wide audience of thousands. True, he did not lure viewers into cinemas with proven techniques, but he waited and waited such that he would find like-minded people who would be struck by the piercing tragedy in the film, by the depth of its expression.

Tarkovsky was not attracted by the honor of being put into the penalty box like the Soviet Union's brightest and most clever artists. He was not among those who sought the laurels of being an outcast. On the contrary, he envied the reception of Bondarchuk's works which drew roaring applause. After the triumph of *War and Peace*, which won an Oscar in 1969, it seemed like it would be hard to surprise foreign audiences. This epic film was shown in a hundred and seventeen countries and baby girls were named Natasha around the world. *Andrei Rublev* remained suppressed, kept away from audiences at home and abroad. As it turned out, however, highly talented and influential figures in the world of cinema were fighting for the film. This meant that Tarkovsky was not walking alone down a mistaken path.

Only in October 1968 did *Andrei Rublev* get a meager run on Soviet screens. Copies were sent to remote cinemas, but even this, together with his great success in Cannes, proved sufficient to win Tarkovsky both enthusiastic fans and bitter enemies. In our time such a scandalous "campaign" surrounding the film would be considered good PR. In this era of stagnation, however, such "promotion" did not help the director. On the contrary, it put him on the list of the unwanted and cut off his access to work. Tarkovsky's applications for new films were denied, leaving him penniless and dependent on the pity of higher-ups. Supporters who rushed to defend the film and its director were denied space in the press. The conspiracy of silence was rigorously monitored: one could either write something bad about Tarkovsky or write nothing at all. There were a lot of bad things said about the film and its director. *Andrei Rublev* was declared the ravings of a madman, a schoolboy's hopeless attempt at making something meaningful and surpassing the masters. The filmmaker was declared an opportunist who wanted to impress the West with his lunatic innovations. When foreign critics got their hands on a copy of the film, they cheered, "Look at what a great artist the Soviets are keeping down."

"What do I get out of all this buzz?" Andrei threw down the newspapers that Olga had brought with articles about him. As he did not speak foreign languages, Olga translated the most interesting bits. But now the enthusiasm of the foreign press angered Andrei. After all, he had been counting on the grand prize at the Cannes Film Festival, which would bring a significant amount of money. He could have used that money now as he sat around for already the second year without work.

While the international film community dined at Cannes and debated the Soviet director, Tarkovsky was facing hard times. Besides his disgrace, he was not happy with events in his personal life. The only positive thing was the marriage of Sergei (the nephew of Larisa Kizilova) to Olga Surkova, although that Sergei was a dubious guy anyway. But Tarkovsky did not have time to bother about all that. He was torn between his family, Larisa who was expecting a child, and a number of fleeting affairs with other women. His hopes of finding a woman who would be a slavishly loyal companion, devoid of any personal interests besides supporting her family, did not materialize. Every woman who crossed his path was initially in love with him and devoted to him with all her heart, but gradually turned cold and did not provoke a response in him. They were basically bitches.

Andrei was convinced of this, not even aware that he himself did not know how to love. He was filled with other drives, toward filmmaking. Frequent and messy attractions came into his life and were just as quickly forgotten.

Two women stood beside him at the end of the 1960s: Irma Tarkovskaya with their son Arseny, who continued to selflessly love the husband that had abandoned her, and the pregnant Larisa Kizilova, desperate to have the director for herself, and strongly counting on the future of his career. Larisa knew how to play dirty and did not hold back from any way of denigrating Irma and destroying their union.

Andrei, who had already fallen in love with Larisa during the filming of *Andrei Rublev*, was drawn into a vortex of little affairs and was not ready to make drastic changes in his personal life.

Larisa fought hard to marry Andrei and turned a blind eye to his affairs, taming him by keeping him at home and by excessive doting. She found ways to get to him through his stomach and the bed, using flattery and maternal affection. She even used overt intimidation — but not by means of the Party Committee; as Andrei was not a member of the Party, he was not vulnerable to such threats. She threatened him with talk of aliens.

She lived at that time with her daughter Olga and her mother at her sister Antonina's home, a two-room apartment on Zvezdny Boulevard. Antonina's two sons Alexei and Sergei were also cooped together with them, and Olga Surkova too, after she married Sergei. Larisa's mother, Anna Semyonovna, a quiet woman in a dressing gown and round glasses with thick lenses, huddled ceaselessly over the sewing machine, as she wasn't a fashion designer, as Larisa would say, but a woman working from home. She not only made and mended clothes for the whole family, but she also managed to make some money from private orders that she kept hidden from the authorities. Everyone loved hardworking little old Anna Semyonovna. Andrei adored her and when he returned from his drinking bouts he would even get down on his knees and ask for her forgiveness.

A frying pan stood on the stove day and night, with fried potatoes, which the same wonderful woman cooked in a steady stream.

They gave newlyweds Olga and Sergei the small room. In the big room, when Andrei was not around, Anna Semyonovna and Antonina, Alexei and Larisa's daughter lived. When the maestro appeared, a bed was prepared for him and Larisa under the kitchen table.

He would appear suddenly, during one of his periodic "maelstoms of feelings". Larisa tried to find out the places he frequented and the names of her rivals, whether by peaceful means or by becoming hysterical and causing a deafening argument. Sometimes, after heavy drinking, her Casanova would call her from somewhere and ask her to come and get him. She would pick him up, give him a scolding, say all is forgiven and go back to taking care of him, because she was sure that her game was worth such hassles.

Olga Surkova has recounted one of the idyllic scenes from the maestro's stay with the family.

Late in the evening, the large family gradually went to bed. Andrei took a bath and put on a striped terrycloth robe, from under which his thin sinewy legs stuck out. On his head he wore a handkerchief with knots tied at its corners, which held back his stubborn wet hair. Below the handkerchief was his sharply delineated and childishly helpless face with his bristling whiskers. Looking like a bankrupt billionaire, Andrei sat cross-legged on the bed on the kitchen floor and majestically invited Olga and Sergei to sit with him. He would then open a volume of Pushkin, Tyutchev or Pasternak, but more often he would read poems by his father. Thus would begin a long evening of conversation.

Peaceful evenings would alternate with savage arguments and festive appearances among society — Andrei would take Larisa to the Dom Kino cinema or the Central House of Writers. Anna Semyonovna sewed stunning "foreign" suits with extremely wide shoulders and bell-bottom trousers. Andrei looked elegant next to his companion, who appeared in her full battle gear with pounds of makeup, eyelashes heavy from mascara, in a fashionable dress (which her mother had also sewn) and always wearing a hat (an accessory she loved dearly). They did not, in any case, match each other at all, looking like people from two different pictures. Larisa looked more vulgar, larger and older than her companion. Next to her, Tarkovsky seemed more like a provincial general and not an extravagant intellectual from the capital.

Larisa's tolerance of Andrei's cheating was not endless. She ecstatically threw herself into her own affairs which Andrei had no idea about. Sometimes it seemed that this vulgar woman was, in reality, indifferent and even unpleasant to him. But something held him fast to this woman bursting with energy. To a large extent it was her practicality, her ability to adapt to every circumstance, to take care of him. Infantile and completely helpless, Tarkovsky belonged to a category of people who could die of hunger next to a full refrigerator. Larisa organized the everyday matters of their life, and it was obvious that the cramped apartment on Zvezdny Boulevard was far from her ideal, but only a temporary solution, which had to be put up with. Her greatest hope was for a prosperous future, which meant that she placed all her hopes on Andrei.

Larisa's efforts bore fruit. At the end of 1969, she announced that she was pregnant and her doctor forbade her from having an abortion. Andrei understood that he had to make a choice.

By that time his relationship with Irma had become even more complicated. The reason was not so much Andrei's affairs and double-life as the growing opposition between them. Andrei was more and more insistent that she forget about directing, as in his opinion this was strictly a man's job. Irma started acting in films, though she had never been passionate about acting professionally. After *Andrei Rublev* she played an important role in *Doctor Vera*, based on a novel by Boris Polevoy. She became however, more and more angry at Andrei for making her give up directing. It was impossible to argue with him about this subject — Irma felt completely untalented. She often thought about Maria Ivanovna and compared her own fate with that of Andrei's mother. Maria Ivanovna told her daughter-in-law that at some moment her husband's talent had undermined her own self-confidence. Next to him, she did not seem especially talented, and she decided to devote herself to her children. Irma could not accept a similar fate. She went off to film shoots, and Andrei also spent a lot of time scouting locations. Ultimately it became clear that their marriage was being torn apart. However, the deterioration of their marriage was long and difficult, since they remained friends and eight year-old Arseny was very attached to his father. Andrei, on the other hand, did not have the slightest idea of how to relate to children. He would philosophize and share with his son his thoughts about the most complex issues, without taking his son's age into account.

The boy listened to him attentively and felt flattered by his father's attention and adult way of talking.

They officially divorced in 1970. Irma was hired at the Gorky film studio, where her good friend Vasily Shukshin was working at the time. She began to make children's films, happy and sunny, as she had once dreamed. Larisa, on the other hand, gave birth to a son in August 1970 and named him Andrei in honor of his father. They would seal their relationship only in the following year.

Surkov, Olga's father, had to leave his post as head of Goskino to become the chief editor of *Iskusstvo Kino*. This was the price he paid for his defence of *Andrei Rublev*. Soon after, Olga divorced Sergey and their relationship with the Tarkovskys cooled.

8.

Thus a boy was born to Andrei and Larisa, and the living situation became even more cramped. Larisa and her mother owned two more rooms jointly with a neighbor on Orlovo-Davydovsky Lane. After the death of their elderly neighbor, Larisa came to own their flat in the old five-story building from the 1930s. Nevertheless, Anna Semyonovna, Larisa's daughter Olga and little Andrei had to live squeezed into the farther room. That gave Andrei his own office, in which only the wide ottoman gave a hint of a married couple's bedroom. In the dining room, with its sideboard and rectangular table, which Larisa covered with fine food on days that guests visited, they could often organize the gatherings which the lady of the house loved.

Andrei seemed like a random visitor, guilty and ill at ease in the new apartment. From time to time he sank into adultery, and sometimes the affairs were quite serious. Through this he almost married a teacher named Daria who lived in Leningrad. Larisa felt obliged to deprecate that unknown woman incessantly in order to pull her husband back. She even demanded that Andrei throw the engagement ring that he intended to give Daria into the Moscow River. .

Tarkovsky, jobless, was having a hard time of it and made desperate efforts to make films. He wrote application after application for various films and got only a succession of rejections.

At the time that he considered an application for *Solaris*, Andrei was fascinated by science-fiction and occult literature. Larisa felt that her impressionable husband was beginning to believe in aliens, magic, spells and fortune-telling. She began to impress upon him her own powers of witchcraft. She told everyone with utter credibility how, in her early childhood, she had been abducted from her baby stroller on the balcony by strange people in spacesuits, and from that time she felt an ability to affect people around her by sheer power of thought, often against her intentions.

For Andrei, watching his wife's frequent transformation from an angel to a demon, it was not hard to believe that he was dealing with a witch. The screenplay that was first entitled *The Witch*, was later called *The Sacrifice*. There was a witch who helped to cure the soul of the protagonist, and he believed in the one that he had at home like a good fairy. More often, however, he was afraid of her.

"Honey," Larisa went into Andrei's office and put her arms around his neck while he was sitting at the desk in an armchair. He involuntarily moved away from her. Larisa sat on the edge of the desk. "I didn't want to tell you too much. You might have thought that it was only the ravings of a stupid woman. But now," she looked at the book he was reading (a collection of Stanisław Lem's stories), "when you have advanced on your path of understanding the complexity of the universe" — she had read the foreword to the book in the morning and knew a lot of right words — "I would like to tell you something. Why don't we sit on the ottoman? Do you have a cigarette?"

After they made themselves comfortable on the ottoman with cigarettes and an ashtray, they began to smoke, enveloping Larisa's story in a mysterious haze.

"So, my dear, you, as an artist who absorbs all unusual details, should know that..." Larisa paused lifting her blue eyes to the ceiling. "Do you remember how the actress Mikaela Drozdovskaya got burned on set? You will say it was an accident? Alas, it was not an accident. She deeply offended me and I was careless, and I was cursing her in my thoughts and wishing her all kinds of terrible things."

"Hmm…" Andrei lay down on the colorful pillows, made from scraps and old neckties by his mother-in-law. "So what? We often think about someone, 'Damn you!' and don't see that this desire has come true, or we tell them to go to hell!"

"Oh, you confuse everything! You are you, and I am me. Remember, when that black horse bolted on you at the set of *Andrei Rublev*? I wasn't there. But right then I was bitterly upset at your relationship with Irma. You praised her and looked at her with implied intent. You desired her…"

"Irma handled her role perfectly."

"I could have done it too! You didn't even think, how your refusal to give me part of Durochka could have hurt me? How much I cried then. Anyway, the black horse and your sudden whim to jump on its back, and your foot that got stuck in the stirrup… Forgive me, Andrei, please forgive me! I keep forgetting what powers I possess. Then I sincerely repented, but it was too late. My being offended was the reason for your fall." Having finished her terrifying confession, she covered her face with her hands.

"Yes, it's strange. But I rode horses before, and nothing like that had ever happened. That horse reared like the devil!"

"Exactly! Like the devil. Trust me, Andrei, you have to be careful." Larisa lay alongside her husband, stroking his hair. "Don't offend me, okay? Darling, I am devoted to you with all my soul. If I have to, I will take a bullet for you. But that unconscious will to defend myself — it's stronger than me! It's as if someone is protecting me from above."

They came to have such conversations often. As soon as something bad happened to someone around Tarkovsky, Larisa broke into tears and confessed that the tragedy was payback for a conflict with her.

Later, when her niece who had worked on the set of *The Mirror*, fell under a train and lost a leg, nobody even had to prove that it was caused by Larisa's curse, as she had long carried a grudge against the injured woman.

"Well, what can I do?" Larisa exclaimed sadly, pressing herself to her husband's chest, as if seeking protection. "It's awful for me too, but that's how it always is! I don't want this to happen, but it doesn't depend on me!"

"That's completely true," Andrei agreed seriously. "Thugs had better keep away from you."

He was not joking. The seed cast by Larisa fell on fertile ground. Naturally suspicious and credulous, Tarkovsky believed in his lying spouse's tales.

Andrei told Olga Surkova about Larisa's abilities.

"I've already heard all of these stories," she answered sarcastically. "I'm trembling and full of wonder!"

"No, no. You shouldn't be laughing. Larisa is capable of anything. I'm afraid of her. It's true. One of our neighbors did something bad to her and he died completely unexpectedly. It's always like that! These can't be just dozens of coincidences! But I am under her protection. She would jump into a fire for me!"

"Why into the fire?" Olga sneered. "If Larisa can do everything, then why won't she deal with Ermash and your enemies?"

"Nonetheless," Andrei frowned, anxiously looked at the door, fearing that Larisa might have heard them.

It is said that when Andrei fell ill with cancer, he talked about how it was Larisa Pavlovna's handiwork. "She did it all to me." Even if she did not directly make him fall ill with cancer, she undoubtedly pushed him toward his illness, by shattering his overly sensitive nervous system and bringing it to a catastrophic state.

During the long hiatus that dragged on after *Andrei Rublev*, Tarkovsky decided to appeal to the head of the USSR, Leonid Brezhnev. He wrote the letter together with Olga Surkova, who had become Andrei's most trusted companion. The idea of writing the letter arose after Olga had read in the French Communist newspaper

L'Humanité that *Andrei Rublev* was the "film of films", just like the Bible was the Book of books, and that Tarkovsky's work ranked among the top one hundred achievements of world cinema. That was high praise, and it came when *Andrei Rublev* was being torn apart in his home country for its supposed inhuman and russophobic tone, and Tarkovsky was treated like an enemy.

"And also the *Cahiers du Cinema* called *Andrei Rublev* the best film of the year, while Fellini, by the way, took fourth place and Bergman sixteenth!" Olga shook some newspapers in front of Andrei's face. "This is an international triumph!"

Andrei frowned. "Complete nonsense! To give rankings to Fellini and Bergman, it's simply foolish and inappropriate."

"The French note the patriotism in your film, its kinship with the best of the Russian tradition!" Olga did not back down. "You should react to this, and the louder the better."

Andrei cut her off, "I won't make any kind of statement to foreign journalists, and our journalists aren't interested in me."

"They are very interested in you, but Tarkovsky is a subject that's off-limits. *Andrei Rublev* is a taboo that they are afraid to get close to. Fine, if they shut the journalists and critics up, let's go right over their heads and write a letter to Brezhnev!"

"You are hung up on this."

"Why? Let him see the film and decide for himself."

"Great, so *he* will see it. And they'll shoot me, I'm sure of it."

"They don't shoot people anymore."

They'll put me in prison.

"They won't put you in prison, you're too famous! Just emphasize yourself that you made an ideologically correct film, which glorifies your native land."

"Yes, well, I don't know myself. I don't know what is hidden there under all those layers."

"You must understand, there can be nothing that would contradict love toward humanity and the effort to make it perfect!"

Their argument resulted in a letter showing a fair amount of loyalty:

> Esteemed Leonid Ilyich:
> Hoping for your sincere interest in the fate of Soviet cinema, I have decided to turn to you with an inquiry to help you solve the difficult, even painful situation concerning our film *Andrei Rublev*.
>
> It has already been three and a half years and this film has still not been approved for release on Soviet screens. During that time, the makers of the film have already redone some parts of the film three times, and all three times the Committee for Cinematography signed statements that they accepted the film and then cancelled them.

They went on to mention that during that time, unbeknownst to Tarkovsky, *Andrei Rublev* reached foreign countries and gained there the most respectful and admiring comments about Soviet art. This was of course followed by a complaint about Tarkovsky's unemployment, connected to the ban on *Andrei Rublev*: "Meanwhile, not having a job, I consequently have no means for supporting myself, though I have a wife and child."

The experience of Mikhail Bulgakov and Anna Akhmatova in appealing to the head of the state had shown that at least the first appeal to the "hangman" was answered and had changed the catastrophic situation that these letter writers faced. Tarkovsky however did not receive any answer from the higher levels of government. The letter was most likely seized by the official channels that filtered correspondence to the General Secretary. But even if Brezhnev had gotten the letter, it is easy to guess what his reaction would be after he personally viewed the film or listened to the opinions of his advisors: extremely negative. That film could only evoke profound rejection in pro-Soviet officials with its foreign nature, incomprehensibility, and most of all, the sense of calamity, catastrophe. This Russia in ruins, even if it is illuminated by the light of the Trinity, clearly spoke not only to the present day, but also to the subsequent fate of Russia. That this was a godforsaken land was the conclusion of many people, even though they noted flashes of spirituality and the miracles of Boriska and Rublev. Hardly any officials saw the film to the end. It was enough for an experienced eye to glance at the screen and sense the "foreign tendencies and slandering of this great nation's history". The church through which snow drifts, the manic slaughter, the reckless and senseless cruelty, the incapability to do anything constructive (even the bell was cast with the help of foreigners) — none of this resembled patriotic glorification of the Russian spirit. It is strange that Tarkovsky hoped that the General Secretary would like his film and would rush to defend it.

Tarkovsky's applications for making films continued to be rejected. The family lived on the earnings of Anna Semyonovna, hunched over her old Singer sewing machine. Larisa, who was on the list of Mosfilm employees, was not keen on the idea of working. However, she soon learned how to find money, but she kept silent about its source. This consisted of poverty loans guaranteed by Tarkovsky's name and his forthcoming royalties. The Tarkovskys consequently ran up huge debts which they never repaid to anyone.

The situation became worse when a debt was discovered, amounting to 1200 rubles. This was an advance from the publishing house Iskusstvo, which Tarkovsky got for writing a book together with the noted film scholar Leonid Kozlov. After the publisher had received nothing before the deadline stipulated in the agreement, it demanded that Tarkovsky return the advance. The director's friends went into a panic and looked for money. The Surkovs gave two hundred rubles. Tarkovsky received considerable support from the critic Neya Markovna Zorkaya, a devoted fan of Tarkovsky's films and a defender of the rights of persecuted artists. Shut out from the Party, this dissident lived on scanty means, but she managed to borrow 600 rubles from Grigori Kozintsev, as well as pawn her Karakul fur coat. Thus paying off the debt to the publisher, Tarkovsky could renew the contract for his *Book of Concordances*. Now Olga Surkova became his co-author on an equal basis, and she immediately gave her part of the advance to the hard-up Tarkovsky.

Tarkovsky's relationships with friends resembled a landscape after a battle. Through Larisa's efforts, all of the friends he had going back to his studies at VGIK were driven away with the most destructive characterizations. It was easy to convince the suspicious and trusting Andrei how envious and mean his former colleagues were. Tarkovsky's mother and sister clearly disliked his new wife, while Larisa was no better and whispered to her husband about their scornful attitude toward him as a son and brother. Andrei increasingly distanced himself from his family.

Vladimir Vysotsky visited Tarkovsky a single time with Marina Vlady. Vladimir, who was "on the wagon" at the time, was quiet and deferential. Marina gently held his hand the entire time. Andrei was in a pleasant mood. He suggested to Marina that he would like her to play the Mother in a long-planned film about his childhood titled *The Confession*. Vladimir sang of course, but Andrei remained indifferent to Vysotsky's songs, giving them only a polite hearing; for him the sound of a guitar remained in the past with his student parties, and delicacy was in general not characteristic of Tarkovsky. An even more gloomy impression was made on the host by Vysotsky reciting his own poems based on *Hamlet*. The way in which Larisa Pavlovna acted politely and friendly emphasized to some degree how incompatible the natures of the host and the guest were. They did not visit again.

It is remarkable that this son of a poet, who had once adored poetry, was completely uninterested in the contemporary authors that fascinated Soviet people. He was not interested in Vladimir Vysotsky, Alexander Galich, Bulat Okudzhava, Andrei Voznesensky or Bella Akhmadulina. It was as if he existed in a world of his own, filled with images from the storehouse of his own memory, his own reflections. Perhaps he firmly believed that his father was the best poet of the age and was jealous of other developments in this field? Most likely, a mechanism of negation was engaged here, which worked in relation to Soviet cinema and film directors — in fact, to everything that was not directly related to his mission of creating utterly special films that did not deal with the superficial aspects of existence, but only with the profound workings of the spirit. A hermit-like mindset, his self-sufficiency, made his various interactions with reality an unnecessary impediment. His lack of interest in the social and political spheres, his childishness in practical matters, and his inability to connect with people — today these are among the traits that make up the disorder called autism. A mild degree of autism along with outstanding talents, even genius, is what a contemporary psychologist would diagnose.

Chapter 6.
SOLARIS, EARTHLY AND COSMIC LOVE

I.

Unable to film any picture, Tarkovsky was bursting with ideas: he dreamt of a film adaptation of Dostoyevsky, of E. T. A. Hoffmann and especially of a film about his own childhood. He submitted a screenplay entitled *Confession* several times (the film would later be called *The Mirror*, but he received only rejections. Giving lectures at the Higher Directors' Courses helped him get by. He became inspired when he spoke about the responsibilities of an artist as a leader for society, about the seriousness of his approach to his duty as an artist.

Faced with the task of "saving the world" either through social reconstruction or by spiritual self-perfection, a dilemma which confronted citizens of the USSR in the 1970s, Tarkovsky clearly preferred the latter. And in this he was at the forefront, allotting the role of leaders to artists, setting himself against the state and society or despising them and breaking ties with everyday thinking, which he saw as dangerous.

Unexpectedly, Tarkovsky broke through with his application for a screen adaptation of the novel *Solaris* by the famous Polish writer Stanisław Lem, which he made in collaboration with Friedrich Gorenstein. Word that Tarkovsky was to make a science-fiction film took many by surprise. Going from 15th-century Russia to a space station? It was all the more surprising because science-fiction is traditionally considered part of popular fiction, designed to attract an audience. Among science-fiction writers, Lem represented a serious, philosophical wing, which did not deprive the novel's plot of its attractiveness and even displayed features of another genre that Tarkovsky had rejected, the gothic novel.

"Among the stars the unknown awaits," was how the author explained the idea behind his novel written on the eve of the Space Age. For Tarkovsky the stellar unknown was primarily located on planet Earth, namely in the soul of everybody living on it.

The reader is intrigued by the premise of the novel: strange reports have come from a space station whose personnel have been trying to establish contact with the planet Solaris, which is covered by an intelligent ocean. The psychologist Kris Kelvin arrives at the station to understand the mysterious events happening there, and decides whether observation should continue, or whether the research should be ended and attempts to communicate with the alien planet abandoned.

Kelvin initially thinks that the personnel living on the station have gone mad. Something utterly strange is happening here, frighteningly obscure. Soon Kris himself becomes the victim of an obsession: he is visited by his former lover Hari, who had died on Earth by suicide. It is revealed that the aliens, which the ocean produces from the human astronauts' subconscious, have visited his colleagues too, embodying their shameful desires and drawing up their repressed feelings of guilt. Unable to ensure his feelings of remorse, one of them commits suicide. The others are on the brink of insanity.

Kris tries to rid himself of Hari, but she is resurrected from the dead three times, and each death awakens the wound in his heart afresh. Even when Kris learns that his former love consists of neutrinos, that is, she is only an illusion of a human being, he cannot hold back his awakened sense of compassion and guilt.

Those who did not care for Tarkovsky concluded that, after the failure of *Andrei Rublev*, he finally took a step closer to a wide audience with this film's captivating intrigue, secrets and melodrama. When Tarkovsky made the application for the film, he himself made it seem like he had learned his lesson after *Andrei Rublev* and wanted a second chance.

"The audience expects a good film in the science-fiction genre from us," he wrote in the application. "The plot of *Solaris* is sharp, intense, full of unexpected twists and exciting developments. We believe, first of all, that the film will be a box office success. The people of the future represent the ideal of moral purity, which our descendants will have to follow, to achieve victory in bettering themselves, in their sense of honor and morals..."

Tarkovsky wasn't too cunning. He had exaggerated in his arguments with Konchalovsky about recognition from the audience. In reality, he knew perfectly well, and with *Andrei Rublev* he felt it in full force, that a film which remains without an audience is an unrealized achievement, as if the film roll is kept in the canister, does not reach screens, and does not even exist. Indeed, audiences should not be afraid of "unintelligible mooing", though Tarkovsky was not going to entertain them either. A serious conversation about serious issues, about the most important thing, does not have to necessarily be presented as a dull lesson.

No matter how hard Tarkovsky tried to make a winning application for a film, he could not change himself, turn himself into a person with a different artistic approach. He had to hear the whispering of rain, the rustle of grass, see a whole array of possibilities in the shadows on the pavement, notice and place a multitude of details into the image on the screen, unnoticeable to an ordinary person's eye. Though the theme of a film could already be a keen one, it did not stop his search for that *terra incognita* in any way, the junction of the layers of creation, where an exchange of higher notions — not completely decipherable — takes place. Any natural phenomenon — fire, water, air, grass — was not just a feature of ordinary existence. It was a message of great meaning from beyond. The rain is not just rain, it is a force connecting heaven and earth, which gives life to the latter. There are many interpretations of the film, and Tarkovsky did not deny an ambiguity to it, a play of meanings.

Lem received his payment for the right to adapt his novel, and the director then began arguing with him for the right to make radical changes. In the novel, all the action takes place on the space station. In the screenplay, on the other hand, the story starts on Earth. Lem was firmly against this and demanded that his ideas be respected, but Tarkovsky insisted on his version. In general, he did not intend to — and was simply incapable of — filming someone else's work, just as he could not shoot a film from an off-the-shelf script. He was attracted the most by a project that was "based on" something, which turned a literary canvas into something of his own. In the end he managed to reach an agreement with Lem on how to implement the opening of the film on Earth.

Tarkovsky assembled a brilliant cast: Anatoly Solonitsyn, Donatas Banionis and Juri Järvet. For the main female role he thought about bringing on Margarita Terekhova, but suddenly another candidate appeared: Natalya Bondarchuk, the daughter of director Sergei Fedorovich Bondarchuk. Mikhail Romadin was hired as the main set designer of the film and Eduard Artemyev as the composer of the film score.

2.

"I bring misfortune to everyone, in love I feel more exhilarated than happy," he confessed to Natalya Bondarchuk after all that had happened between them.

During filming Andrei Tarkovsky was 39 years old, while Natalya Bondarchuk was 21.

The romantically-minded young lady had fallen in love with Tarkovsky already during the audition from the stern, boyish face of the nearly 40 year-old director, his stylish shirts from patterned fabric, masterfully sewn by Anna Semyonovna, and the piercing, somewhat strange look in his eyes. He gave cues to Natalya, who was standing in under a bright light.

"Please don't interrupt me. I'm a woman after all," she said resentfully, reading from the script.

"You're not a woman, and not a human being. Understand that," not quite correctly pronouncing the letter "l" in Russian, he argued relentlessly. "You're not Hari. You're just a reproduction, a mechanical reproduction. A copy. A matrix!"

"But I am becoming a human being. I can feel just as deeply as you. Believe me!"

He believed her. Natalya was cast in the role. His rather strange choice of actress generated some debate. She clearly was not entirely consistent with what was in Andrei's imagination. Natalya had to undergo complicated makeup, and another actress had to read her lines because of the mismatch in the timbre of her voice. But Tarkovsky rejected Terekhova and went with Bondarchuk's daughter. Was this sudden burst of interest in her coming from Tarkovsky the man? A desire for some kind of revenge against his rival director, laden with honors, by filming his daughter in a major role? In any case, he later told Natalya that with his "opportunistic choice" of actress had caused discontent among his colleagues. On no account could Tarkovsky be accused of opportunism and self-interest. On the contrary, he lacked the skill and tact to maneuver through the pitfalls of the cinema world. It is difficult, however, to ascribe his selection of Bondarchuk's daughter for the role of Hari merely to chance.

Shooting began in Yalta in the spring. Everyone rushed to the seaside. Tarkovsky was in high spirits and tireless in telling stories. He told jokes and delighted in the work before him after six years of inactivity. Also the presence of this girl that looked at him wide-eyed, and the anticipation of a love affair, inspired him and gave him courage.

"The judas tree is blooming," Andrei mused, stopping at a small cercis covered with purple flowers. "This is the kind of tree that Judas hung himself from. Only then it probably didn't bloom."

Suddenly he began to recite some lines of poetry:

And you walked through a small, trifling,
Naked, trembling alder grove
Into the ginger-red forest of a cemetery,
Which was aglow like stamped gingerbread.

One of the crew asked, "Did you write that poem, Andrei Arsenyevich?"

Tarkovsky laughed, and then suddenly became serious and looked straight into the eyes of his interlocutor. "If only I could write poetry like that, I'd never make films. That poem is by Boris Pasternak."

After he saw the set that had been built, he grimaced and hissed to the frightened set designed with suppressed rage, "What is this, a pioneer summer camp? What have you been doing here the whole time? Sitting on the beach sunbathing with the girls? God knows what you've been doing!"

"We'll finish it," came a timid reply.

"Finish it? You'll finish this cardboard bullshit?" He looked ready to start a fight and smash the set before him to pieces. Glancing at Natalya, who had become frightened, Andrei suddenly grew calmer. "This is a hack job. I'm not shooting until everything is how I want it."

Natalya looked wide-eyed at the raging director. Later she would have to face his hot temper many times.

Andrei opened the newspaper. "Listen to what they are saying about us in *Pravda*: 'Tarkovsky has started shooting his new film *Solaris*. On a cape, silver rockets are directed toward the sky. Astronauts Donatas Banionis and Natalya Bondarchuk are ready to take their places. Space awaits them.'"

In the evening he sat with Natalya along the seashore.

"Here I am making my fourth film. I have three left to make."

"How do you figure?"

"It's a prophecy, an especially accurate one. Pasternak said it, the ghost of Pasternak. Once I took part in a séance. I managed to call up the spirit of Pasternak and ask him, 'How many pictures will I make?' A firm reply came, 'Seven!' 'So few?' I asked. 'Seven, but good ones!'"

Natalya held back laughter, but Tarkovsky had a very serious look on his face.

3.

By the summer he was ready to film the Solaris space station at Mosfilm. Tarkovsky went far beyond the minor changes he promised Lem: the Earth is the starting point of everything that happens in the film. The Earth is one's home, the source of human passions, its heights and falls.

The film includes a symbol of modern human civilization, a long journey through a maze of highways that was shot in Japan. Set in contrast with this industrial world is a world of living nature, peaceful human existence.

Kris meets earlier with a living witness of the mysteries of Solaris's ocean, the pilot Burton, and comes to understand how dangerous his assignment could be. For this reason, his farewell to Earth has a nostalgic ring to it.

Andrei found a location for the opening scenes, the terrestrial prelude to the vast mysteries of space, along the river Ruza. There are swaying underwater plants, autumn leaves on the slow surface of the water. We see a man's legs as he walks among huge silver burdock plants. An unsaddled horse rushes by, its hoofs clopping on the ground. Rain comes down with a rustle on the open terrace of the summer cottage.

As Kris leaves his world, perhaps forever, he is keenly aware of the fullness of life: the drizzling of rain, the dawn chorus of birds, the dampness of the garden, the living flame in a bonfire, his father's stooped back. The small details of his father's house are slowly imprinted in his memory, to be stored for the rest of his life: the photographs, napkins, books, shells, stones, things accompanying an existence on Earth.

The great success of Stanley Kubrick's *2001: A Space Odyssey*, which had in a way become a model for the space genre, pushed Tarkovsky to reject established techniques. There is no feeling of imitation, artificiality, no straightforward interpretations of what is going on. Tarkovsky was accustomed to speak in code. A fortunate meeting in this approach was making the acquaintance of the composer Eduard Artemyev, who had made experiments in the field of electronic music. After Eduard's first conversation with Tarkovsky, it shook his imagination, he willingly followed the director on his course. Artemyev left traditional film music behind and took care of all the sounds of the film score on his own, endowing them with the music of life. Artemyev combined processed natural sounds with variations of synthesized sounds. The musical setting included various noises, sampled sounds and excerpts from pieces by Bach, which Artemyev reworked.

He recorded fifteen different sounds of the ocean for different episodes. These are not meant so much as an accompaniment to the visual image of Solaris's ocean outside the porthole (which was specially developed in a laboratory), instead the special, pulsating sound represents the constant presence of the unknown outside the walls of the space station. The ocean, the space station and the Earth are three realities in contact with one another in many ways thanks to the complex score that Artemyev composed.

The main action in the film takes place on the space station. Tarkovsky strove to remain as far as possible from the typical "alien" interior. In Mikhail Romadin's beautiful sets, there is not the slightest hint of props. Tarkovsky insisted that there be a handmade Armenian carpet in Gibarian's room. Furthermore, the station's library does not fit with the space setting with its antique furniture, candles in bronze candlesticks, paintings by Brueghel, Pushkin's death mask, old tomes and a porcelain Chinese dragon — the space is kept warm with the culture of Earth.

The people living on the space station have tried to establish an Earth-like atmosphere. The library is a reconstruction of earthly coziness. Tarkovsky chose the various details himself: the porcelain Buddha and a rocking chair are signs of home. Thanks to these, the floating of everyday objects and people in freefall is perceived more strongly. It is a miraculous moment and a reminder that their real home is incredibly far away.

The artistic staff relentlessly aged the details of the surrounding technology. Tarkovsky wanted a sense of dilapidation, the abandonment of this hopeless and outdated space station to be easily noticeable. In fact, he strove to make the viewer believe in the reality of what was happening. The final shot — the tiny island that is a memory of Earth receding into the endless ocean, with the home, Kris's father and Kris in front of him on his knees — touched the hearts of audiences and inevitably evoked applause.

Tarkovsky, tormented all his life by nostalgia for his village childhood, could not leave out this sequence that embodied the harmony of human existence. His characters, through catastrophe, did not aim for peace, but for harmony. They could not make contact with the ocean because they did not have a clearconscience; rather theirs were stained with secret intentions and sins. Kris's beloved, who had died on Earth, comes back to him in order to allow him to understand the cornerstone of the laws of the universe: the observance of ethical standards. He acts according to his conscience after he has gone through Hari's death and resurrection twice. He does not want to destroy her anymore, even though he knows that she is a construction of neutrinos. With her love and her desire to become a human being, Hari awakens in Kris a feeling of reciprocal love and a keen sense of guilt. The scene is shocking where Hari experiences an insuppressible need to be with Kris and breaks through the locked metal door of his room. Fatally wounded, she comes back to life. Her wounds heal before his eyes, and with a guilty smile, Hari again follows after Kris. Hari learns the redemptive bitterness of love, learns suffering and compassion, and carries Kris away with her.

"I am already human and I love you!" she pleads with him. "I have learned to love!"

His fellow astronauts avert their gaze. Kris's love for this ghost, which is doomed from the start to suffer, must be destroyed. Only one fate is possible for Kris in this story: insanity and suicide.

Agreeing with the arguments of his colleagues, who had already experienced similar situations, Kris agrees to undergo an experiment: his thoughts are transmitted in a powerful burst of radiation to Solaris's ocean. The ocean responds to the memories in Kris's heart, the bitterness of his nostalgia, in which his dead beloved one, his guilt and redemption are forever inscribed. His home and his native planet, its sounds and smells, will always be with him. Hari disappears from the station, annihilating herself.

During filming, Tarkovsky told his actress, "Just sit there and don't say anything." Preparing Natalya for long takes, Andrei whispered as if uttering a spell, "Don't act, don't act, just live, breathe!"

He appealed to those present on the set, "Look how beautiful she is! She's an angel."

As Natalya later recalled, "Andrei generally liked to look at me. I was like a painting for him; he constantly decided where to put the brush strokes in order to make the picture perfect. He studied me in order to decide what the female character in *Solaris* should be like."

Natalya had to spend a lot of time in the makeup chair, and the lighting technicians spent a lot of time on her in order to achieve what the director wanted. Tarkovsky had a completely different approach with Solonitsyn. He pushed the actor into overdrive and extreme exhaustion. He often scolded and deliberately humiliated Solonitsyn, which was unbearable for a man who adored Tarkovsky.

"Look at how you're walking! What are you doing, competing in the Olympics? Your coach is filling you up with hormones? You're an old man, worn out, on the verge of despair, deeply submerged in your own anguished inner world. Really, Anatoly, can't you do better?" Only after he had brought Solonitsyn to tears did Tarkovsky begin shooting.

He never sat down when an actor was at work, and would stand very close to him or her. The "warm-up" techniques that some directors applied were not very gentle and could even be cruel. For Tarkovsky, an actor was just raw material, and he achieved his desired result by any means necessary, sparing neither himself nor the other participants in the making of the film. It was not easy to please Tarkovsky. He completely rejected traditional acting methods in constructing a character, demanding unclear pronunciation from the actors, illogical stresses when reciting the lines, a total lack of acertain demonstrativeness in the shot.

The crew was barely given enough Kodak film. The cinematographer Vadim Yusov had to do everything without any reshoots. The single shot ready for editing was taken at the end of a shift, when everyone was already exhausted and could barely speak a word. The necessary effect of naturalness was reached.

4.

Tarkovsky once told Natalya, "You know, many people have stopped greeting me because I chose Bondarchuk's daughter and Gerasimov's protégé for the main role. Stop looking at me like that, Natasha. They don't execute people any more for family connections. Children were once made to denounce their parents. And you know," he suddenly switched to another topic, "I feel like I've given birth to you. No, not as an actress, but as a human being. Maybe that's how it was in some other life."

"Doesn't a person only live once?"

"This depends on what one wants and what one is capable of."

As she later said, "For some reason he let me get close to him, and I felt that this was a man who was infinitely close to me spiritually."

Tarkovsky's belief that one cannot properly film an actress if one has not had an affair with her, happened also in Natalya's case. They began a serious affair.

They shot the scene where Hari tries to kill herself by drinking liquid oxygen.

"Do you know what it's like to drink liquid oxygen? She has no insides left! She is no longer able to talk — everything is burnt up!"

When they were alone in Andrei's empty apartment, Natasha sat quietly with her hands around her throat.

"What happened? Have you caught a cold?"

"I can't…" she said hoarsely, with big tears pouring from her eyes. "I can't live without you."

"Stop making those hoarse sounds, otherwise I will feel like I have been strangling you."

"It would be better if you strangled me." She fell exhausted on the sofa, just like Hari had lain a few hours earlier on set and slowly thawed and come to life. "I've learned to love you. And I cannot live without this feeling. I dream of appearing everywhere next to you like Hari."

As she later recalled, "For me, like for many of his favorite actors, Tarkovsky was the center of the universe. If he commanded me to throw myself into a fire, I would do so unquestioningly. But in Tarkovsky's world I was like something ideal, unearthly, that's why a physical relationship between us was impossible for a long time."

"You are my woman," Tarkovsky said. "And that means… That means that I love you. Don't think that I haven't noticed; that I don't understand how you feel about me. True love does not go unrequited."

"I know how often this happens between an actress and a director. They work together, get to know each other and feelings develop. 'Fish in the same sea,' like Marina Tsvetaeva wrote."

"It's normal. If a director does not love his main actress, then he cannot make a film about love, or a film about anything."

"I decided that if I could give you some portion of happiness, I would throw myself into love head first."

As she later recalled, "We lived in the moment and did not think about what would happen to us next. When we talked, it was always about something important, divine. 'Oh, this world hasn't been created for me, it's much worse than I am,' I sighed. Andrei disagreed. 'No, that's not true,' he said, 'it's better! Everything is arranged here wonderfully and wisely. We are bad, sometimes very bad indeed, but we must perfect ourselves and the world, but one must always start from himself.' Finally we became intimate."

"Oh God, what will we do now?" Natalya sobbed into his shoulder.

"It's great that we are surprisingly compatible with each other," Andrei said as he sat down and lit a cigarette. "Could you really sleep with me forever? All our lives, in the same bed?"

"It's the most beautiful thing imaginable."

"Swear it to me."

"On what? You want me to swear it to you on my blood."

"Listen, it's a silly confession, but… You know, I am still somehow afraid of women, especially in my bed."

"What with your two wives and various mistresses," Natalya reminded him.

"Yes, I'm always taking risks in my search for the woman for me. I go through fear, through suppressing my uncertainty, and I hope I'll find the right one. Now it's clear, it's you."

"What are we going to do? It will hurt my devoted Nikolai Burlyayev, and you're married," Natalya's eyes, fixed on her lover, filled with tears.

He bit his fingernails as he made a difficult decision. He thought for a long time, then looked down over her tear-stained face and answered curtly, without hesitation: "I'll get a divorce!"

5.

The time came when Larisa should hear of his decision.

The apartment peacefully smelled of dinner, Andrei junior peacefully slept in his crib, and only from the back room could one hear the sound of the sewing machine. (Olga Surkova had by then divorced Sergei and returned to live with her parents.) Larisa was wearing a pale-blue quilted robe and her hair was gathered into a pitiful bun. There was fear in her wide eyes, which were somehow naked and defenseless without mascara.

"What happened? Don't stay quiet, I beg you, I can tell that something has happened!"

They went into the bedroom that was his office. Andrei sunk into a chair and drooped. "I'm tired, very tired." He felt sorry for this devoted woman and all the comforts of home that she had made.

"Maybe you'll eat first, Andryushenka? The *solyanka* soup is just like in the National Hotel."

"Sit down, Larisa. I don't want to dance around the subject." He jumped up and moved around the room, picking up a book here or a notebook there. He stopped and looked up. "Natalya Bondarchuk and I are getting married. Forgive me, Larisa Pavlovna, but we will have to end our marriage."

"What?!" Her blue eyes rolled back and she collapsed unconscious on the quilt. She was capable of throwing an old-fashioned tantrum. Many people even believe that in his film *The Sacrifice*, Tarkovsky used Larisa's fits as a basis. After she pretended to faint, she moved on to her usual routine: screams, taking drugs, waking up the house, throwing down her wedding ring and cursing.

But when she almost hadn't noticed that Andrei was going to leave, Larisa froze in a Medea-like pose and made the tragic decision. Her voice could reach the back rows of a vast auditorium and send a chill down everyone's spine.

"Leave me for whoever you want. But remember, you will never see your son again!" It was impossible to bring a more powerful blow down on Andrei.

The next day on set he was met with the smiling eyes of Natalya.

"Today we're rehearsing the scene where Hari breaks through the door. Imagine, I'm walking through the halls of Mosfilm in a torn dress and covered with blood. Cranberry juice is running down my arms and my dress very realistically. Guess who comes toward me: Stalin in a white tunic covered in medals! He was taken aback and just stared at me. With blood running down and torn clothes, I apparently represented a victim of his terror."

"That was Zaqariadze. He's playing Stalin in *The Great Battle*."

Without even a smile, Andrei looked thoughtfully at the battered Hari. A difficult scene stood before them. The actress would have to give her utmost. So, it was now or never.

"Natalya, let's go have a smoke."

They went out onto a staircase with a full garbage bin and clouds of smoke. He took her hand, blood-stained with cranberry juice and kissed it. He held it for a long time without letting go and without raising his eyes.

"My girl, I love you, and I'm ready to spend the rest of my life with you. But I can't betray my son a second time. Larisa said that if we divorce, she will keep little Andrei away from me forever."

Natalya looked at him for a long time, as if she felt that she was slowly falling from a height. Falling from a miracle that had almost come true into a deadly, ice-cold hopelessness.

"Of course I understand," she muttered. "I understand." She put out her cigarette and went on set. The scene was beautifully shot and the following takes also went well. With tears in his eyes, Tarkovsky filmed the scene of Hari's voluntary self-annihilation, her irrevocable exit from Kris's life.

When it became clear that the material was filmed without problems and Hari's part went to the stage of adding sound (some other actress gave her voice to Hari), Natalya tried to take her own life. As she later recounted, "With bitterness and shame I remember how I once tried to end my life. My temples were pounding with the thought that I didn't need a life without Tarkovsky, but what could I do? I was married, and he wasn't free. My head was in a fog, my thoughts were confused. I went into the bathroom. Hardly aware of what I was doing, I grabbed a razor and slashed my veins with it." The suicide attempt was unsuccessful. Natasha returned to life and her family managed to cover up the unhappy episode.

Tarkovsky told Larisa that everything would be the same as before. Natalya receded from the scene.

Larisa was not a naive woman. She knew that women who hear wedding bells approaching rarely give up without a fight. For that reason she invited Natasha to a café, telling her that she had to relay an important message from Andrei. She looked like a caring and loving mother.

"Natashenka, you've got your whole life ahead of you. And you've got a husband, Nikolai Burlyayev, such a sweet, caring guy. It doesn't matter that you are just cohabitating! And he's so talented. I understand that you're attracted to Andrei. It happens to everyone that has been in his films. Just look at me, I got caught up too, and so many tears have followed it. You can't rely on him, that's the most awful thing. I live each day like I'm on top of a volcano."

Natalya was pulling at a handkerchief and thinking that she shouldn't have agreed to meet this woman with the eyes of a liar under her fluttering eyelashes covered with clumps of blue mascara.

"He wanted to convey something to me"

"Andrei Arsenyevich is ill, but I have learned to deal with his horrible disease. Earlier binges have happened quite often."

"Andrei is ill?!" Natalya could not believe her ears.

"I'm afraid so. He's a very sick man. In general, Andrei is not what you think he is. He's a very difficult person. He is fond of women and he knows how to drink, how to go on week-long binges. Not long ago I found out that one of my friends is pregnant," Larisa took a drag from her cigarette with a tragic demeanor. "Pregnant with Andrei's child! What could I do? I paid for this silly girl's abortion. Yes, I have a hard time of it. But I forgave him for this; it's my cross to bear. My lifelong obligation to a great man. It is my responsibility to save him so that he can make films. For history, for eternity."

Larisa shed tears with a long-practiced ability to not spoil her make-up. "My girl, he's not for you. You could not bear such a man."

6.

"Wet snow was falling outside the window. Andrei softly told me, 'I bring bad luck to everyone, even you!'" Natalya Bondarchuk recalled, and she added, "Behind those words was a hopeless pain and responsibility for the people who believed in and followed him and were faced with a terrible lack of understanding by Goskino."

More than thirty changes to *Solaris* were demanded of Tarkovsky, and the film reached screens only half a year later. The premiere took place in May, in the Mosfilm hall and then in the Dom Kino cinema.

Sergei Fedorovich Bondarchuk attended one of the showings. After being impressed by the film and at the request of Natalya, he went up to congratulate Tarkovsky. The twenty year-old Natalya was so happy at this meeting of two people dear to her that she blurted out, "You should collaborate on a film of Dostoyevsky's *Humiliated and Insulted*!"

Bondarchuk, taken aback, only nodded, while Tarkovsky said, "Maybe not the novel. It would be interesting to make a film about Dostoyevsky himself."

Alas, no collaboration would result between these two directors. The mutual repulsion they harbored for one another would only intensify in many respects because of Andrei's distrust, for he suspected his colleagues of envy and underhandedness, to some extent because of their incompatible creative approaches, and because of Bondarchuk's completely understandable dislike for his daughter's seducer.

Tarkovsky's new film played to full houses. Audiences mainly saw *Solaris* as a film about immortality and about love proving victorious in outer space. They saw it as a film about eternal questions. After all of Kris Kelvin's suffering, the protagonist muses, "Maybe we're here in order to experience people as a reason for love."

Positive reviews and audience feedback appeared in the press. "*Solaris* is a trial of love. Love is the test for humanity. It is thanks to love that we become human beings. Without love and compassion we are not human. Only love makes a human being a human being!"

"Love is a feeling that one can experience but which cannot be explained. One can explain a notion. You love what can be lost: yourself, your wife, your country. Kris initially rejects love, he is afraid of love, because love is our conscience. Hari is his conscience that never lets up. Thanks to Hari, Kris understands that love is more important than science, love is more important than everything!" So viewers wrote about the film, watching it over and over again.

"'The universe is a woman, it is Hari! Hari is the eternal feminine! Almost every man dreams of a woman like her. She is the personification of every man's dream about an ideal woman…' Here, read what we got," Natalya Bondarchuk put newspapers with reviews in front of Andrei. "My Hari is every man's ideal."

Andrei guiltily looked down and changed the subject. "We'll go to Cannes with some others. You know that?"

"Of course!" she grinned and turned away. The film had been an ordeal for her.

7.

In May 1972, *Solaris* was shown in competition at the Cannes Film Festival. Few doubted that it was a contender for the top prize. Tarkovsky attended the showing with Donatas Banionis and Natalya Bondarchuk. The film was received with great enthusiasm. The final scene, where Kris is on his knees in front of his father, was met with thunderous applause. Then the camera began to rise higher and higher, and Kris's home and everything with it dwindled to a point on a small island, yet another illusion created by Solaris.

The film did not receive the Palme d'Or but the Grand Prix Spécial du Jury, the Ecumenical Prize and the FIPRESCI Prize again. Andrei however was counting on the first prize with the money attached to it, and felt wounded and dejected like a child.

"Now I know this is all a conspiracy. Some people jealous of me can't lay off. I don't want to point to a specific person, but I have no doubt that forces known to me are at work here," he said during dinner in a restaurant and looked suggestively at Natalya.

"Are you thinking of my father? He was in the jury, but he would not hurt a film in which his daughter was playing a leading role."

"You don't understand people well. Someone could sacrifice his own daughter in order to hinder a bastard like Tarkovsky," he said, throwing aside the knife that he had been nervously fiddling with and hurrying away from the table. Over the time of her relationship with Andrei, Natalya understood that his hypochondria sometimes took the form of a persecution complex. He had hallucinations about plots weaving around him. In each failure he saw the malice of those close to him. Later Natalya wrote, "I do not know if I could have lived with Tarkovsky. Nikolai Burlyayev and I lived together in tranquility for 18 years, united in many respects by our admiration for Tarkovsky. Admiration from afar was best for any fan of Tarkovsky. The people around him often had to recall the Japanese proverb that 'A genius is a problem for those close to him.'"

In the airport, Andrei and Natalya were slightly delayed, found their companions furious and on the plane.

"They thought that you would stay behind," whispered Banionis who had been sitting quietly.

Andrei was outraged. "How could I stay behind? It's absurd! I could not live or work here, but only in my own country," he turned toward the window and an expression of disgust for a long time there lingered on his face for all who give up their homeland for "paradise in the West".

The rights to *Solaris* were bought by many countries. For the premiere in Italy, a country which Andrei was very fond of, he was sent with Natalya and Donatas Banionis.

In Rome they happened to see Fellini's new film *Amarcord*, which was playing to a half-empty little hall. Tarkovsky loudly expressed his delight and made comments, as if he had created this masterpiece himself.

"This is how you should never cut a frame," he shouted. "What is he doing? He is butchering his own work!"

The next day Fellini invited the visiting Russians to his office. He greeted Tarkovsky simply and warmly and talked about his intentions for his next film *Casanova*.

"I saw your film, Andrei, but not the whole thing. It's very long, you see. But what I saw was brilliant."

"The film is long?" Tarkovsky was outraged. "And what do you have, a lot of short films? But I've watched them all to the last frame."

"Don't worry, we are geniuses, you and I!" Fellini smiled. "You Russians are a totally brilliant people. How do you all manage to make your films? What about? They don't let you make films about anything! I couldn't make any of my films in your country, because all my films are about prostitutes. And then again, I'm not a serious man. A director should be a bit of a child. You are very concerned with a search for truth, but you are also a child!"

"Well, no! Cinema is too important to treat it like a toy, for me at any rate."

"You know what I say?" A look of doubt passed over Fellini's face. Is it worth saying?? "I say that your child-like nature consists in your exceedingly deep and, in my opinion, naive belief in the absolute power of art. This way you can burden yourself with the role of a messiah."

"I aspire to be a preacher, and they close my mouth. Even if my films reach cinema screens, there are few who understand them."

"The works of a great artist don't necessarily have to be accepted by everyone and accepted unequivocally. How many stones were thrown at me!"

"But why did you stop using professional actors?"

"They're expensive, and then movie stars get the right to dictate their terms!"

"Even to you?"

"To everyone! They get the right to control absolutely everything, even how many and what shots I have a right to film. And they expect me to pay for everything!"

"Money, money! Damned capitalism!" There was no sarcasm in Tarkovsky's voice.

"It's hard to work these days. Producers don't fork out anything for 'great cinema'. Give them box-office hits. Distributors go bankrupt with my masterpieces. It is hard, brother, but you and I are geniuses, of course!"

Andrei ran into Nikolai Burlyayev at the Dom Kino. Tarkovsky greeted him in passing, as if *Ivan's Childhood* and *Andrei Rublev* had never happened.

Nikolai rushed up to his director he worshiped and invited him to his place. He was alone at home and was eager to watch *Solaris* together with Andrei on the latest wonder, the VCR.

"You know, in your film Natasha turned out, really, unearthly, neutrino-like. I don't think that anyone will ever film her better than you have!"

"She has a big career ahead of her," Tarkovsky said, fidgeting in his chair and looking for an excuse to slip away. Such sentimental enthusiasm for the film, especially coming from this cuckolded husband, was painful for him.

"Look, this is Natalya's strongest scene! You constructed it masterfully!" Tears shone in Nikolai's eyes. "When Hari breaks through the metal door to the man she loves. It can hardly fail to touch people!"

"Many people think that *Solaris* is a film about love," Tarkovsky said smiling. He was desperate to end this childish talk about "love". "Sadly, melodrama is not my genre. What can I say to a woman? 'Who untied you? Go on, lie down in your place!'"

8.

In 1974 Tarkovsky wrote in his diary, "A woman's nature consists of the following: subordination, humiliation in the name of love!"

In an interview with the journalist Irena Brezna, Tarkovsky was even more explicit: "A woman does not have her own inner world and should not have one. Her inner world should be completely dissolved into the inner world of a man."

Brezna recounts a remarkable conversation with Tarkovsky:

"I think that you demand of a woman what you are yourself incapable of. You are unable to love."

Tarkovsky stroked his mustache:

"I think the verdict is partially true. Love… I find this feeling very difficult, in the full sense that you mean. Love involves self-sacrifice for the sake of another, right? It's very hard for me to love, as it is very hard for me to sacrifice part of myself. Anyway, I feel rather more exhilarated than happy in love."

By nature, a great lover of the female sex, he in fact did not understand women and was afraid of them. The reason was a lack of self-confidence. Only a slavishly devoted woman would pose no threat to him. No such creatures can be found in the jungle of the film world. Andrei's devotion could only be a brief episode, a prelude to offering his hand in marriage. How could he not suspect members of the fair sex of self-interest and the desire to gain a famous husband? Tarkovsky, who had been so poor and had become so famous at the age of 40, a perennial winner at the Cannes Film Festival, was now apparently a desirable match.

Sadly he was a complicated man, difficult to communicate with, no matter what relationship he had with those who happened to be close to him. Besides that, the concepts of "family" and "love" were not equivalent for him. Having a dependable life companion and a child, Andrei Tarkovsky reserved the right to be above the family in the name of the principle he proclaimed, that "a director's work requires intimacy with the actress". He would not limit his own freedom in many other contexts that were unrelated to filmmaking.

Tarkovsky himself wrote about this aspect of himself in his diary: "I'm no saint or angel. I am a selfish person, who is afraid more than anything else of causing pain to those he loves." There is a clear contradiction here. He could not have failed to notice that with all his desire to avoid bringing suffering to his loved ones, he was hurting them nonetheless. Where does the truth lie then, was he afraid to hurt someone or did he simply think that he, with a personality that did not stand for limits, had a right to be unfaithful?

His first son was abandoned, and the second was almost left behind were it not for Larisa's efforts to hold on to her husband. Tarkovsky, in turn, made the mistake for which, to the very end, he could never forgive his father. And who knows if it wasn't Larisa's firm grip that stopped her unfaithful husband from making many other similar mistakes?

Irma Raush-Tarkovskaya admitted that seven year-old Arseny took their divorce as hard as any kid. Holding a grudge, she made the mistake which Maria Ivanovna had managed to avoid. After Andrei married Larisa, he asked Irma to allow Arseny to visit their home, but Irma forbade the boy to have any contact with his father. "When he gets older, he can decide himself," she thought. She recalled all too well the expression on Andrei's face when they went together to visit his father. It had probably come to him in his childhood and stayed with him, this paralyzing fear of being abandoned, of being unwanted, of not being loved enough, as well as his secret longing to prove his own importance, his right to get love and attention from the "best poet of our time". And his grudge, his wound that would not heal also came from this. As a result, neither warm feelings nor male bonding developed between father and son. In the end, Andrei had almost no contact with his son Arseny. Visiting Irma's house, as he himself said, was hard for him. In the end Maria Ivanovna interceded — she simply took Arseny by the hand and brought him to his father. However, by that time Arseny was already in high school. His relationship with his father proved complicated, like that of Andrei himself and Arseny Alexandrovich, despite the fact that each had a great love for the other. They loved each other. It would be right to assume that for Tarkovsky, love was something mental, arising from the intellect, and not something emotional.

"Olga," he guiltily confessed to Surkova, "Children are an awful thing. A family, they make you vulnerable, defenseless. It's awful. It's so horrible and you can't do anything about it, right? Isn't that true? It's like they tie your hands and feet. They surround you. Help! It's awful, haha."

He said this with a little nervous laugh as if to give it a humorous tone, but it was a cry from the heart, and one incapable of strong parental feelings.

Tarkovsky did not have warm feelings toward his fellow directors either. He considered some traitors and others hacks. He was sharply critical of the most prominent films of those years: Khutsiyev's *July Rain*, Talankin's *Day Stars*, later Alov and Naumov's *The Ugly Story*. He was harsh on Talankin and Kutsiyev, viewing them as people with an unfair view of society who did not support Soviet ideas and principles. "I am encouraged by the highest and purest thoughts, but they slap me on the wrist. They should rather slap the people who don't do anything at all," he repeated often, having noticed incentives, bonuses or recognition being given to those who were clearly not ideologically correct enough.

It is true that Tarkovsky's thoughts about other directors sometimes changed. Though he denounced *No Path Through Fire* with a vengeance in the year of its release, he later grew close to Panfilov. Only when he was in the West would Tarkovsky develop a serious attitude toward Iosseliani, whom he had simply not noticed before. Andrei had a great appreciation for Sokurov's *The Lonely Voice of Man* upon its release (he did not see any other films by that director). Sokurov, however, considered Tarkovsky one of his teachers.

Even the best exemplars of so-called Soviet art were alien to Andrei Arsenyevich. Voznesensky, Yevtushenko, Lyubimov and Vysotsky — idols for the progressive community of that era — left him indifferent. "They are too journalistic and political, thus they are not deep."

However, among the directors whom did not interest Tarkovsky, he also had some open enemies, which made for his excessive suspiciousness. The most extreme suspicion in the "Rublev affair" fell on Sergei Gerasimov.

"Don't you see," he explained to Surkov. "Gerasimov was behind everything that happened. He's a real Salieri. He's a smart guy and deep inside he knows that he's got no talent. That's why he's full of hate. The main thing with Gerasimov is his lust for power. For the sake of that lust for power, he tramples on everything around him while smiling and saying wonderful things."

Surkov agreed. "One can understand his resentment to some

degree. You got in his way with *Ivan's Childhood*. His *The Men and the Beasts* was entered into competition at the Venice Film Festival. Your *Ivan's Childhood* was playing out of competition and nonetheless won the Golden Lion!"

"What about Bondarchuk? It was he who ruined the chances for *Solaris* at Cannes. He was on the jury for expressly that purpose."

"All of the hype around *Andrei Rublev* ruined the triumph of *War and Peace* somewhat, you see. And what's more, you had something going on with his daughter. You surely promised you would marry her."

"How can I leave such a wife?" he thought and said firmly, "It just wouldn't happen."

"Of course, you've got a small boy. That's a serious thing."

"That's not the point. Larisa is endowed with great power. Don't smile like that. She promised to put a curse on my enemies," Andrei said seriously.

"This sounds," Surkov smiled, "somewhat ridiculous."

"She'll do it, you'll see! For me she'll bite everyone's throat!"

Tarkovsky was supported by this feeling of being protected which the resourceful and belligerent Larisa provided for her ambitious, but actually not very capable husband.

"Do you know what happened?" he said after returning home from yet another trip to the Central House of Writers. "It's incredible! I stood with Larisa at a taxi stand — we had to wait like always — and some jerk, some idiot, can you imagine? He comes out of nowhere and wants to get into our taxi. Of course I rushed to get in first, but then Larisa comes up and slaps him in the face with all her might. Do you understand? She's got a wrought metal bracelet. Just imagine how this lout went flying."

"My hat is ruined!" Larisa tried to fix the smudged brim of her thin blue headwear. "Now I have to send it to the cleaners. Or should I soak it in persalt?"

Larisa made noises in the bathroom, trying to undo the damage to her hat. Andrei whispered warmly to Anna Semyonovna, "Your daughter is an exceptionally devoted wife. I'm sure that if I needed it, Larisa would kill for me."

In everyday life, as a cocky and impulse person, he really needed protection. He couldn't interact well with the outside world, as if he saw through thick glasses with fogged lenses. His relationships with his crew were mediated by Larisa. That's why anyone who did not cater to Larisa failed to stay on with the maestro. She had enormous influence. At the very beginning of their relationship, Larisa had won a major victory: she managed to persuade her husband lacking in self-confidence that he was an incomparable sexual titan and virtuoso in the erotic arts.

Larisa unwaveringly pursued her goals. If, in the beginning, she was attracted to Tarkovsky out of a desire for a wealthy and influential husband, now her aim had changed: she sought to go down in history with him as a tireless wife, a genius assistant and even a movie star! The husband and wife were joined in a love/hate relationship, something typical of Tarkovsky and not only with Larisa. Yielding to her suggestions, he could easily change his attitudes toward people and thus lost long-time friends and collaborators.

"I can make him believe anything!" Larisa boasted. But even her influence was not unlimited when it came to a role in one of his films.

Larisa fought desperately to be seen as an actress. Without batting an eye, she told everyone that Fellini and Paradjanov dreamed of filming her, and then turned to her husband for confirmation.

"Is that true, Andrei?"

He mumbled something affirmative, though he himself did not see an actress in his wonderful spouse.

Larisa had intended to play Gertrude in Andrei's production of *Hamlet* at the Lenkom Theatre, as well as Kris's wife in *Solaris*. Now she aimed for the role of the Mother in the autobiographical film that Andrei was planning.

Chapter 7.
THE MIRROR,
CAPTURED TIME

I.

The idea of an autobiographical film had been maturing in Tarkovsky from the very beginning of his work in filmmaking and would become the fullest expression of his intentions as an artist. None of his other films had such a complex history, none absorbed so much of his personal experience and professional skills, none brought such satisfaction and such pain.

Even before applying to make *Solaris*, Tarkovsky had collaborated with Alexander Misharin on a script entitled *Confession*, which was not accepted by the studio. His crew also reacted to it negatively. The screenplay weaves together three storylines. The main, basic storyline would consist of a frank and in-depth conversation with Maria Ivanovna, filmed without her knowledge. By means of a hidden camera, he intended to capture a kind of psychoanalytical session, where an unsuspecting woman talks about the most intimate things: her worst misdeeds, an especially happy day, her husband, her love or resentment.

Andrei proposed the role of the Mother to his first wife. Irma refused on ethical grounds. The use of a hidden camera in those days was considered immoral. After reading the script for *Confessions*, Vadim Yusov called Andrei to talk.

"I think a hidden camera is better used for catching criminals."

"It's a powerful way to make a person open up. It has enormous potential."

"Can you imagine how much this spying will offend your mother?" Vadim hoped to reason with Andrei, his friend and collaborator since the time of their graduation thesis *The Steamroller and the Violin*.

"She's no fool. She should understand that anything I film, whether openly or secretly, will be in her favor."

"Oh, I don't think so. But remember, you will ruin your relationship with her forever." Vadim paused for a moment. "Anyway, I've decided that I will not film anything with a hidden camera. Find another cameraman."

With his inflated ego, Tarkovsky could not stand ultimatums. He was irritated by Vadim's failure to obey him unquestioningly on the set.

"You're mistaken if you think that you can give me advice. Anyway, two geniuses on set is a bit too much." He turned away, letting Yusov know that the subject was closed.

A new variant that Andrei conceived was titled *A Bright, Bright Day*, but he did not succeed in getting through the blockade of officialdom, which rejected his application. Andrei felt humiliated and trampled on; what he had proposed as a canvas about the things most precious to him was not considered worthy material for a film. But there was one more obstacle, an inner one, his doubts about the result. He was unhappy with the imperfection of his filming equipment, which did not allow him to capture the pictures in his imagination, to fully realize his ideas at a modern level of filming.

He returned after yet another rejection, clenching his teeth, going back in his head over the words of suppressed indignation that he had not said. He crumpled up his application, where the pages with the script were scribbled over, and in a fit of anger used it to wipe the dirt from his thick soles in the hall.

"Well, what is it, Andrei, do you have bad news again?" Anna Semyonovna was in the kitchen feeding little Andrei porridge with grated apple. "Look what a bad boy he is, he's spitting out his porridge!"

"They're spitting something out too, the officials. They don't want this film," and that's that. He sat on the stool next to him and relished the smell of the semolina porridge, mimicking the carelessness of a child. He saw the frowning face of his mother, young and strong, through the veil of time.

Anna Semyonovna patiently picked up the spoon that little Andrei had spat out onto his oilcloth bib and put it back into his mouth.

"Eat, eat! You're stubborn, but I'm more stubborn. This is *A Bright Day*, isn't it, that they've torn apart again?"

"Yes, that one. About my childhood, mama, father, Marina, about all of us. I want everything to be as real as it was then."

"I've been thinking, why doesn't your mother come to see her grandson? Your relatives have never once come to visit us. They are like strangers. Do you want to see your other grandma, Andryusha? He wants to, but you and Larisa don't invite them."

"That's silly, I think about them all the time, about my mother and father, about this film. I'm racking my brain to find a way to bring back the past."

"Oh, Andrei, if only one could turn back time."

"But I have it all right here!" He rapped his knuckles on his head. "Here everything is still alive! I can't just take the things that are most dear to me and bury them, can I?"

"Don't bury them. Keep them with you until you can get through the officials."

"I will get through."

"And how are you going to turn back time?"

"Have you heard about holography? It's when you make a three-dimensional image and project it without any screen."

"Is this science-fiction?"

"It's real! For the present only individual devices have been created that are capable of transmitting three-dimensional images, but there will be more, there certainly will! No cameras or screens! And even better, you'll be able to put on a helmet and transmit everything that you have in your memory, like real life…"

Andrei was constantly thinking about how to get around the complicated process of recording an image on film that had been artificially recreated and not reproduced from the storerooms of his memory.

He initially decided to get rid of artificiality by using a hidden camera. Later he did not stop thinking about his most precious project during his first hiatus and when he filmed *Solaris*. The fact that this "science-fiction film" was full of life on Earth was caused by Andrei's aim to create an autobiographical film, inseparable from the breath of our planet.

In 1973, Tarkovsky returned to the script *A Bright, Bright Day* with an epigraph from his father's poem:

> *A stone lies by the jasmine.*
> *Under the stone is a treasure.*
> *Father stands on the path.*
> *It's a bright, bright day*

His application to make the film, after many changes, was finally approved.

When Andrei was already preparing to shoot *A Bright, Bright Day*, on his birthday April 4, it was finally decided to invite his parents to the apartment on Orlovo-Davydovsky Lane and introduce them to his new family.

"I know they don't like me. No one can forget Irma," Larisa was rolling dough, preparing for a "lavish reception". "And, apparently, they don't miss you much either. Their grandson is already two years old, but they haven't been able to see him. They haven't even met my mother and my daughter."

Andrei gave a vague explanation, "That's just how things happened," and hurriedly left the kitchen. Needless to say, he did not get on well with his relatives, but now the time had come to improve the situation.

Arseny Alexandrovich came with his wife Tatyana Ozerskaya, a woman of high society, well-groomed and a frequent guest at the Central House of Writers and writers' retreats. Ozerskaya was a famous literary translator, which brought her closer to her husband.

The reserved Maria Ivanovna, putting out one cigarette after another, thin, stern, dressed extremely modestly, with a bun of gray hair, still seemed to feel love for the father of her children, calling him Arsyushenka. The presence of these people together at the table, including Larisa with her daughter Olga and Anna Semyonovna, made for such a volatile situation that everyone was trying to stay quiet. Olga Surkova, who was among those invited, has given a detailed account of what happened that day.

Everyone noticed how Andrei flew off the handle after he had been drinking to give himself courage. Nobody had ever seen him like this before, nor would they after. Andrei sensed the importance of this moment, the intensity of his relationship with these people close to him. By his nature, he was already tightly strung, and now he was in a state of nearly hysterical excitement, recalling Prince Myshkin with his extremely intimate straightforwardness.

With childlike exuberance, he offered a toast in honor of his mother. "Mama, you have no idea, I'll take you to our old house in the country! The foundation of the house we lived in is still there, and on that foundation I will build exactly the same house — you know, as we lived in. And only then will I bring you there, and you'll see it yourself. You can check yourself if I remember everything correctly. You'll see it, it will be our house! Do you understand me?"

He had recently thought so frequently about recreating the film reality of *A Bright, Bright Day*, that now he was experiencing a sense of time standing still. He felt like a demiurge capable of returning to the past. He was already filled with vague images of the childhood that had come back to him. It seemed that it was enough to step over the threshold and then everything could be brought back! This is where the euphoria that took over him on that memorable evening came from — and, of course, the fact that he was quite drunk, and alcohol had always liberated the reserved and self-contained Andrei.

Most often he addressed his father, whom he openly worshipped, suffering at the same time from the unrequited love he had for him as an abandoned child. His father had remained for him an ideal, the worthiness of being related to whom he always had to prove to himself.

Andrei's feelings that had cumulated all his life burst free at that strange gathering. He literally made a declaration of love to his father:

"Papa, you should know that here, in this house, everything belongs to you. Everything has been designed just for you. Papa, you are the master of this house. My eldest son is named Arseny — in your honor, papa! Look, your youngest grandson Andrei also belongs to you."

That evening was an attempt to rewrite their lives from scratch. It was a hasty and clumsy attempt. Andrei had the feeling that precisely *Bright Day* would be the best way to express his feelings to his father. He did not cease to urge him:

"Papa, you'll see what a film it will be! You'll all see…"

"Calm down, Andryusha," Marina tried to stop her brother's outpouring of enthusiasm. "We're sure you can do it, and we'll see."

"He suddenly calmed down, sat at the table and, deep in thought, began to pick at his plate of pilaf that had grown cold."

"And if I can't. If I can't do it, eh, sister? You and mama have always considered me the strongest person in the family. You've considered me to be stronger than you. But I was the weakest one. It's just that you never realized this. You don't even realize now how difficult it is for me…"

2.

The new script focused on the story of his mother and his childhood. The script began with a funeral at a cold and snow-covered cemetery in winter. Of the scenes which relate to his mother, an image emerged of a proud but, at the same time, a sadly abandoned woman. Later half of them were left out, but the film contained the reflection of her story in the relationship of her grown-up son and his wife, Natalia and Alexei, which, repeating in a mirror-like fashion, the split between the parents. The film now took the title *The Mirror*.

Larisa naturally made a claim on the role of the Mother, but Andrei already had his eye on another actress. Once, when he was still working on *Solaris*, he ran into Margarita Terekhova in an elevator. She had come to audition for the role of Hari.

"What wonderful hair you've got," Andrei remarked.

"Oh, I've got amazing hair," Margarita said as she let her entire mane out from under her collar.

Tarkovsky didn't cast her in *Solaris*, however. Then on the set of *The Mirror* he said, "If I had cast Rita, it would have turned out a completely different film."

When auditioning for the role of the Mother, Terekhova asked, "When are we going to make a film of Bulgakov's *The Master and Margarita*?"

Tarkovsky knitted his brow. "Well, I'm pretty sure who Margarita will be. And who will be the Master?"

"What do you mean who? It will be Smoktunovsky, of course."

Tarkovsky shrugged. "I don't know, I don't know. And if I played the role?"

He decided to give the role to Terekhova and did not even bother to inform Marina Vlady, who had previously auditioned for the role and was already planning to make a film in Russia. Maria hoped to get some kind of official employment in Russia and thus be allowed to remain together with Vysotsky. As a director, Tarkovsky interested both her and Vladimir. "We spent several days calling Andrei, but each time his wife answered, and with her usual courtesy, she just hung up. I felt that it was pointless to call, as the answer would be no, but Vladimir didn't want to believe it. When Tarkovsky's secretary told us a few days later that all the roles had been cast and thanked me for auditioning, Vladimir flew into a terrible rage. For two long years,

Vysotsky broke off contact with Tarkovsky. The friends they had in common tried to reconcile them, but in vain."

Marina was perhaps unaware that Vysotsky's offense at Andrei had deeper roots. Tarkovsky respected Vladimir as an actor and wanted to shoot him in his films. However, with all his love for Vysotsky, Andrei was forced to give up working with him. In *Andrei Rublev* Vladimir should have played the role of the centurion taken by Nikolai Grabbe, but he got drunk twice, and twice he let him down. Tarkovsky could not forgive him for this. In everything concerning his profession, he was an unbelievably jealous and pedantic man. Only after Vysotsky's death did Tarkovsky admit, "Vladimir Vysotsky was a unique character. I have the impression that he was one of the few artists of our time, in a genre I can't quite identify, and who managed to evoke his era like no one else."

Marina Vlady said with exasperation, "I tried out for the role of the Mother, and then he took an unknown actress." More than Vlady, the emergence of "a certain Terekhova" enraged Larisa, who had put herself forward for the role and could already see a potential temptress of her husband in the beautiful actress. Hatred flared up with a glaring flame from the very first day, especially when the "unknown actress" amazed Tarkovsky with her precise insight into the character and clearly satisfied the director. He glowed with inspiration behind the camera, shooting close-ups of Terekhova (and then cutting them from the film). Her splendid contempt for the rich lady next door and the humiliation of being forced to sell her earrings pierced her every sigh, every line of her face, which he strove to capture.

"All right," Andrei said with praise, not daring to extend the compliment under the loathing eye of Larisa, as it was her whom he had given the part of a big-bodied miserly woman who bought the earrings from her poor neighbor — the only worthy thing. ("And in addition to that," Larisa complained, "he made me hide all my hair under a headscarf!").

The episode with killing the rooster established a clear relationship between the two women. The quick mistress of the house (Larisa) cruelly mocks the mother for being terrified at killing the animal:

"In Moscow you must have eaten dead ones… This is what our feminine weakness means. Maybe, if you can't do it, then let's ask Alyosha?"

"No. Why ask Alyosha, I'll do it myself." Margarita grabbed the axe.

There is no way back now. The axe is in her hand, a man with a sack of roosters is standing by her side. "Are you really going to chop them with the axe?"

"No, I won't," Terekhova categorically says.

Tarkovsky looked from behind the camera, "What do you mean, you won't do it? What will happen to you?"

"I'm going to be sick"

"Great, let's film it!"

Terekhova stood on quivering legs outside the shot. Without turning around, she said, "I think that if you filmed *Andrei Rublev*, you don't have to make any more films."

"Right, that's it, turn off the lights!" and to Rita, "Let's go out and have a talk."

They went out into the sunshine and lit their cigarettes behind some fir trees. Andrei was seething with fury. Finally, trying to remain calm, he said clearly, "Just to let you know, I'm presently making my best film!"

Rita looked at him with his rigidly outlined wrinkles. His jaw bones moved under the skin of his face.

"The answer is still no," she said, and walked off toward the field.

In his diary Tarkovsky wrote, "Today disaster struck: Rita refused to chop off a rooster's head. But I also feel that something here isn't right…"

He did not try to persuade Terekhova, although with this episode he had to show how people can be broken by circumstances and are made to do things that are unthinkable for them. Instead of a horrible naturalistic scene, the inappropriateness of which the director himself felt, they filmed a simple scream of a rooster and threw some feathers into the air — it was as if the murder had happened, and after that Andrei made a close-up of the main character's face, the face of a person who had overstepped the boundary of the impossible.

He demanded that Terekhova bear within her, like in Leonardo da Vinci's portrait of Ginevra de' Benci, something beyond good or evil. The heroine should be charming and somewhat alarming at the same time, through a kind of inner cruelty, not subject to the softening effect of femininity.

Margarita tried to learn more about her character from Andrei's mother and father, who were present at the shooting.

"Arseny Alexandrovich, I heard that you intended to go back to Maria Ivanovna?"

"Maybe I wouldn't have left at all… But she has such a character!" He waved his hand, without going into detail.

Marina recounted how during the war, she and Andrei, constantly hungry, managed to steal cucumbers from somewhere. Happy that they had done something to support the family, they took out their loot. Their mother took the cucumbers out of the children's dirty hands and left the house. She returned sullen. "I threw your trophy into the ditch so that you'll always remember that you can't take someone else's things."

She was indeed a complicated personality.

3.

The Mirror was shot in Tuchkovo. In the summer, the whole Tarkovsky family —Larisa's daughter Olga, little Andrei and Anna Semyonovna — was housed in a rustic cabin not far from the set. It may have seemed that his caring wife was creating an ideal environment for his creativity, but underneath this cozy rustic atmosphere, dangerous conflicts were brewing.

Larisa despised Terekhova. Their constant fights turned the set into a hell. Andrei rushed to try to prevent fist fights. In the scene with the rooster, which was shot at Mosfilm, he was literally torn between the two women boiling with hatred.

Larisa's daughter Olga was becoming a more and more attractive young lady. Red-haired and with full lips, maturing early, she had mastered the art of seduction since childhood. Andrei, in a clear masculine way, favored his stepdaughter and jokingly flirted with her. She jokingly acted coquettishly with him. He even filmed the red-headed beauty in two scenes of *Solaris* and *The Mirror*. However, Olga speaks about her stepfather without any reverence, "He had plenty of those women. He constantly cheated on my mother. He changed his underwear and then left the house. My mother raised scandals, but it was useless."

The appearance of Olga in these scenes encouraged Larisa. She dreamed of her daughter having a career as an actress and pushed Andrei to help her get into VGIK. His support did not help and Olga did not become an actress. When she understood this, Larisa did everything to keep her daughter away from Tarkovsky.

In the meantime the family lived in the cabin near the set of *The Mirror* and a very different story was playing out. The core of it was Larisa's uncontrollable jealousy of Terekhova and her aim to constantly keep her husband drunk and with a lifestyle that would preclude any affairs. She herself, who loved to drink, did not limit her intake.

Raging from the proximity of Terekhova, Larisa managed to turn the little house into a haven for heavy drinking. They drank after the day's work into the next morning. Who knows how the filming crew got on with their work, and what was happening in the director's head after he got carried away with drinking. In any case, Tarkovsky did not resist the way of life that his wife had arranged and was inspired by these surroundings. Constantly flirting with his stepdaughter, and calling her a redheaded beauty, he patted her on the knee and in his drunken stupor he apparently perceived mother and daughter as a single woman.

One might have thought, that such a lifestyle was unacceptable for Tarkovsky, who preferred solitude. But no matter how strange it may seem, young energy and euphoria from the work on his "most important film" allowed him to maintain a constant creative high and inspiration. It was a special state of getting through to the depths of his subconsciousness, his intuition. He filmed and filmed, not motivating his visions, his imagination, entrusting the editing assistant with the function of putting it all together conceptually.

The editing process proved torturous: 15 different versions were made and none of them were right. The film did not hold together, the scenes did not want to come together into a whole. The long shots and unexpected junctions, so essential to Andrei for building a work that rang true, did not hold the frame of the entire structure. Finally, after another reshuffling of parts, the film was brought together.

The Mirror begins at a time when the break between the mother and father has already occurred and only the formalities of saying goodbye remain. But there is also a prologue consisting of a doctor treating a stutterer, shot in a documentary fashion. This liberation of speech, of sounding words, is a metaphor for the liberation of the human soul from the bondage of silence, an impulse for confession.

Immediately after the prologue we see a rickety willow fence next to a rustic cottage. The mother peers into a path that runs away into the forest. When she notices a man's silhouette, she thinks, "If he turns from the bushes toward the house, he's their father. If he does not turn, he's a passer-by." He turns and heads toward the house. The woman does not move. She has already understood that an accidental passer-by is walking toward her, that she has nothing to wait for any longer: her husband will not come back.

The man in front of the young and beautiful woman is Tarkovsky's favorite actor, Solonitsyn, an odd fellow with a big forehead, with a slightly flirtatious grin as if hinting at a better life. She puts a stop to any possibility of further acquaintance with deliberate strictness. Terekhova did not even smile to the nice passer-by; the choice has been made once and for all: uncompromising loneliness and raising the children.

The narrator's voiceover monologue (in the film this is Alexei, the grown-up son) was read by Innokenty Smoktunovsky. It was a story about his childhood, his life, which reflected the life of his parents, like in a mirror.

In real-life, an elderly mother is present on the screen and there is a young woman by her side, Alexei's wife Natalya. Terekhova plays both roles: the grown son's wife, a woman of the present day, and the boy's mother when she was young. They are two embodiments of the same kind of female faith, female character, fused from the most rare charm and a deeply hidden grudge. The prewar and postwar women follow similar paths. The former one — in a linen dress and a heavy bundle of braids on the back of her neck — is proud, self-reliant, graceful and irreversibly lonely. The younger "emancipated woman", regardless of her air of bravado and independence, her hair let down according to fashion, and her efficiency, also breaks up with her husband and moves to her son's home.

Tarkovsky was never moved by romantic themes. They are just an element in the canvas of a more general subject here, namely the inevitability of loneliness in the course of generations. Each generation that goes through life faces the same question: Why is love so fragile? Why can one not hold on to happiness? Why do our loved ones leave us, why do children, brought up by their lonely mother, also go away, leaving their old mother with her unfulfilled love?

There are no answers to these questions. Alexei would not be able to point to any straightforward reason for his parents' fights, just as he cannot explain the reason for his breakup with his wife. His parents' experience does not help keep the family together, avoid guilt in front of their son and wife. Guilt does not extinguish the longing for eternal love. Thus the family history becomes a parable.

Arseny Tarkovsky himself read lines off-screen, piercingly lyric ones:

> *We celebrated every moment*
> *Of our meetings like epiphanies,*
> *Just us two alone in all the world.*
> *Bolder, lighter than a bird's wing,*

You hurtled headlong
Down the stairs, leading
through the wet lilacs to your own territory
From the other side of the looking glass.

As night fell, I was blessed
With grace, the altar gate
Opened, and in the darkness
Your nakedness shined and slowly reclined,
When I awoke I said "God bless you!"
And I knew my blessing
Was daring: you were fast asleep,
The lilac leaned toward you from the table
To touch your eyelids with its universal blue,
Those eyelids brushed with blue
Were peaceful, and your hand was warm.

And in the crystal I saw pulsing rivers,
Hills wreathed in smoke, glimmering seas;
Holding in your palm that crystal sphere,
You dozen on the throne,
And — praise God! — you belonged to me.
Awaking, you transformed
The banal lexicon of human beings
Until speech was full and running over
With resounding strength, and your revealed
The new meaning of the word: it meant king.
Everything in the world was different,
Even the simplest things — the jug, the basin –
When stratified and solid water
Stood between us like a guard.

The mother, played by Terekhova, lives under a shower of poetry,
like in the scene under the lashing rain. She is soaked through with

the uniqueness of her feminine happiness with Arseny, happiness destroyed by parting, but still sounding at any moment of her life, in every movement of her body. This strange, secret happiness, closely bound with tragedy, is portrayed by Margarita Terekhova.

Losing a man and losing a husband who is a poet are different things. Maria Ivanovna was a spiritual invalid, who had suffered an irreparable loss of love. The poems read off screen with their rhythm, their mood, permeate everything that appears on the screen. Poetry, art, high spiritual construction — everything is vain in the face of an unknown danger that destroys one's feelings.

The film has many layers and many "mirrors". The fates of characters overlap, a person's memory wanders in a labyrinth of recollections. Tarkovsky captures the loop of time: the still young mother (Terekhova) looks into a mirror and sees there another, older face, that of Maria Ivanovna in the present day.

Memory is conscience and memory is guilt. The memories in which poems echo was the true crown of the love between Andrei's parents, even though it was ruined.

4.

Tarkovsky was inclined toward a means of storytelling, where the general plot is unveiled through the perception of an ordinary person, through everyday events. Thus in a novella about typography, the latency of the fears of Stalinist times is communicated through a silly mistake, which in the end turns out not to even be one. And in the stories of family dramas, one can see a philosophy of a metamorphosis of human feelings that link the generations.

Tarkovsky liked to work with juxtapositions of different images and time layers. Boys and their military course instructor are playing war games at their school's rifle range. Immediately afterwards there are rumbling shots of a chronicle: soldiers pulling artillery through muddy roads to endless, tormenting music. The music by Bach and

Purcell adds rigor to the scenes of the chronicle, a slow and heavy motion. There is then a cut to a boy standing on the top of a hill, and a bird lands on his head — and suddenly there is a victory salute, and Hitler's corpse is briefly shown in documentary footage.

In everything that Tarkovsky created for depicting childhood, he is exceptionally precise and thorough. The audience recognizes details of the everyday life of their post-war childhood, which live on in their memory, the dark walls made of wood, smelling of wood sap, the lace curtains blown by the wind, the kerosene stove with a sooty flame, the glass bottles with the delicate stems of meadow flowers.

Tarkovsky tries to bring back the moment that had been imprinted in his memory in his childhood, and capture it on film. To drink cold milk from a pitcher covered with drops of condensation. A gust of wind knocks the pitcher from the table and the white milk slowly spreads over the dark wood. Slowly, ever so slowly the flowing whiteness turns into a miracle captured on film. That's it, that's just how it was! Tarkovsky savors the moments: the wind roars outside the window, the lace curtains swell, we see the figures of shaven children. That's how it will always be now, whenever one turns the projector on.

He is led by his aspiration of relaying facts, without getting into the labyrinth of film parables. For this, he thinks it is enough to bring together documentary techniques and concrete images from one's own life.

Art and chronicle are the two opposite poles between which the director sets the world in his films. In *Ivan's Childhood*, Dürer's threatening engravings, as if by accident, force their way into the film. In *The Mirror*, the boy is leafing through a thick volume of reproductions of Leonardo da Vinci to the sound of Bach and Pergolesi. Parallel with Leonardo's reproductions there is a chronicle: Spanish children leaving their home, bombs exploding in Madrid, then the first zeppelins in the skies over Moscow — all of this brings back the unrepeatable taste of time, its breathing is captured on film and interwoven with the present day and with eternity.

In the final scene the reflections are multiplied. A young woman, expecting her first child, sees a path going off into the distance in a field and herself in old age, leading her shaven children by the hand during wartime. At the other end of the field, she sees herself as a young woman, but already abandoned, looking at a future that has not yet come to pass. One's memory likes to play with such slices of time intersecting one another. These moments, captured in the language of film, become a deeply philosophical thing, an image of the course of one's life.

Tarkovsky rarely managed to get into such contact with audiences and hold their attention for the whole film, as if he were transmitting his images into the viewer. More often, in the best case, there occurred moments of being right on target, hitting the bullseye of the viewer's perception, which Tarkovsky refused to see as rational or emotional but rather as something magical that focused the flow of energy emitted by the screen. His aim was bring one's soul to a state of concentration, a task that is difficult and the way to achieve it is unclear. However, such cases of being right on target made a deep impression on the subtle workings of the audience's reception. Alas, only an elite among the audiences possessed this capability.

The "capping of the film", as the crew called the banquet celebrating the end of production, was lavishly organized by Larisa.

It was not a joyous occasion. Andrei was awaiting the verdict after the first screening of the film for the higher-ups. In the meantime they could sigh with relief at the table heaving with delicacies, remembering days bygone.

"It was awfully hard work, but now at least there is something to remember," said a cheerful young woman, the director's assistant Maria Chugunova who had been devoted to Tarkovsky since *Andrei Rublev*. "Do you remember how we sowed a whole field of buckwheat by ourselves? The secretarial staff went off to farm work for the whole autumn, planting potatoes and digging the fields. By the time of shooting, everything was green, and someone had said that buckwheat won't grow in Podmoskovye — it does really well!"

"And we did a lot of good carpentry," said a lighting technician who was a jack of all trades. "We bought two old shacks that were supposed to be demolished, and we used them to build the house that Arseny Arsenyevich imagined, just like in the picture. We followed the photographs exactly."

"Yes, we were all armed with those photographs," boasted the costume designer. "We copied the costumes to the smallest detail — button for button! — and we washed them to make them look worn. It wasn't easy."

"I have the feeling," Solonitsyn quietly broke in, "that Andrei reached a certain stage with this film, one important to him."

"Exactly, Tolya," Tarkovsky said. "I'm free from my debts to myself and to my memories. Now I don't have to carry it all with me, I can leave it with people."

"You'll make a hundred more films about childhood," Larisa assured him.

"No, I have three films left, Pasternak told me," Andrei was serious, in spite of the many shots he had drank.

"Why have you stopped loving your good-luck charms? Did someone's spirit tell you that too?" Larisa was already drunk and laughed at him. "You used to try to get Ogorodnikova into at least one of the scenes, and you had to have apples and horses too. And here they told you, 'Put a rotten orange by the bed, and replace the horses with dogs.' Have you changed your style?"

"I was hoping that the film would have more luck with the distributor, treated like a bold experiment."

The composer Artemyev nodded and said, "For me, everything in working with Andrei is an experiment. In the beginning I was surprised by Andrei's ideas. I thought that they were going to work. And now I'm making noises that become music and vice versa. Do you remember how a stain from a hot glass slowly disappears on a varnished table? Andrei demanded from me a sound of such intensity that it would hit everyone like the smell of ammonia and maybe clear their heads. Andrei is a demanding taskmaster in general. You never get bored working for him. I had to record the creaking of trees for him. All of the trees broke before he found what he was looking for."

"Andrei Arsenyevich checked every branch, every object," Maria continued, enchanted by the director. "He could not stand anything unintended in the shot. Here he made it darker, here he added a silver cast to it, all to make it look real. One guy from VGIK took Andrei Arsenyevich's notes from me to read. He said, 'What an amazing man, he writes that you have to film things spontaneously, and then he does the complete opposite.'"

"Spontaneity, just like improvisation, should be prepared well in advance. I love simple things like wooden boards, and I must have pebbles and bottles. Bottles have to be carefully chosen first, since they will shine differently in the shot."

"And he even arranges floral bouquets himself," Larisa said. "Isn't that right, Andrei? I look and I see my genius walking around in the meadow at dawn. He picked the flowers himself and dried them in bouquets, which this *auteur* later put all over Smoktunovsky's apartment. Well, why are we just sitting here? Whose funeral is it? Fill up the glasses! I will give a toast, although I regret that I turned down the role of the Mother, but it still turned out pretty well. Nothing turns out badly with Andrei Arsenyevich, because he's a genius. Everyone sitting here, we'll all go down with him in the history of world cinema. Little Andrei will open an encyclopedia of cinema twenty years from now and we'll all be in it, with photos and long entries. He'll even found a museum. To your contribution to world cinema, Andrei Arsenyevich!"

"Why are you so solemn, my dear Larisa? You should speak at official meetings."

"And I will, and at the end I'll shout, 'Let's honor comrade Tarkovsky, a deserving fiogure in the arts, a People's Artist and winner of state prizes.' Well, let's wish him this." She expertly downed her drink and looked carefully to see that the plates were not empty and she did not have to bring out more food. Andrei had a caring hostess.

5.

The final cut of *The Mirror* was released in 1974. The film was seen by various departments which tried to answer the same questions from the time of *Andrei Rublev*: Will the film make sense to audiences? Will the people understand it? What exactly is this slippery "genius" trying to say in all of this?

At one of the preliminary screenings at Mosfilm, Andrei defended the film with his characteristic obtuseness, as he had to explain some very complicated issues. He in fact had to explain the unexplainable. He talked in general terms with poorly concealed irritation:

"Since film is an art, it cannot be more accessible than other art forms. I cannot see any sense in popular cinema. A myth has arisen about my inaccessibility and unintelligibility. The only film which can be discussed seriously is Shukshin's *The Red Snowball Tree* — there is nothing incomprehensible from an artistic point of view."

He did not even notice how he denied what Stalin, the immortal leader, had put forth about the "accessibility of the arts", and he accused all of his colleagues of lacking true artistic value.

The film annoyed people with its absence of straightforward storytelling, its eschewing of a clear theme. The need to make an effort to decipher the film irritated the authorities. Well, fine, a simple engineer could not grasp anything, he was ashamed to ask other people leaving the cinema hall. He saw that there wasn't even anyone he could ask for an explanation, but he was touched by the film and had tears in his eyes! By why this was, he wasn't going to ask. What can you expect from an ordinary filmgoer? The officials responsible were supposed to be no less qualified in matters of cinema than the critics who knew the subject. They hand down ready ideas which determined the stylistic approach and put the given field into an historical or a world context. So what then, should we send an interpreter to every showing of this Tarkovsky's film? It's mockery, hidden mockery. This director acts in an extremely loyal fashion, but he's defiant and his eyes burn with hatred. Who comes into a government office like this? They should come in with a smile and in high spirits, and express their readiness to follow their older comrades' advice. He comes in like a hedgehog, in his black-market outfit, and looks with disdain on your Soviet necktie. He's a foreign element. And he has become skilled at playing tricks on the authorities. Every film raises a scandal!

This is more or less what Filipp Ermash and the decision-makers at Goskino and the Union of Cinematographers thought. Nor did his fellow directors have much love for Tarkovsky, as he treated their work with total disregard.

At a joint meeting of Goskino and the Union of Cinematographers, four films were deliberated: Yuri Karasik's *The Hottest Month*, Andron Mikhalkov-Konchalovsky's *A Lover's Romance*, Andrei Smirnov's *Autumn* and Tarkovsky's *The Mirror*. With regard to the last of these, among all of the different evaluations of the film, the most justified criticism was formulated by Vladimir Baskakov, who was then the first vice-president of Goskino:

"The film raises interesting moral and ethical issues, but it is hard to grasp. This is a film for a small circle of filmgoers, it's for an elite, but cinema cannot be just for an elite."

Grigory Chukhray, one of the secretaries of the Union of Cinematographers, proved Tarkovsky's suspicions that he was biased against the director's work. He stated simply, "This film of Tarkovsky's is a failure. The man wants to tell something about time and about himself. Maybe he succeeded in saying something about himself, but not about time."

The first two films were given as examples of the greatest achievements of Soviet cinema, showing directions for further development. They debated *Autumn* for a long time and eventually shelved it, and they thought deeply about the fate of *The Mirror*.

Outside the film studio, a division of defenders and critics of the film, which Tarkovsky inevitably experienced, was especially clear.

Maybe the reason for this was his bare depiction of his private confessions, which was uncharacteristic for traditional Soviet cinema. Or maybe the viewer was attracted by the poignant childhood theme which they could not understand, which annoyed them. The vague nature of the plot had an effect also on the audience; no one wanted to be called a fool. The viewer wanted to understand and to feel something, but Tarkovsky fought against this and wanted to dig deeper to people's deepest emotions. Nonetheless, he did not often manage to break through the growing irritation. The Academy member Likhachev claimed that Tarkovsky's films were difficult and people should be taught how to appreciate them, that is, a lecture should be held before showings — and it would be better to allow the press to publish articles about his films. But there was a strict ban that only a few voices could break through.

The rumors circulating around the film, as we would think nowadays, proved an excellent PR campaign.

At the first showing in the Dom Kino, the filmmakers so wanted to see the film they had heard so much about, that they broke the glass door at the entrance to the hall.

On that day Andrei's dream came true: it was the first time that his father appreciated his son as he deserved. Arseny Alexandrovich sat at the banquet table after the premiere at the Dom Kino, his eyes shining from tears, quietly said again and again, "Andrei, was it all really like that? I didn't know that. My God, how talented you are."

Finally, Arseny Alexandrovich gave a toast and said the words that his son probably found the most precious. "Andrei, I drink to you. You have made a remarkable film about how a child becomes an artist. I didn't think that you could have felt everything so deeply."

Later he learned of his mother's serious illness. Andrei sat by her bedside, lowering his head with his hair falling over his forehead. He clenched his teeth from nervousness and one could see his jaw muscles move. He tapped his fingers quickly, as if crushing crumbs on the edge of the bed. He already knew the verdict, and this meant that the end was near.

"This time everyone is praising your work. Arseny told me."

"Well, not everyone. But I get letters from people who had seen the film."

"Do they swear at you?"

"Not necessarily. There are a lot of good letters, which show an understanding of the film and say that their memory was shaken by it. They even remember the shirts they wore as children."

"I remember that whenever I had just managed to wash your clothes, you already made them dirty again. You either fell into a hole or got into the blackberries."

"We all remember everything together." He placed his hand on hers and noticed how that dry hand, which had washed mountains of laundry, resembled the feet of a bird.

His mother would die of cancer when Andrei was far away, in Italy.

6.

Tarkovsky was undoubtedly comfortable hiding from the world behind Larisa's wide back. Without getting into things in detail, he let her arrange everything in their lives and deal with their business affairs. If he asked her anything, he would get a tangle of lies in response. Or maybe what she said was true? It wasn't worth finding out. It was undoubtedly more comfortable for him this way.

Andrei always dreamed about a house in the country. Through Larisa's efforts they bought an old, dilapidated house on the Para River in the nearly deserted village of Myasnoye. Larisa took care of their living space, getting herself so into it that the brick house miraculously appeared on the riverside, with wood shutters and an enormous glass veranda. Here Andrei had a separate office of his own with a fireplace. Of course, building such a mansion required a great deal of money. Andrei was pleased with the house and constantly complained about the debt that he had racked up. Guests rarely visited, as few could stand a journey of 300 kilometers without a car. Olga Surkova often visited with her new husband Dmitri. In the evenings their customary conversations took place beside the fireplace.

"It's great," Olga said, stretching her legs closer to the fireplace. "Here we are sitting in the maestro's own manor."

"We're sitting in debt, and up to our ears," Andrei illustratively held his hand up against his throat and his expression, which until now had been content, quickly turned angry. "Just think," he went on. "No, really, just think, what foreign directors in other countries are counting their pennies? Just one film like *Ivan's Childhood*, if it got a normal distribution, could bring huge profits. The film would pay for itself and I wouldn't have to beg."

"Oh, dear Andrei," Larisa said as she added wood to the fire. "If they didn't keep you without work, you would have already made ten films. And not just any films, but ones that win at festivals. We are sitting in the middle of nowhere and we're happy. You can't get out of here without a car, it's an ordeal, and we don't have any hope of getting a car. But over there, every teenager has a car. Here, Peredelkino is booming and on Nikolina Gora all the distinguished people have their villas, and cars. They even go to those resorts for filmmakers."

"Getting to a resort is nothing. I could also get a pass there, I've just never asked for one."

"You never ask anyone for anything, especially those monsters."

"They make me angry with their prohibitions, their rejection of my applications and their derision. They are not letting me work! Sometimes I think I'll spit on it all and leave. I will make films abroad in peace and get my rewards."

Olga had doubts. "So that's where you want to go! It's not so easy to get out of here, running away or making a fictional marriage like Iosseliani."

"That's true," Larisa said, growing into a rage. "You should get away on a business trip and then apply to reunite the family. Let them throw a tantrum here. In the West everyone knows your work and appreciates you. Here they aren't even allowed to write a positive review of one of your films. Let people realize for themselves that Tarkovsky is a genius, and they do understand! Look at the sack of letters you got after you made *Solaris*. Audiences want to see Tarkovsky's films."

"Exactly. This is exactly why I can't go anywhere. You see, I understood that I have my audience and I have no right to betray them." Andrei looked into the fire without blinking. The bright rays of the fireplace reflected off his cheekbones and little flames danced in his dark eyes. "If you want to know, after reading those letters I realized what my mission, my destiny is. Now I know for sure that I mustn't leave. My real audience is here."

He was being honest both when he dreamed of escaping the Soviet Union and when he claimed a deep attachment to his native land. Inside he was seething from contrary impulses. His nerves were on edge. He bit his nails almost to the quick after every rejection of one of his scripts, after every humiliating screening of the film for officials, and he fell into a deep depression. To hell with this place! And this river, this Russia with its forests and meadows, his upbringing in the countryside, what should he do with all that? Leave it behind? His heart was simply torn in two.

This profound expert on the human spirit, who carefully studied the conflict within mankind between the spiritual and material worlds, really liked to live in idleness and plenty. Like his father, he strove for comfort and the good life. With Arseny Alexandrovich, his craving for comfortable living resulted in building more bookshelves, whereas Andrei managed to get for himself a better life under the Soviet system.

Thanks to Larisa's efforts, the Tarkovskys traded two apartments they had in a brick building on Mosfilmovskaya Street — a two-room apartment and a three-room one on the same floor. The three-room apartment formally belonged to Larissa and Andrew, while the one-bedroom apartment belonged to Anna Semyonovna with little Andrei and Larisa's daughter Olga. Prior to leaving for Italy, Tarkovsky fought for the right to put a partition on the landing, connect the two apartments and redesign and renovate everything. Andrei decided to make a large dining room. They bought a massive sideboard carved from oak, from which he removed the paint so that it would look like living wood. In the same room there stood a massive table and the chairs from the early 20th century.

It was necessary to furnish the rest of the space with stylish and exclusive furniture. The heads of a chain of furniture stores visited the Tarkovskys, ate and drank and built their own exclusive import furniture. Tarkovsky was only slightly concerned about the money. He knew his debts and his meager earnings well, he carried the names of his creditors in a notebook, but Larisa's arguments were reassuring:

"Don't trouble yourself with this. I'll find the money! You'll still win awards!"

One of the sources of money (besides Zorka's fur coat and "loans" from kind people) was known for certain.

One day Larisa urgently called Olga Surkova:

"We must get a loan for an Arab-style office for Andrei immediately! But we're unemployed and they won't work with us. They will only give it to us with your salary backing it up. Can you imagine how wonderful it will be? Can't Andrei work in a decent environment?"

Olga agreed, "Of course! More than anyone else. What do I have to do?"

She was ready to immediately come and help the build the office.

"Your job is to help get the loan. The rest is nothing! Buy the furniture under your own name. You'll pay ten percent of it each month for one year. Of course I'll give you the money."

Olga's salary was 110 rubles a month, but it turned out that the monthly payment was 44 rubles. She didn't want to tell her parents about what she had done and she lived a hand-to-mouth existence for a year. Larisa didn't even think to pay her "friend" back.

After the housewarming they organized a dinner again.

Now Larisa could walk proudly. She covered the expensive tables with food and received Andrei's fervent thanks.

"I want to propose a toast to Larisa, who saved me and to whom I am forever in debt," he clumsily sought to express his appreciation, and he did it from the heart, because he didn't know how to pretend.

Larisa acted embarrassed. She looked down and interrupted him, "What are you saying, Andrei?"

"Yes, yes, Larisa! Everyone ought to know that without this woman, I'd be totally lost. I want everyone to drink to Larisa, to this saintly woman."

Someone suppressed a grin, wondering what the price of "saving" Andrei was. He could not act. At that moment he believed he had been saved by Larisa, by Irma, by Natalya, from a beggarly and miserable existence. After all, this "saintly woman" provided her unemployed husband with a decent living. The sources of Andrei's income were not clear to him. She made up a series of things, "I got it from somewhere", "I pawned a watch", "some kind people wanted to support your new film". Andrei's diary entries from those years are full of complaints about his growing debts. Probably, after he had put his concerns down on paper, he pushed the problem to the back of his mind. How could he work under such a burden?

After the feast, the guests proceeded to dance until they dropped. Their host could stand no more and quietly retired to his Arab-style office, giving the obligatory speech. Tarkovsky always gave long and thorough toasts, touching on issues of civilization, spirituality, problems in filmmaking, often voicing elaborate ideas in an inspired tone, unaware that he was alone in all of this.

"Larisa, where is everybody?" Suddenly he looked around the empty dining room, as if he had just awoken.

"Andrei, we're in here," Larisa said with an innocent look from the office, where she had secretly been having another drink.

"Larisa, are you all drunk?"

"Me?" Her voice shook with anger. "Me? Well, Andrei, look here, my glass is sitting on the table completely untouched. You always want to hurt me somehow."

The predilection that the author of *Andrei Rublev* had for beautiful things and self-indulgence is hard to understand. For some reason, one is inclined to think that an artist who fights for the spiritual and against base material things, would have a completely unassuming life. He would work without noticing what he eats and what he sleeps on, with his eyes always fixed on the absolute. The Soviet style, alien to the aristocratic, manor-bred tradition of the classic writers, and even to his life in Florence, most likely did not appeal to this artist.

Clearly it wasn't the Soviet predilections that already revealed themselves in the teenager from a poor family, caught up in the pursuit of stylish clothes. Clearly poverty in an attic and a ragged sweater were not Tarkovsky's style. He needed to be in comfortable, prestigious surroundings which paid attention to what he was wearing. He wanted to keep choice things around him because he thought himself entitled to be surrounded by comfort and beauty, just like those who had lavish gardens in Nikolina Gora, in the Alps or on Lake Geneva. He loved the material world such as stones, driftwood carefully collected and stored, this pristine part of creation. And also little things "with a history, with a suggestion of the stamp of time", this was a passion for him. Andrei had exceptional taste.

The Rothschild-like urge, which had taken ahold of the teenager who played *rasshibalochka*, had not abandoned the older Tarkovsky, who sought to put the spiritual first in his films. Later, when he reached the hated "capitalist world", he was desperate to get rich, not by robbing banks, of course, but thanks to his art which was considered worthy of prizes and high fees.

When *The Mirror* was almost finished, the director of the Cannes Film Festival, Mr. Bessy, visited Moscow to make the official choice of films. However, Goskino and Filipp Ermash personally had already decided against allowing the film to be shown abroad. Ermash wove a web of intrigue and ridiculous laws to stop Bessy from seeing the film. When Bessy had not managed to see *The Mirror* due to all these tricks out of a spy novel, he decided to take the film on any terms. Ermash was categorically opposed. The affair ended with the Soviet Union, for the first time, not taking part in the festival.

After a test screening with a hall full to capacity, it was announced that "the film was a flop, it couldn't attract viewers". *The Mirror* was put in a very low category of distribution and only three or four copies were sent out. Any mention of the film was removed from the press by the censors.

Andrei lay on the couch, his hands across his chest. He thought it would be better now if he were in his grave: his beloved film — the confession of his soul — was held back from an audience hungry for it!

"They've buried *The Mirror!* They've buried me! That stupid bastard, I know this is Ermash's doing." He jumped up and darted across the room, breaking his fingers. "The bastard! I'll leave the country. Yes, I'll leave!"

"Dear Andrei, where are you off to?" Larisa arrived with a steaming mug of coffee. She understood him perfectly and accepted his aim to leave the USSR. "Drink your coffee while it's hot. I put two spoonfuls of sugar in it."

"Leave the coffee! Think about it, I have only one way of showing my strength: make films where they won't hide them away and deny them."

"Andrei, it's obvious. They should understand who they've been bullying for so many years! Whom they wouldn't let work."

"I'm completely helpless! At three screenings they wanted to shelve it! And who's responsible? It's Ermash, and I'm just his slave. The studios and critics are under his control. It's disgusting."

Another hiatus began as he received rejections for making a new film. Tarkovsky's application for an adaptation of *Hamlet*, which he had long dreamed of, was returned to him. In 1977 however, he put on a production of Shakespeare's play at the Lenin Komsomol Theatre with Anatoly Solonitsyn in the main role. Tarkovsky claimed that there was a great mystery in this play for him. He said the tragedy of Hamlet in the "obligation, before committing murder, of accepting the laws of this world, of acting according to its rules, that is to say, giving up one's spiritual aspirations and becoming a common killer. That's where the tragedy is!"

Gertrude was played by Margarita Terekhova, who again grabbed a role intended for Larisa.

The play's run was brief. Tarkovsky proved an unwelcome figure in theater.

Chapter 8.
STALKER, A CONFESSION TO DRAW ENERGY FOR LIVING

I.

No matter how deep the wound, how great the insult, the need to work was more important than anything else. They did not let him film *The Idiot*, they flung aside the *Hoffmaniana*, they turned down his *Hamlet* — in every possible way they prevented him from working with the classics. He did not want to make comedies. Perhaps science-fiction would save him?

Indeed, Tarkovsky's application for a screen adaptation of a book by the Strugatsky brothers was accepted and Tarkovsky began work on the new film. He had taken notice of Boris and Arkady Strugatsky's story *Roadside Picnic* and began to work with them on the screenplay. Gradually, the original idea was completely reconsidered. Arkady Strugatsky said with delight, "We wrote eighteen versions of the script, because Andrei demanded it."

The genre was pretty profitable and the Strugatsky brothers were at the peak of their popularity. *Roadside Picnic* was read by almost the entire adult population of the Soviet Union.

The plot of the novel is gripping. After the invasion of the Earth by an unknown spaceship, somewhere on the territory of a foreign country a mysterious Zone emerges, which attracts human visitors but at the same time hides a certain danger. The laws of the unknown civilization are in force there, different from the ones on Earth, and they transform this slice of ordinary territory into a trap. Special military forces guard the Zone. The most important thing attracting people to the Zone is the mysterious wish-granting Golden Sphere. However it obeys only one's deepest subconscious desires, granting the true, innermost wishes of whomever comes to it. The Zone is constantly visited by scientists, adventurers, people who think they can save the world. But nobody manages to achieve his goal. Even the illegal profession of a guide to the Zone, the Stalker, emerges. The novel talks about a Stalker who combines adventurousness, romanticism and a passion for the unknown with a mercenary cynicism. As he leads yet another group of people into the Zone, the Stalker pursues his own aim: to sacrifice his companions to the Zone, get to the Golden Sphere and plead that his invalid daughter be healed.

While they worked on the script, the Strugatskys changed the structure of the plot right off, going in a new direction. Now two people headed for the Zone: the Professor and the Writer. The Stalker sacrifices his companions and reaches the Golden Sphere, but instead of his daughter's health he only gains wealth, cursing his perennial subconscious yearning to become rich.

Tarkovsky was not satisfied with the material he received. He kept purging the script of its fantastic elements, transforming the risky escapade into the Zone into a discussion. Nobody died or gave up, but nobody reached the chamber they sought either. All three of them stop on the threshold of that place, not courageous enough to make a wish. Each of them was afraid of the impurity of their secret thoughts.

2.

The location was found in Tallinn. The territory of a neglected power plant looked suitably creepy, a waste ground with the remains of industrial structures.

Larisa hired herself as the assistant director and she began organizing her own little kingdom. Only her people stayed long on the set. The Tarkovskys moved into a two-story house on location that had escaped destruction. There parties with "their" people took place each night, with those who pleased the "lady". Those who treated her negatively, were turned away forever.

Larisa employed a certain Araik, an intern at the Higher Directors' Courses as the second director. This man was supposed to take on all of Tarkovsky's organizational matters. Araik however knew nothing about filmmaking and ended up helping Larisa in her household duties. Conjectures about some "other" help that the young intern gave the lady of the house are only speculation. Therefore, Andrei had to solve a great deal of practical issues and financial problems himself.

Under Larisa's influence, Tarkovsky broke up with the artistic director Alexander Boim, accusing him of "coming drunk to the set". From that moment the duties of artistic director fell on Andrei's shoulders too. Next was the excellent cameraman Georgy Rerberg, a clever and intelligent man who did not yield to the feminine charms of his "hostess". A coincidence helped Larisa to get rid of Rerberg. The entire footage material turned out to be unusual, a disaster! Later it proved that Mosfilm had purchased discounted Kodak film. The testing of the film, performed in Moscow, was insufficient and Rerberg did not check it afterwards. Tarkovsky was furious. Clenching his teeth, he attacked Georgy, "How can you explain this defect?" Andrei had a talent for being hard on people. "It's a fishy story."

One could see that Rerberg, who was standing in front of Tarkovsky with his girlfriend, was slightly drunk. "I have nothing to do with it," he said, "though I deeply regret what happened of course."

"You should have checked the tape in addition!" Andrei yelled.

"But it had been checked by the Mosfilm experts. Rechecking it is not my job." Rerberg was handsome, women loved him, and in this particular case he was right.

"Oh, so it's not your duty? But drinking and hanging around with the girls is?"

"It's my business whom I spend my free time with and how. That's it, Andrei, I'm not working with you anymore!" Rerberg took his girlfriend by the hand and stormed off.

"You behave like a drunken, unrestrained lout! Get out, get out of here! I never want to see you on the set again, get it?!" the infuriated director shouted at the operator.

It was said that the fight with Rerberg and the spoiled footage had undermined Tarkovsky's health — he suffered a heart attack. Larisa did not hold back from blaming the "drunken lout" Rerberg.

In reality, Tarkovsky's extreme egoism had been struck another blow, and not from Rerberg but from his superiors. One might have expected him to have gotten used to the fact that in Soviet cinema, he was allotted the role of an exile. This was especially insulting in the case of the country's number one film director, which Tarkovsky undoubtedly considered himself to be. The situation was typical for the USSR, which not only suppressed everything that did not fit into an orthodox plan, but also took privileges away from obstinate people who could not "find a common language" with the authorities.

The naive Tarkovsky had applied to the Union of Cinematographers for a pass to one of their artist retreats, but against all his expectations, he was refused. Tarkovsky could not stand refusals. He became so furious that he suffered heart palpitations from this overt humiliation and denial of his merits from the Union. The doctors, however, did not diagnose a heart attack, but they advised taking valerian extract. An old doctor, after he had listened to Tarkovsky's confused, rambling story about getting a pass to the artist's retreat, smiled at his patient with pity and said, "It would really do you no harm to take some rest, my friend. In the past in such cases we used to recommend going to Capri, and now we prescribe valerian. Oh, just don't use a tincture. Better to infuse the root yourself. My advice to you is to be more careful with alcohol. How many young people from your artistic circles have we lost prematurely: heart attacks, strokes linked to alcoholism. They keep putting people down!"

The impressionable Andrei gave up drinking for good. He could not think about dying, afraid even of a temporary inability to work.

The footage of *Stalker* was ruined and he had other plans seething in his head. The film had to be immediately reshot with the remaining money. In fact, he thought himself lucky to have the opportunity to make everything different this time around. There had to be a different twist to the action, totally different! In this case the entire film turned out to be a "rough draft".

The place of Rerberg was taken by an outstanding cameraman, Alexander Knyazhinsky, a gentle and compliant person.

Few people were admitted into the little residence of the Tarkovskys. Knyazhinsky, who surprisingly had no inclination for drinking, joined them. Thus Andrei, who had given up drinking, gained someone sober to talk to.

Larisa herself was secretly imbibing. She was protected by her faithful assistants, who did the job for her and Araik. Soon, however, Araik found something he could do; he became an independent manager of the house in Myasnoe, organizing the arrangement and construction, thanks to whom there soon appeared a banya on the bank, a sturdy fence, that separated the "manor" from the enraged, drunken, enviously peeking "masses".

3.

Tarkovsky was making a new film, having changed the emphases with regard to the main character and intensified his attention to the border between "the possible and the impossible in the shot". The reworked depiction of the imperceptible danger of the Zone was close to mysticism, a paranormal experiment on set.

As he had become the artistic director of the film, he rejected all the traditional elements of science-fiction, lemon-colored sky, mutants, and as he had lost his assistant, he had to arrange the "mosaic" at the bottom of the stream in the Zone by himself, making the trees the way he wanted them, and making the walls in the Stalker's home look old. Every detail in a shot, as usual, did not escape Tarkovsky's attention.

Fortunately, a wonderful man from Kazan appeared, a true, selfless fan of the director. Andrei called him Rashid, or Rashidik. He appointed him the artistic director's assistant. A teetotaler constantly finding DIY solutions for the film, Rashid proved himself an indispensable jack of all trades, who did all the work with textures in the shot. Now that he had relieved the director of some of the burden, he painstakingly scratched the walls or made them dirty, imitating cracks and mold. He planted or rooted out, at Tarkovsky's request, any vegetation that could get into the shot. He worked silently, without fuss and not saying a word about remuneration. This was the kind of enthusiasm with which Tarkovsky had dreamed of making *auteur* films.

The Zone began to breathe with its secret, satanic essence. Dead sands suddenly gave way to streams of water, a unused railway writhed dimly, crushed bricks stood silently about the terrible event that had occurred, half-destroyed buildings, deformed reinforcement, ruins of structures with gaping "eye sockets" of broken windows.

The Zone terrifies us with its monotonous lifelessness. A terrible trial called the "meat grinder" (which is just a long metal pipe that one can only go through with extreme mental effort) makes one believe in its bloodthirsty nature. The Zone, just like the mysterious Solaris, is something that thinks. It accurately "tests" those who reach it. That is why the "meat grinder", after it "scans" a person, immediately makes its verdict: to execute or to pardon. It is also why the traps of the Zone, which Stalker has explored, have been so far kind to this regular visitor to the unknown.

The Zone enchants the three men who come to it and keeps them and the audience in constant suspense. Tarkovsky had guessed at the mechanism of fear: it was not a bloody massacre with rows of realistic flayed corpses, but rather it was the anticipation of the unknown, when one is frightened and alarmed even by a slight shift into the unexplained. In the deadly emptiness, an element of everyday life — an old telephone ringing in the long-abandoned ruins — seems more frightening than a series of shots of unseen horrors. Even the appearance of a lively black dog that sticks by the Stalker in the deserted Zone, leads one to alarm: why is it black, where did it come here and who or what is it?

Every detail bears a seductive mystery in the debris that remains after an unknown catastrophe. But is it debris? Or it is a "mosaic" put together with some unknown intention? Aquatic plants float threateningly, while, below them, under the water, there are shattered tiles, springs, bundles of wire, syringes. The image of the Saviour on a prayer card looks up through the water among shimmering little fish. Tarkovsky put together this "canvas" himself and for some reason placed a page from an old calendar offhandedly among the debris. The date on it is December 29th, the last day of his life…

There are no digressions in the film, no flashbacks or side plots. The running time is compressed by the viewer's suspense. The risky game with death becomes a spiritual journey where the three characters come to discover themselves, their basic truth. There are many close-ups here, of Anatoly Solonitsyn (the Writer), Nikolai Grinko (the Scientist) and Alexander Kaidanovsky (the Stalker), who stand in a tense relationship with the Zone, with each other and each of them within his own self. The main changes in the second version of the film affected the Stalker: he turned from an adventurer and a cynic into a servant of a cause.

The Stalker's face and his figure reflect the collapse of the hopes and vanities of his past attempts. He is tormented by being unable to understand some important meaning that he strives to grasp, as well as the riddle of the Zone. The Stalker is obsessed with the attempt to bring his companions to the miraculous room and provide them with the opportunity to make their wishes come true. Maybe this time he has not gone astray and these people's wishes will manage to change the world for the better? But the way to the Zone reveals the true nature of the Scientist and the Writer: they are superficial and vain. The Stalker's hope dies slowly. He already has doubts about the very idea of improving the world by human willpower, in the possibility of finding great thoughts corresponding to the Creator's plan in the best of people.

Finally, they reach the ruins and the mysterious room they have long awaited, which looks like a laboratory that has been blown up and then flooded. The time has come to make their innermost wishes. However, the Scientist begins to hurriedly assemble a bomb that he has secretly carried through the Zone, risking his life. His aim is to destroy the Room, to avoid someone's insane wish coming true. He has tried to reach this place for this. But by destroying the possible danger, he will also destroy any hope. The Stalker fiercely defends the Room, saying "I want unhappy people, just like myself, to have this little piece of happiness in their lives, this Room…"

After a fierce fight the Scientist throws away the bomb, but he refuses to make a wish as well. The Writer too decides not to use the opportunity. No one on whom the Stalker hoped dares test the mysterious powers of the Room. The Zone has torn off the mask from these self-confident, successful people. After they have made the arduous journey and reached the Room they longed for, where wishes come true, the protagonists of *Stalker* do not dare step across its threshold. During their journey they have gained sufficient grounds for doubting the sincerity of their own intentions. Each of them admits to himself now that, deep in his heart he is not pure enough and lacks a strong wish to change the world for the better.

The Stalker is disappointed again. He is an eternal apostle, who fails to find his Christ. When he returns from the Zone, the exhausted man says to his wife with grief, "The only thing they can think about is how to sell themselves not too cheaply!" His wife — no longer a young woman, who lives in pitiful slums with the strange guide to the Zone, delivers a monologue, addressing the film audience directly: "You've probably noticed already that he's not of this world. All our neighborhood laughed at him. He was so clumsy, he looked so pitiful. My mother used to say, 'He's a stalker, he's doomed, he's an eternal prisoner!' … We had a lot of sorrow, but it's better to have a bitter happiness than a dull, gray life. He approached me and said, 'Come with me' and I did, and I never regretted it."

The wife's monologue is the most powerful part of the film, as it is the center-point of the film's hidden meanings. She is the only sincere, deeply feeling person. Unlike the seekers of meaning, she is driven by an unchanging, simple feeling, and the only one that really matters: love.

When Alisa Freindlich delivered that monologue at the audition, Tarkovsky begged his crew to save the recording. "It's impossible to repeat it! That's right to the point, it's exactly what I wanted!"

"What are you talking about, Andrey Arsenyevich? I'm an actress. I'll repeat it as many times as I have to."

In the final scene of the film, the camera stops before Stalker's ill daughter sitting at a table, who possesses great inner strength. Deprived of the ability to walk, she moves a glass full of water by the power of her thought and in her thin girlish voice carefully reads poems by Fyodor Tyutchev, "And through the downcast lashes, I see the dull flame of desire."

The key to it all has been found! Everyone who went through the trials of the Zone lacked this flame of desire, a yearning for achieving their goal. Without it, a man is sucked into the mire of trivial material needs. His soul is alive as long as three eternal values exist: love, poetry and art. The poems by Arseny Tarkovsky, sound in the background with the refrain "But it is not enough", as if assuring us that the Stalker will not cease searching for his Christ, to bring a person into the secret Room who will manage to fix what sinful "free men" have done by his willpower and desire. However risky his encounters with the Zone, exhausted but not deprived of hope, he will not deny the purpose of his strange existence.

4.

Stalker is probably the most integrated of Tarkovsky's films. The central idea of the film is the trial of fundamental moral values in the face of a new and inevitable catastrophe. Tarkovsky presents his main concern with utter clarity — humanity can be saved only by its spirituality overcoming its material aspirations. The logic of the development of this core idea required an extensive, clear form, an asceticism of texture. The film lacks that fragmentary discreteness that created a polyphony of colors in *The Mirror*. There are no lively textures such as apples in the rain or horses, and there is almost no color. Gray and monochrome completely prevail in the film. The work of the composer Eduard Artemyev is something other than music in this film. The sound is abstract, something that makes one uneasy. This is how a film depiction of the landscape after the Apocalypse could look.

As Tarkovsky explained:

> To me it was very important that the script meet three conditions, the unity of time, space and action. If in *The Mirror* it seemed important to me to work sequentially with chronicles, dreams, reality, hopes, assumptions, memories, the fuss of circumstances that the main character faces with the relentless problems of existence, then in *Stalker* I wanted there to be no break between editing clusters. I wanted it to be as if the whole film was made in a single shot.
>
> Only the external situation can be called fantastic here … But from the perspective of what happens to the characters, there is no fantasy whatsoever. The film was made in such a way that the viewer has the feeling that everything is happening now, that the Zone is somewhere here.

At the time *Stalker* was finished, Tarkovsky turned 48 years old. He had put three years of his life into that film which, as it turned out later, was not to last so long.

Even many years since *Stalker* was made, after the Chernobyl disaster, after the death of its director, the film carries within it a visceral impression of the reality of what is happening in the plot. This film once more highlights the fact that in the case of Tarkovsky's work, we are dealing not only with a rich imagination, erudition, non-standard thinking, and the courage to innovate, but also with some kind of breakthrough into a world of secret knowledge that he himself could not always understand. Tarkovsky's prophecies are the evidence of how close he was in his search toward the main source of truth, toward the understanding of the higher laws of the universe, to put it simply, toward the Creator by whom he was led.

Years will pass and the word "zone" will enter the dictionary as referring to a deadly, deserted land. The designation of the fourth reactor of the Chernobyl nuclear power plant corresponds with the fourth section destroyed in the Zone of *Stalker*. Also the diameter of both exclusion zones — in the film and in real life — is the same: 30 kilometers. And the terrible prophecy of the page from the calendar lying amongst the underwater debris, a page showing the last day of Tarkovsky's life, would be brought to pass. Death came on December 29.

His colleagues called Tarkovsky's gift of insight into the hidden meaning of things an incredible sense of intuition.

The editing assistant on all Tarkovsky's films, Lyudmila Feiginova, was incredibly devoted to his aesthetic. She literally broke down every frame into its smallest details and claimed that "Tarkovsky had some secret insight, which told him all the tricks. He had a talent to receive signals from outer space." Otherwise, one would not be able to explain the sudden flashes of insight that he had on the set, the spur decisions he made to change the script and the set. The film crew was exhausted by his delirious dreams, as if he were driven by some higher powers, his extreme neuroticism, his sudden persistence in that which was vague, his impulsiveness, his extreme megalomania that made no exceptions in any situation at work.

"All of us who worked with Tarkovsky found our endurance, fortitude and patience tried. At work he was merciless with himself as well — nothing was trivial for him and he demanded the same from us. He indulged neither himself nor anyone else."

Even those who shared his views found it difficult to work with Tarkovsky. Many of them left him. However, the reason was not only Tarkovsky's sharp character and the spontaneity of his creative methods. People were disgusted by Larisa lording it over them. She thought herself the "lady" on the set. The habits of a merchant's wife were apparently in her blood, and the methods that she used to deal with undesirable people disgusted many.

This was also the case with Alexander Kaidanovsky, an actor who was in every respect close to Tarkovsky's aesthetic. However, Alexander established a friendship only with Solonitsyn and cursed the moment when he got involved with the film. He suffered under the venomous atmosphere in the group, under Larisa's petty tyranny and the servility of her team. Nor did the maestro himself raise the spirits of those helping to realize the film, as he was in a continuous state of neurosis, capable of screaming at people and insulting them.

It is difficult to understand how Tarkovsky reacted to his wife's behavior. Did he really notice any of that? Or did he not want to know, wishing to maintain his usual lifestyle? But Tarkovsky didn't know how to act, adapt to a life that he couldn't accept. Does this mean then that he saw no problem with manipulating people? Was Larisa doing the dirty work and he stood apart from it?

One should not forget that this film poet wasn't a man of this world, who combined within himself very different personalities and psychological models. Genius or a high level of talent are always an anomaly, a hypertrophy of some abilities in turn for suppressing others.

Indeed, he was an example of nonconformity and honesty in his work, a knight of high ideals. Within the territory of film he felt like a warrior for eternal truths, a defender of moral ideals. His battlefield was the world, and his goal the salvation of the human race.

However, his deep elaboration of the structure of personality has a slight shade of a dissector to it, to cut up, to study the mechanism, to reach the essence. The man himself, with his ordinary existence, his everyday life, was of little interest to Tarkovsky.

5.

Stalker was received without particular objection and it reached screens in 1980. The film was honored with wide distribution and the money for production went not only to Andrei as the film director and artistic director, but also to Larisa, as Tarkovsky's second assistant director.

It came to win the Italian David di Donatello Award and received the special Luchino Visconti Award.

Dreaming of future projects, Tarkovsky applied again for filming adaptations of *Hamlet* and *The Idiot*. Ermash however stuck to his principles: to categorically suppress any opportunities for Tarkovsky to work with classical masterpieces. He hastily gave the green light to Alexander Zarkhi's film *Twenty Six Days from the Life of Dostoyevsky* with Solonitsyn playing the main character, and he shrugged to Tarkovsky, who was going mad from the constant refusals, saying that he would be happy to give Tarkovsky permission for *The Idiot*, but he could not allow two Dostoyevsky films to be made at the same time.

A cunning practice existed in the USSR: shunned film directors who could reach screens in their home country only with difficulty, but who were popular in the West, were given incentives to keep them at home, and if they did leave, they would have nothing to complain about, as they got the recognition they deserved from their country. In 1980 Tarkovsky was awarded the title of People's Artist of Russia. Not under any illusions about the seriousness of the incentive, Tarkovsky had little hope for being permitted to work on his new film — and he wanted to work like never before.

"I feel so strong now, so high in artistic terms, my urge to work is so strong, but where, where is that work?" Andrei said to Tonino Guerra, who was visiting Moscow from Italy.

Cinephiles and lovers of literature were already aware then of the busy Tonino's incredible energy, the boundlessness of his great love for people and the world, the magnitude of his contribution to cinema.

He had started writing as a young man in a Nazi concentration camp. After the war he immersed himself in the world of cinema, which was booming then in Italy. He authored scripts for films that have entered the canon of world cinema classics, working with the most prominent directors. For Michelangelo Antonioni, Tonino wrote the scripts for the following films: *L'Avventura*, *La Notte*, *L'Ecclise*, *Il deserto rosso*, *Blowup*, *Zabriskie Point*, *The Mystery of Oberwald* and *Identification of a Woman*. Together with his close friend and compatriot

Federico Fellini, he wrote the play *Amarcord*, which was later turned into a famous film. After that came *And the Ship Sails On*, *Ginger and Fred*, *Orchestra Rehearsal* and *Fellini's Casanova*.

Tonino and Lora, his beautiful Russian wife, had lived among the mountains of Tuscany for many years, in a little house in the town of Pennabilli, surrounded by dogs and cats, with a pottery workshop, paintings and drawings — Tonino was full of ideas and realized them, if possible, by his own hands. (A monument to Tarkovsky would appear in the garden of sculptures next to Tonino's house as well, in a form of a chapel with its doors closed forever.) On the walls of the town the poet hung ceramic tiles with philosophical aphorisms, which he had collected all his life. Tonino Guerra's poems were translated into Russian by his close friend, the poet Bella Akhmadulina.

In Rimini, to commemorate his friend Federico Fellini, who was born there, Tonino opened a restaurant, which he decorated with his drawings.

The most prominent people from the art world gathered regularly in Tonino's home, and he knew about Tarkovsky, had seen and valued his films. They had now known each other for a long time and Tonino once offered Andrei to make a film together. His visit to Andrei in Moscow was informal. Tonino came to offer his help.

"I understand, I understand…" Tonino spoke a little Russian, and in general it was Lora who served as interpreter. "They are keeping you here on a starvation diet. Am I right? They won't let you make films."

In a pink shirt and one of his favorite multicolored knitted vests, Tonino was picturesquely handsome and impressive as usual. He reminded Andrei of his father, though both the happy expression on his face and his voice, as well as his excessive gesticulation were different from the strict and reserved manner of Arseny Alexandrovich.

"They don't," Andrei sighed expressively.

"They have completely worn him out!" Larisa threw up her hands as she finished setting the huge table with pickles and home-made dumplings. "Years without work, and every film issued is a real torture."

Lora translated to her husband what had been said.

"I understand, it's a torture. That's bad," Tonino said and narrowed his eyes teasingly. "You must defeat them! You should go and film in Italy, Andrei. We will make it a joint production!"

"They won't let me go."

"Why? We'll work together!" Tonino crossed his fingers. "Russia, Italy. I will make the papers."

"They are cunning."

"I am bigger cunning," he said in broken Russian. "I remind you that Guerra means 'war'. It's better to keep peace with me."

"He never fights!" Lora laughed, her golden hair shaking.

"He fights, he fights!" Tonino protested, "I wanted to put on this shirt and I put!"

"He's joking, I made him wear it. Tonino is fighting for clean water in the local river, for the environment. He tries to save our region."

"I am an official myself, and a big one, the 'president of the river'. Yes, now it's clean there. Can drink water. The superiors listen to me. You will give me document, that I tell you. Many paper. We will fight. Did I say it right, Lora?"

The preparations for a joint production of the film *Nostalghia*, the script for which had been written by Guerra, took two years, although some major film figures were involved on the Italian side. But also Soviet officials resisted and in every way dragged out the preliminary negotiations between Soyuzeksportfilm and the Italian television company RAI.

All this time Andrei was tormented by one question: will they let me go or not?

Larisa, who had readied herself to leave for Europe, was developing her own plan in parallel: simply run away at the first opportunity, ask for political asylum and then demand that her family be reunited with her. An opportunity soon came their way: Tarkovsky was assigned to go to a festival in Sweden.

"What are they doing?" Andrei was puzzled. "They've decided to appease me? They're trying to make me content with a week-long getaway instead of letting me shoot *Nostalghia*?" He was sitting at the fireplace in Myasnoe. It was here, since the preparations for leaving for Italy had begun, that all their conversations took place — they were afraid of the KGB bugging their home.

"Andrei, you must understand, it's a chance." Larisa's face acquired a resolute and authoritative expression. "It's absolutely obvious that they won't let you go to Italy. We must run away."

"Run away?" Andrei dropped the heavy poker which he was using for stirring the coals. "I haven't watched spy films. I don't know how people 'run away'."

"I know. We will write down the plan in steps. You'll just have to go through each step carefully."

6.

In Stockholm, Andrei nourished his ambition and vanity, which had been trampled on by Soviet officials. He remembered all the humiliating episodes where his films were deliberated and banned, all the abuse he had taken from hired critics. Ready for a fight, as it had all been planned before, he informed the right people among the local authorities about his intention to stay. They supported him and promised to help. Now the escape had to be organized.

Andrei acted neatly: he left the hotel secretly so that the careful eye of the Soyuzeksportfilm member who had been keeping him company (obviously a Soviet snitch) did not see him.

Out of naivety, he left a note on the table asking his chaperone not to wait and not to look for him, "don't worry". The note, of course, had the completely opposite effect and was immediately sent to the Soviet embassy.

The Swedes, as they had promised, quickly drove Andrei away from Stockholm to a house in the country. There, under the hospitality of a kind woman, who did not understand a word of Russian, he spent a couple of days. Oh, what an ordeal that was! Andrei had never been attracted to the political thriller genre, his impulsiveness and unwillingness to yield did not imply courage at all. He felt as if he had already got himself into a room at KGB headquarters. The terror consisted entirely in the fact that the poor "non-returnee" was overwhelmed by fear of being tortured by the KGB and at the same time he experienced great grief for his homeland, which ached like a wound. He increasingly panicked, for Larisa was not with him and she would have known very well how to manipulate him to get what she wanted.

"I am a complete foreigner in this country," he thought, trembling. "My home, little Andrei, Arseny, Russia. Without them I won't be able to live."

Those feelings were so strong, that even the fear of the Soviet authorities did not stop Tarkovsky — he rushed back to Stockholm. There, stammering and looking down at his feet he explained his disappearance to his "companion" as simply going for a walk. Thus he successfully returned home.

"Can you believe it, Lara," the "non-returnee" beamed. "I got away with it! They pretended that they didn't notice anything."

"Well, thank God." Larisa tried to hide her fury. "It's not like you to carry out such actions on your own. Oh, If I had been with you…"

In March the contract with the Italians for shooting the film *Nostalghia* was signed and Tarkovsky began preparations for the trip. A day before his departure, on April 4, 1982, Tarkovsky celebrated his 50th birthday. The big day turned into an excruciating insult: once again people in authority had made it clear to him that they did not take any notice of the director and his work.

No one called to officially congratulate Tarkovsky, as was the common practice. No books were published for the anniversary, not even the smallest formal celebration at the Dom Kino was organized. Tarkovsky looked with hope at the silent telephone the entire day.

"If only I could get out of here as soon as possible," he said to Larisa, nervously pacing from one corner of the room to another. "They are deliberately humiliating me: Goskino, the Union of Cinematographers, Mosfilm. It is them who always observe without fail birthday ceremonies, they honor everyone, no matter what their positions or titles are! I can't stand it!"

One might be surprised how deeply a person of such prominence was hurt by the lack of attention from the authorities, but Andrei suffered terribly from the unwillingness to admit his contribution to cinema.

He became excessively nervous and impulsive, beating Larisa severely a few times. There was an incident with Larisa's daughter Olga, then 18 years old, who was beat by her stepfather with a belt for coming home late. After that he started a fling with a simple country girl named Olya from Myasnoe, who was the same age as Larisa's daughter, in order to "regain his inspiration". Larisa put up with it, as it was not the first time such things had happened in the family. It was not in her own interest to start a fight just before her cherished dream was about to come true.

7.

Preparing to leave, Tarkovsky was overjoyed: he had an interesting script and the opportunity to work with an excellent crew. His palms were itchy from the eagerness to begin shooting. This mood at least in some way might justify the terrible negligence that he had committed. More probably, however, the reason was much deeper — it was in the paradoxical makeup of this apostle of philanthropy's nature. In his diary Tarkovsky wrote, "As long as there is an inclination for sacrifice, a human personality lives." These words may seem like mere fluff, since in the director's films there are few examples of a deeply Christian worldview, i.e. a universal love that defeats everything.

The inability to love, to feel compassion, to empathize, was a serious disability that impeded Tarkovsky in his creative work. He was not endowed with an understanding of the real essence of the substance he studied, call it what you want, spirit or even soul. Nostalgia, sacrifice or the task of being human are not possible without love, and this means love not for oneself, not for an abstract human race, but for one's fellow person, which is often not very pleasant or "necessary". Tarkovsky talked more and more insistently about the need to take upon oneself the burden of suffering in order to save the human race. He wanted to speak to people through his films about the most important thing indispensable for salvation. However, he was missing something very important to ensure that people would follow him instead of criticizing him for his coldness, his detached air, his unwillingness to take a step toward mutual understanding. This lack of warmth can be particularly observed in his last films, where we find his most exalted and messianic ideas, and of course in his real-life relationships with those close to him.

At the time when Tarkovsky was already preparing to go to Italy, his "good-luck charm", his favorite actor, a man that had been inseparably faithful to him, was dying a painful death from lung cancer. Anatoly Solonitsyn considered Andrei his spiritual father, his love was overflowing and timid.

Andrei looked on Solonitsyn's work for other film directors with jealousy. He was completely incapable of being happy for Solonitsyn's success in the films of Gleb Panfilov, Larisa Shepitko, Nikita Mikhalkov, Alexander Zarkhi, Vadim Abdrashitov and, of course Sergei Gerasimov. He didn't say a single word, did not give any friendly nod to the actor who had played a significant part in his work. His disregard was total and clear. Solonitsyn, in turn, was embarrassed by his "betrayal" and, of course, did not count on his mentor's support. Nonetheless, deep in his faithful eyes there hid an almost a puppy-like yearning for the approval of his master.

Andrei never showed an interest in other people's work, especially when it was successful. He did not notice even the success of those close to him, not understanding how it could hurt them.

Perhaps he had seen love, attachment, as a pitfall fraught with pain and humiliation from the very moment when, crying, he pressed himself to his father's uniform, hoping for him to come back. But his father would leave, leaving behind his mother, wracked with pain, and two crying children. Love hurts. And if such a man as your father could not manage to maintain a love with his family, then this superficial matter of existence (and not in the mysterious depths of the spirit) is so ephemeral, that it is not worth being taken into consideration. Andrei was always reserved and cold with his mother and sister. He could not, in an outburst of feelings, throw his arms around his father, or a woman whom he loved, or his own child.

Thus it would be even more difficult to expect him to sympathize with the dying Solonitsyn, for whom the main part in *Nostalghia* had been written.

Solonitsyn, a shy and modest man, burned himself out. He drank heavily, did not eat well, smoked incessantly, and in addition to that there was his first wife, who also drank her fair share and deprecated him. She had had enough of wandering with her loser husband from town to town and from one provincial theater to another, and so she abandoned Anatoly, leaving him with a broken heart. Tarkovsky, who had been invited by Mark Zakharov to stage a production of *Hamlet* at the Lenkom Theater, gave Solonitsyn the main part. Anatoly was living in a dormitory and drinking terribly. Nonetheless, he coped with the part pretty well, although the play's run was soon ended.

Tarkovsky was infuriated by Anatoly's dependence on alcohol. Later he would say, "Solonitsyn built his life on a disrespect for his talent. In real life he played some kind of idiot. He had this irresponsible lifestyle. Artists can't do that! One should be aware of one's mission".

During the shooting of *Stalker*, Solonitsyn met a wonderful woman who eventually became his second wife. Svetlana adored him and soon she bore him a son. On the money that he had borrowed from Andrei, Anatoly bought a tiny co-op apartment and for the first time in his life, got a chance to arrange an acceptable existence for his beloved family.

It was already too late, though: the removal of one lung did not bring relief and the end was already inevitable. He could hardly lift himself from his bed, looking like a skeleton covered with skin. A photo of Andrei hung over his bed, to whom the dying man frequently spoke in his thoughts. A role in a film, shooting in Italy! Maybe fate, after it had scared him a bit, would now take him away, grant him a tiny bit of more life? His dim hopes for a miracle helped keep the dying man alive.

The Tarkovskys knew about Anatoly's state, but over a couple of months Andrei and Larisa, who had been living only a 15-minute walking distance from Solonitsyn, visited him only once. During the visit, apparently unsure how to behave, Andrei repeated the same phrase over and over again: "Tolya! You fool! Hey, what's wrong with you?"

Solonitsyn felt guilty before his mentor, as he was supposed to play the main part in the film. He was unaware that the role had already been assigned to Yankovsky.

As he was leaving to sunny Italy for an extended trip, Tarkovsky did not even think it necessary to pay a brief visit to Solonitsyn and comfort the dying man, to give at least the false assurance that he would manage to get better before the shooting started. Comforting a dying man is a tiring job, and Tarkovsky was not characterized by either warm-heartedness or sentimentality.

In one of his interviews, the film director said among other things, "Freedom does not exist as a choice, freedom is a state of mind." This is an excellent position when fighting for one's artistic principles, but as a means of liberating oneself from personal responsibilities of charity and sacrifice it is flawed. It borders on an anarchic disregard for moral standards. He left without saying goodbye to his favorite actor, his "good-luck charm", knowing for sure that he would never see him again.

When Anatoly was told that Tarkovsky was already filming Yankovsky in Italy, he lost feeling in his legs. He asked the nurse to take Tarkovsky's photo off the wall and he never rose from his ottoman again. "He sucked all my blood dry," he muttered. Solonitsyn died before he reached his forty-seventh birthday.

Andrei was leaving a city that was empty for him as well as his own home, where he did not love anyone. He left in June, and Larisa followed her husband only in August.

PART III. "From confession to sacrifice"

Chapter 9.
NOSTALGHIA. FROM CONFESSION TO SERMON

I.

He was heartily welcomed to Rome and placed in a cozy old apartment on the top floor of a house dating from the 15th century. Tonino, ever attentive to him, made sure that everything was organized just like in his new friend's Moscow apartment: there was old furniture made of dark wood against the white walls, on which the still life paintings so loved by Tarkovsky hung, as well as reproductions of photographs. There were dry flowers in great transparent vases on the floor, woven baskets with fruits and books on the shelves and windowsills. There was also a multitude of little antiques which warmed Tarkovsky's soul, and a fireplace which reminded him of the remote house on the Para River.

In August, Larisa arrived and picturesque garlands of garlic and onions appeared in the kitchen. The apartment began to smell like a home.

Andrei looked tired, but at the same time lively and young, enthusiastic and excited, as if preparing to make a decisive leap. He went with Tonino for a trip around Italy, enjoying the warm climate and the grandeur of its nature. Tarkovsky and Tonino would later make an attempt at a documentary about this trip under the title *Voyage in Time*.

However, Tonino Guerra's efforts to charm Tarkovsky with the sunny Tuscan landscapes were in vain. The grandeur of this blooming land, which Tonino had so glorified in his poems, was alien to Tarkovsky's aesthetic. His choice for the film fell to a little resort town, Bagno Vignoni. Here, in a rundown hotel, behind high, dilapidated walls, the waters of the healing pool of St. Margaret lie in a bed of pitted, porous stone. In the hotel he found a room with a window looking out at a brick wall. It is here that the director placed his protagonist.

Tarkovsky positioned himself as an advocate of an art which contained within itself "the yearning for an ideal that gives a man hope and faith". One way or another, the theme of longing for this ideal persists through all his films in the form of echoes, subtexts or hidden thoughts.

In *Nostalghia*, produced abroad, the spiritual core became the plot. This time it was not merely a spontaneously shot film, but a conceptually constructed one. The protagonist of *Nostalghia* was meant to be a Russian peasant composer (based on Dmitry Bortniansky), sent to study in Italy. However, the idea was quickly abandoned and the composer was replaced by a contemporary writer, Andrei Gorchakov (played by Oleg Yankovsky).

"I wanted to tell a story about Russian nostalgia," Tarkovsky commented, "about that peculiar mood which we Russians get into when we are far away from our homeland." Preparation lasted for three years and shooting took three months. For Tarkovsky this work progressed in stages. "Only in *Nostalghia* did I feel that cinema is, to a large degree, capable of expressing the artist's mood," he said in an interview. "In the past I did not suspect that this was possible."

Tarkovsky fundamentally changed the screenplay that he had initially written together with Tonino Guerra. The story of the writer Andrei Gorchakov, searching for traces of the peasant composer Pavel Sosnovsky in the company of a female interpreter — a golden-haired Italian woman — was overshadowed by the projection of the protagonist's mental state as he is overwhelmed by an apocalyptic mood and seeks a way to save humanity. Trying with all his means to express the depth and complexity of the main character's suffering, Tarkovsky failed to notice that Gorchakov's mental state resembled not so much an aspiration for "spiritual heights" as mental illness. The evocative image of a weak-willed intellectual's depressive state was reconstructed with Tarkovsky's usual mastery. After he saw the first cut of the film, the director exclaimed, "I didn't even think that we would get such a dark film!" He must have realized that he had tried a bit too hard to intensify the melancholy. Furthermore, it was not longing for one's homeland (Gorchakov is not an immigrant, he is on an artistic excursion and can return home whenever he wants) but rather "universal grief", resembling more a medical diagnosis.

There is no doubt that the artistic approach and the mood of *Nostalghia* were strongly influenced by the fact that with this film, Tarkovsky was finally going to win at Cannes, that is, receive the Grand Prix, which would change not only his financial situation, but also his status as a professional. It would finally confirm his right to be the winner of a European film festival, irrespective of the Soviet higher-ups' opinion.

The victory placed certain demands on the filmmaker, however: not only did he have to reach the level of the latest tendencies in world cinema, but also he had to surpass them. Tarkovsky tried to ensure the highest level of meaning and artistic value and avoided the slightest contact with commercial themes or strategies. To be harsh, gloomy, deep and tragic — this was pretty much in compliance with Tarkovsky's worldview and in accordance with the moods of mainstream society in this age of triumphant existentialism. Apocalyptic visions, messianism in a world moving toward catastrophe were considered signs of the artist's sophistication and the power of his intellect. The demands of the times coincided with the director's artistic aims and abilities. The trick with turning Tuscany's sunny texture into at least a Russian province, if not Hamlet's Denmark, "a prison, and a goodly one" was representative of Tarkovsky's style.

Darkness and rain invaded Tarkovsky's Italy. Guerra's screenplay was deprived of its positive, life-confirming component. In turn, it came to abound in Tarkovsky's favorite techniques: a frozen pace, fragmentation of the plot line, intertwining of dream and reality, poetic fantasy and everyday prose, as well as the absence of the slightest trace of "entertainment films" — irony, humor, real human feelings (unsuppressed by mental illness).

The film begins with a Russian landscape in black and white and a prolonged Russian lamentation. A blackened wooden house appears on the screen, an unsaddled horse in tall grass, a woman and a boy moving through the morning fog. This image of Russia emerging in the protagonist's imagination might have been labeled a metaphor for his disposition, had the director himself not strongly deny any such "artistic" tricks. The scene was shot on the outskirts of Rome, but Tarkovsky managed to convincingly reconstruct the "Russian soul", sufferer and martyr.

This introduction then gives way to the action proper: after arriving in Italy, Gorchakov drives his car along a mountain road and complains with irritation to the female interpreter — the blond-haired beauty Evgeniya, "I'm sick of all this beauty!" However, he hasn't been invited to tourist attractions (and neither has the audience). And as far as the blond beauty accompanying this Russian is concerned, one must not be under any illusions — Gorchakov is not capable of anything more than squabbling and rebuke with this liberated woman in love with Russian culture. Just as Tarkovsky was afraid of sunny landscapes, he was afraid of the terrible "viruses" of joy and humor, which might have sprung up in contact with the reality of this lively Southern European country. Thus, the shots are full of rain, mud and darkened sets, recalling the Russian province and insistently drawing the viewer into the main character's depressive mood.

Only the procession of women with candles, carrying out the statue of the Virgin Mary, patroness of women in labor, brings local color back. It seems that light will break out in a moment! But Gorchakov will not enter the ancient chapel for which he has come to Italy. He will not watch the moving ritual when hundreds of birds fly out from inside the Madonna. This Russian intellectual will not be moved by these simple women's belief in the miracle. He will not even be touched by the fresco of Francesco del Piero on which the camera focuses for a long while. There is a strong refusal to allow the tender emotion, cordiality or joy that naturally emerges when a man encounters masterpieces of world culture, or the sincere dedication of simple people believing in miracles.

Evgeniya carries with her a collection of poems by Arseny Tarkovsky. For Gorchakov this is a symbol of the untranslatability of cultures and the impossibility of a mutual attraction between these two people. The young woman is attracted by Russia, Russian culture, she likes Gorchakov, but for Tarkovsky romance is inappropriate and love is impossible. Gorchakov is irritated by the presence of the woman, preferring to experience his emotional turmoil alone in the discomfort of the hotel. The level of symbolism increases here, giving film scholars, who try to decipher the figurative structure of the film in various ways, the opportunity to explain Gorchakov's behavior from a philosophical perspective, even to the point searching for Freudian motifs. Experts in the field of cinema get carried away with deciphering Tarkovsky's "codes", while he himself categorically denied their suspicions that any shots or aspects of the plot were not spontaneously constructed. "Captured time", this is how it looks like here: depressing, painful, a torment for the soul. The swimming pool is empty, dark, and dirty, the protagonist does not take off his coat even while lying in bed. His refuge reminds one of the hovel in *Stalker* — ruin, mold, dirt.

The part was written for Solonitsyn. It is easy to imagine him, battered by life, in the impenetrable darkness that envelopes the main character. Yankovsky was too young, handsome and in the prime of his life to play the role of one worn out by psychological torment. Gorchakov suffers from not understanding the symptoms of his illness. He is overwhelmed by grief for the whole world. Finally, he finds a person who is ready to undertake the burden of responsibility for degenerate humanity and show the way for sacrificial redemption of his sins. The half-insane Domenico (played by the Swedish actor

Erland Josephson) came to Tarkovsky's mind as a new character — the redeemer of all human sins. The Stalker had not met such a person with pure intentions and desires, but Gorchakov does. It is not Evgeniya who becomes the center of gravity for him but this crazy old man, hanging out by the pool with his dog. Gorchakov asks Evgeniya to take him to Domenico's dwelling. An impoverished, half-homeless existence prevails here, where an old mug, a ragged lace curtain and dry flowers create an atmosphere of dying life, depicting the triumph of spiritual asceticism in a world of capitalist money-grubbing.

Domenico reveals a secret to Gorchakov: in order to save the world, one must carry a burning candle across St. Margaret's pool and make a wish (one can see here an analogy to the secret room in *Stalker*). A fragment from Beethoven's *Ode to Joy* with Japanese motifs highlights the importance of the revelation as Gorchakov perceives it.

Gorchakov's dreams, as is always the case with Tarkovsky, are equal in status to reality, if not even surpassing it. The film interweaves reality with half-hallucinations, half-dreams. Reality thus resembles illusion and illusion is almost indistinguishable from reality.

Suddenly a color shot breaks in: the back of the main character, who is walking through the town. Here elements of previous films and his father's poems are woven in, and the girl in rubber boots, Angela, appears in front of the main character like a minor angel.

The film consists of self-quotations, the reuse of previous motifs, which complies with postmodern tendencies, encompassing all artistic strategies: allusions, self-allusions, echoes and roll-calls of motifs and images. The camera brings it all together at a very slow pace, in a rhythm unusual for Western viewers.

Domenico decides to take the last step in his fight to free people from their sinful material passions. He preaches on the Capitoline Hill after he clambers up the equestrian statue of Marcus Aurelius. His passionate address to the healthy and sated does not move any-one: "What kind of a world is this if a madman tells you that you must be ashamed of yourselves!" After he finishes his speech, Domenico orders, "Music!" One of the madmen around him pours gasoline on

Domenico from a shiny canister and he awkwardly strikes a match. His old clothes cannot catch fire and after that only his back flares up. The old man is in flames in an awkward and painful way; a restrained dog wails pitifully and strives to rescue his owner. Finally, Verdi's *Requiem* starts at full volume from a loudspeaker. The scene is filmed brilliantly and makes the impression of a culmination, which in fact still lies ahead.

While Domenico is dying, Gorchakov comes to Bagno Vignoni and hurries to the pool, to perform the ritual of saving the world.

Andrei Gorchakov's "way of the cross" plays out just as exaggeratedly mundane as Domenico's sermon. The pool has already been emptied, he has to walk through watery mud. Andrei's Golgotha proves tiresome. The first time the candle goes out. He goes back and lights the candle stub again. It turns out that carrying a candle requires deep concentration; he covers the flame under his coat and walks carefully, but the candle goes out again. Exhausted, the poor man swallows a sedative and again trudges back, taking out his lighter. The scene is deliberately slowed down, as if the author wishes to drag the viewer into the whirlpool of this excruciating movement, make him enter the rhythm of this sacrificial self-torment. This time Andrei carries the candle, protecting it with his entire self. Finally, his shaking hands attach the candle stub to the edge of the pool. There is a sound of a fall and screams… The death of a martyr is perceived with a relief, a *requiescat in pace*. And there is peace.

In a still black-and-white frame, we see a modest Russian landscape over which towers a gigantic Roman church. Andrei sits on the street and with him is Domenico's dog. Snowflakes flutter down slowly. Again a woman's voice begins to wail and the credits appear: "To my mother, A. Tarkovsky." It is an extremely beautiful and deep film, despite Tarkovsky's attempt to get rid of the artistic structure of a shot and the meanings inherent in it.

Afterwards Tarkovsky admitted, "I placed a Russian house and the walls of an Italian church in the final scene. This is a constructed image, the simulated mental state of the protagonist that does not allow him to live in harmony, or his new wholeness which encompasses both the hills of Tuscany and the Russian countryside."

In reality, the film allows multiple interpretations. One of them would later be formulated by Tarkovsky in an interview: "As they say in the West, Russians are bad immigrants. Could I have known that the state of aching melancholy that fills the screen would later become reality in my life?"

The processes that have taken place in the world view and aesthetics for the last 30 years since *Nostalghia*, have changed our perception and feeling of the tragic, presented with forced dark significance. Gorchakov's death doubles the death of Domenico, but if history repeats itself, first presenting the events in a tragic key and again as farce, then in Tarkovsky's film everything happens in reverse. A crazy old man dies in an awkward manner and in the name of high ideals. Verdi's *Requiem*, which Tarkovsky intended to be the accompaniment to the grand finale, sounds with a delay, mixing the sublime with the ironic. The viewers feel pity for the old man and his dog, they are ready to sympathize with the sacrifice of this half-insane messiah.

Gorchakov, the gloomy fighter for perfecting the world, is seen today with a humor that the author did not want. It is true what they say: if you don't want somebody else to laugh at you, do it yourself. The post-modernist world is especially critical of "beautiful impulses of the soul". Gorchakov, in his long black coat, making his way several times through the mud of the neglected pool with a candle, is far less impressive than a laughing Baron Munchausen rising into the sunny sky.

2.

When Tarkovsky applied for a visa extension, journalists began to pester him on every occasion, asking "If you claim that a Russian in a foreign country is doomed to suffer from nostalgia, then why don't you go back yourself?" Tarkovsky was always annoyed by this and answered either: "I have said everything in my film and I have nothing to add to that" or "Why are you identifying me with the character from my film?"

While Tarkovsky was working on the film, he felt how futile his hope was to integrate into a foreign society, a foreign culture. He was tormented by the ambivalence of his feelings: the world was attractive, but not for him. This world annoyed him with its alien beauty and repulsed him with its yearning for material things, but at the same time he was attracted by it and admired it.

At that time he had not yet realized that he should demand money for interviews. Journalists kept clinging to him. Some of them pretended to be his friends (or did they really want to be his friends) and asked for an informal conversation at a table in some quiet café.

"It's not bad here," Ron Shebbort looked at the view from the wide window of the café. He spoke good Russian, as he was a second generation immigrant. "There's a lake, a small forest behind it, stables, a racetrack. There are such great races here sometimes."

"It must be an expensive place," Tarkovsky said, taking the wine menu with trepidation. "I'll have just a double coffee."

"That's true, it is an extremely expensive place, but only during the racing season. Right now it's quiet here and prices are low. Besides, you're my guest and fellow countryman. My grandmother was brought from Odessa after the war and my mother married an American. I work at a respectable newspaper, we don't slander people or spread rumors."

"I know." Andrei had found out beforehand about his interlocutor from Tonino and had received a good recommendation. Tarkovsky was very afraid of scandals, as they could cause a negative reaction on the part of the Soviet officials — he was still a Soviet citizen and did not intend to change his citizenship.

"Apart from that, I will show you the material of the interview when it's ready and it will be printed only after your approval." Ron flashed his white-toothed American smile.

"How do they manage to maintain such an immaculate smile?" Andrei thought. "He must be around sixty."

"My dear Mr. Tarkovsky, I'll be frank with you, hoping for mutual concessions, only between the two of us, out of my personal curiosity. I have seen your films and I am convinced that you are the number one director within your stream in *auteur* cinema."

Coffee was served, glasses with cognac and a plate with strawberries. "Not too luxurious. Quite Soviet, don't you think?"

"Well, almost. Only the strawberries, I guess, are an unnecessary luxury."

"I promised to be sincere. I noticed that you were surprised by my teeth," Ron smiled again. "The thing is that in our country it is usual for people in the public eye to get their, err, second teeth. It's like a cover."

"I know, I used those in the films and on the stage, when we had to alter the actor's appearance, but they found it terribly annoying."

"It's extremely comfortable. And if you lose your own teeth completely, our prosthesis wizards for a significant sum will make you a whole new mouth."

"Thank God, I don't have this problem yet." Andrei took the journalist's detailed explanation as a hint at his own, not very good teeth and his lack of means to see a good dentist. "What is your question?"

"I don't understand: you're not a rich man, how did you manage to make such expensive films?"

"In our country the government pays for the filmmaking process. Once, when we were filming *Stalker*, I had to shoot the film again two times because of a technical defect. Everything was paid for, the film crew received their salaries regularly."

"What an amazing country! But why then is a successful film director not wealthy?"

"Because my films are not being shown."

"They pay for the production and they don't want to make a profit? The same people?"

"All our cinema officials are interconnected. They did not make any profit from my films and they suppressed all my new ideas. Here, for all those years, I could have made twenty films!"

Ron was lost in thought. "I think it would be difficult. To find a producer able to finance non-commercial films, films for a narrow audience, is extremely difficult. Fellini, even after he had won his Oscars and had old friends in producer circles, had to look for money for every new idea he had, and sometimes it would take years."

"But audiences forced their way in to see my films in some provincial cinemas in the USSR, where the films had been pushed away by the distributors."

"You say yourself that there were few screens allotted to your films, while here, in the capitalist world, a distributor chooses for itself what to make money on. And, you know, the Americans flood us with their action films, thrillers, horror films, fantasy. A show for the masses brings large profits. They have also, I must say, developed pretty good technology and they have good actors. Of course, it costs a huge amount of money."

"I understood all that when I was working on *Nostalghia*. It's difficult to work here, everything is converted into money, and I had to make the film on very little means. For the first time I've found myself in unusual circumstances which I have been inwardly opposing. There is a system of putting pressure on the director's thoughts here. The question is always put this way: is there money for it? I had to give up shooting certain scenes in Moscow, because I was exceeding the budget… It's difficult to maintain the necessary creative focus under new circumstances, many things get in the way."

"I'm afraid that you wouldn't have been able to make the films here that you did in your country."

"Maybe… And it isn't just a matter of money. I've gotten used to working with my people. Here my usual way of communicating doesn't work. I have to explain ideas in much more detail to the set designer and the cameraman…"

"Of course, they are used to a completely different level of artistry, to greater simplicity."

Tarkovsky frowned. "My films are very simple. But you're right, the quality of the mainstream of films here is extremely low and our profession is of a very low prestige here."

"But is it easier to live here? In terms of strawberries year-round."

"There are many temptations here that are completely absent in our country, or they are very primitive there, a bit higher than the average — a car and a dacha are as much as people wish for."

"You, of course, have all that?"

"I have a little house in the countryside. I don't drive a car."

"You have a driver?"

"Soviet people don't have servants. And I don't have a car."

"Nonsense! I shouldn't write that, should I?"

While he was making this film which overwhelms the viewer with its joyless doom, Tarkovsky left out many moments of content about life in Italy. Andrei had always wanted to live comfortably in a beautiful country, like any ordinary person who was suffocating behind the Iron Curtain and not inclined to asceticism. But he fought for having the bare minimum and for eschewing materialism, unquestioningly advocating for the primacy of spiritual values. So what? If in his younger days Andrei could not be reproached for preferring stylish new clothes to those of the Soviet masses, how then could one be surprised at the desires of a Soviet citizen who found himself among capitalist temptations, and who had a wife going crazy from the "beautiful life" that had appeared before her? They wanted many things, and for that reason the Tarkovskys in those days were most of all depressed by their lack of money.

They were desperately pressed for funds because Andrei did not manage to hold back Larisa's appetites. First of all she had bought herself an expensive fur coat and afterwards kept sending packages of clothes to Moscow. Other cravings came up too.

Still before the festival, Larisa found a house in the village of San Gregorio, located in the mountains close to Tivoli. This unbelievably beautiful village was huddled around a castle that towered over it.

It was like something out of a fairy tale, a dream. Andrei, following the old keeper of the keys, looked at the walls of the castle halls, full of family portraits. He stared at the wrought iron chandeliers, the suits of armor, the gaping, blackened fireplaces… This was no longer a minor place ennobled by the "dust of centuries", but an entire vault of frozen time that could become his property. When he thought of this, Andrei grimaced, "Eventually someone will buy this castle, some fat guy who sells commodes."

"Or perhaps a successful film director?" Larisa looked at her husband with a meaningful glance.

"But where will we get the money? I don't understand what you're saying."

"Don't worry, Andrei. We'll get the money." Larisa calculated in a business-like manner, "The castle requires an expensive renovation and maintenance, that's why it only costs 1.5 million dollars."

"Only? We'll have to rob a bank."

"It's an ordinary amount of money for a top film director… Don't shake your head, we'll see who will become the owner of this castle."

In the meantime, waiting for Andrei's career to quickly take off, they bought a tiny bit of that luxury: a dilapidated "tea house" in an abandoned garden. Even this was enough to make Andrei start dreaming about the renovation of the property and even make attempts to build a swimming pool.

Cannes, Cannes… Cannes and the Grand Prix would to change everything.

3.

The aim for victory at the Cannes Film Festival had a long history. *Andrei Rublev*, which had every right to compete for the Palme d'Or, was shown only out of competition and thus was not eligible for the Grand Prix. *Solaris*, which was officially presented in competition, did not win the Grand Prix but the special FIPRESCI Prize.

The Mirror never got out of the Soviet Union, and *Stalker* was in wide distribution, but it did not do well at the festival, because Tarkovsky was already preparing to leave.

With *Nostalghia*, which Italy presented at the festival in 1983 hoping for the Grand Prix, Tarkovsky was going to finally get his revenge.

Tarkovsky undoubtedly deserved the prize for his entire career and after all he had suffered. He waited with great expectation, under extraordinary tension, with his nerves stretched taut.

In Cannes he was struck by the news that the eldest of the classic French directors, Robert Bresson, who Tarkovsky adored, had decided to participate in the competition. Truly, fate is sometimes inventively cruel to those who aspire to great heights. For Tarkovsky to have the director he respected most as a competitor, this was too much, even for an ambitious egotist.

Andrei was taken aback. "What? Why didn't anyone tell me about this? Did they want to leave me vulnerable?"

He was bewildered and panicked, suspecting that this dirty trick had been plotted by someone with diabolic intentions.

Bresson, who had never competed with anyone, had come to Cannes in the year of his 75th birthday to take the crown! He announced as much in every interview he gave. Fate had brought Tarkovsky into a battle with almost the only idol he had. This was a trial even for a propagator of high spirituality.

When the showing of Bresson's film was scheduled, Tarkovsky announced his decision. "I will see that film with an objective attitude and if it's the next masterpiece, so be it. But if I don't like the film, I will defend myself."

Bresson's film *L'argent* (*Money*) based on Tolstoy's novella *The Forged Coupon* did not bowl over Tarkovsky and his friends, which gave a certain hope that *Nostalghia* would prove victorious.

The next day, Tarkovsky's film was shown and Andrei participated in the press conference in the same hall. He spoke about the issue that was important for him in the context of the film, about the disharmony between the spiritual and the material in modern life and that the purpose of human life consists of the development of the spiritual element. "When this purpose is lost, society inevitably degrades."

Tarkovsky's speech ended with applause. However, when the journalists had already started for the exit, this advocate of salvific moral power stopped them: "Wait, ladies and gentleman of the press, I have an announcement!" The audience strained to hear. "The thing is, that I have been told that Monsieur Bresson allegedly made a statement that he had come here only for the Grand Prix! But, if this is true, then I must tell you that I too will settle only for the Grand Prix!"

An excited buzz swept over the audience — a scandal had appeared within the intrigue of the festival.

Tarkovsky's statement seemed odd after he had rambled about the need for a person to develop his spiritual qualities. His challenge to the classic director and grand old man of cinema clearly cost Tarkovsky some of his dignity, but he did not notice this. The odious material element in the form of the monetary prize had made him forget about the principles he had been declaring. And he forgot about them easily. One might have expected Tarkovsky's statement to have sounded differently: "I think, that the competition between me and a classic figure of French cinema is inappropriate and unethical. In this situation let's leave the right to decide for the jury." This would be quite an acceptable position, especially as he could not influence the situation in any way. But Tarkovsky acted differently, claiming that he was ready for a fight. It is surprising how this advocate of spirituality did not understand a simple truth, that it was better to save face than show too much self-confidence and a disrespectful attitude toward a cinema veteran. The decision would be taken anyway, irrespective of his ultimatum. By what means would he fight with Bresson?

A couple of hours after the conference, wishing to smooth the blunder, Bresson, who was well acquainted with Tarkovsky, invited his competitor for lunch.

Nervous and twitchy, Tarkovsky set off to the meeting. After he returned, he no longer expressed his admiration for the "genius of the screen". He did not change his position concerning the prize, but he also did not say anything more about Bresson's virtues as a director.

At the festival Tarkovsky, after a long break, met with Otar Iosseliani and Krzysztof Zanussi, who was a member of the Ecumenical Jury. These leading figures expressed their appreciation to the Russian director and delicately passed over the matter of the competition that had arisen.

4.

Andron Konchalovsky, who had also come to Cannes, decided to talk to Andrei.

They sat in a small restaurant, as far as possible from the festival public. They looked at each other carefully, deciding the tone of the conversation.

"Look," Andron started simply. "The situation with Bresson is really nasty. The idol and the terror of the French, celebrating his birthday, the patriarch... Who could have expected such a coincidence!"

"I announced that I would fight," Andrei clenched his teeth. "I'll show them."

"Well, I wish you luck..." Konchalovsky muttered without enthusiasm. "I've seen Bresson's film and I've seen yours too."

"And?"

"I think it's not the best of your achievements."

"And your *Asya Klyachkina* is any better? That's why you shredded it like the officials told you to." "That's our Soviet business, you know that yourself. I cut some parts and gave the film the possibility to reach screens."

"Good job! You satisfied your superiors! And they sent Bondarchuk to the jury to bury me." Andrei had flown into a rage. "They know how to hunt a person down. When I was still working on the film, Bondarchuk rushed here and made a statement to the press that he didn't like my films at all."

"Don't take it personally, but it's not just him. You shouldn't turn a blind eye to it."

"Maybe you'll even tell me I should follow Ermash's tastes? It's him who sent Bondarchuk here. Of course, Oscar winner Sergei Fedorovich is respected everywhere!" He smirked caustically. "This is exactly why you invited him to play the part of Astrov, to secure your position in case there were difficulties with the film."

"Listen, if we keep talking like this, we'll end up in a fight. Remember, we used to be friends after all. I consider you a great film director, but why do you continue to play against yourself? Why are you being so insistent? To spite yourself?"

"As I understand it, you were starting a discussion about the 'monotony' of my films? I remember your cow. You claimed that I moo unintelligibly like a cow, about something important, but what about, it's not clear."

"And you don't want to make your ideas more clear no matter what!"

"To whom? More clear to whom?"

"To your viewers. I think, the idea about there being different audiences for films has already reached our leaders. They understand now that films can be different! Just not with an anti-Soviet message. By the way, your film is very loyal to your country."

"I've never been anti-Soviet."

"You have another *idée fixe* and you cling to it insistently. Listen, Andrei, I've watched *Nostalghia* with great effort. You can't make someone look at Raphael's paintings tied to a chair. Maybe your film is worthy of Raphael, but still, you shouldn't tie the viewer up in order to make him watch it. I had to pull myself by the ears trying to figure out what was going on in the film. I don't consider myself an idiot, but I wasn't keen on deciphering your puzzles. You can make people watch whatever you want, but you won't win anything with this coercion. And your slow motion is coercion of the viewers!"

"Of course! I should entertain them! Like you. You absolutely must be liked and you're ready to do anything to achieve it!"

They were already talking loudly and people who were sitting at other tables looked at the arguing Russians.

"The viewer *must* like the film." Konchalovsky was trying to stop himself as he could from telling Tarkovsky to go to hell. "You have many ways of going about that, from low-grade techniques to ones that reach the level of great art. Look, in Fellini's *8½* there is quite a similar situation — the artist has a creative crisis and he's depressed. But the film does not dwell in blackness, it glitters with all colors! Federico's self-irony works better than weeping!"

"It shines with buffoonery. Self-irony! Ha! Why should I meet the needs of morons and laugh at myself?"

"Of course, blackness and gloom have a far more positive effect on people's spirituality… OK, let's leave the impenetrable darkness and the colors of your masterpiece alone. They fit logically with what the film is trying to say. The pacing is what I would change in your film. You should absolutely speed up the music. With this slow motion you violate the very nature of perception."

"A slowed pace is my main principle. It sharpens one's attention."

"It is good for the climax of the film, but you cannot make a fetish out of a principle."

"If I want to entertain people, you mean. I have never treated cinema like a show, and even less like entertainment. It should become a spiritual experience, which improves a person." Andrei make such a claim seriously and strictly. "I think that one must have no dignity at all to be led by the nose by the audience like that. It's about you, Mr. Konchalovsky."

"And I think, you must have no dignity if you announce in public that you are competing with Bresson in the fight for the Grand Prix!" They hurried off in opposite directions and never again did they try to come to an understanding.

5·

On the day of the announcement of the jury's verdict, everybody gathered in Tarkovsky's hotel room: Larisa and Olga Surkova, Oleg Yankovsky, Otar Iosseliani, Tarkovsky's interpreter, a professor from

Grenoble and representatives of Italian television. Tarkovsky paced around the room, wrung his hands, bit his nails. People tried not to look at him, just like one tries not to look at a handicapped person. The television in the room was on and journalists crowded in the corridor.

When it was announced, the result hit them like a bolt of lightning. The Palme d'Or was awarded to a Japanese director, while Tarkovsky and Bresson received special jury prizes. Andrei had received honorary prizes before, but alas, they had no money attached to them. He collapsed into an armchair, and then started again to pace around the room like a hunted animal.

"No, I won't let this happen! I came here for the Grand Prix and I don't need these miserable handouts!"

Someone reported that Bresson had made a similar scene.

They tried to calm Tarkovsky down and it soon turned out that the special prize was accompanied by the FIPRESCI Prize and the Prize of the Ecumenical Jury.

Andrei slowly started coming to his senses. Nonetheless, in the evening, when the prizes were handed out, he looked demonstratively offended. He came to the microphone after Bresson, shrugged his shoulders and said with difficulty through clenched teeth: "*Merci.*"

He communicated to journalists that he was indignant at what, he believed, was the unfair distribution of the prizes, and blamed Sergei Bondarchuk, who was in the jury, for supposedly being against awarding *Nostalghia* the Grand Prix. A series of worldwide premiere screenings of the film followed, along with countless interviews. Tarkovsky answered the interviewer's questions, either becoming truly angry or falling into pathos. In America, after he had given an inspired talk about the mission and the vocation of an artist, a young person who saw the director as a guru asked him naively, "What should I do in order to be happy?"

At first Andrei completely failed to understand the question and turned to the people that accompanied him, saying "Who is this man? Why is he asking such idiotic questions?"

He then gave an entire philosophical monologue. "I can only laugh at this question that has been posed to me. The feeling of happiness cannot be absolute, just as there can be no absolute freedom. One must first think, what are you living in this world for? What is the purpose of your life? Why did you appear on the Earth at this particular moment? What role has been predestined for you? Try to figure all that out. You must understand that man is not born to be happy at all. I believe that we are born for hard work. Life is given to us for spiritual growth, spiritual perfection. And in the first place, I don't understand, who said that we should be happy? A man cannot live only for the sake of pragmatic aims, even in a very well-organized herd. He will simply degenerate. Christian love begins from the love of one's own self. But such love for oneself does not mean being egoistic but being able to make sacrifices for the sake of others."

Tarkovsky was then asked, "And what is suffering necessary for?"

"Of course, it's silly to assume that one can or ought to aspire toward suffering. The person does not have to realize that he is making a *sacrifice*. I'm talking here about the readiness to sacrifice as the natural state of the human soul."

Another question: "What do you think, who is art created for?"

"For me there is no doubt that art is a *duty*, that is, if you create something, you feel that you must do it. But only time will tell if I managed to be a *medium* between *the universe* and *mankind*. In summary, I would like to tell you that one cannot comfort himself with the illusion that *spiritual* and *mundane* issues can be *combined*. Unfortunately, I am a megalomaniac, and I would rather make you watch my films than take at least one step toward you and, to your delight, help you understand them!"

In the discussion with American journalists, one can notice Tarkovsky's disregard for their spiritual poverty and his stubborn affirmation of his principles of communicating with the audience. It often seemed that Tarkovsky was trying to convince not only others, but also himself, of the need for higher spiritual values to triumph.

However, as the years went by, Tarkovsky's contradictory personality clearly did not undergo any progress toward sanctity. The more he was seized by the craving for material wealth, the more his didactic approach developed.

Standing up for disinterested art, the maestro himself desperately fought for his royalties. Long before the festival he had arranged the staging of *Boris Godunov* at Covent Garden with the help of stage manager Nikolai Dvigubsky, with whom he had worked together on *The Mirror*. Nikolai had married a Frenchwoman and had long been living in Paris. According to the contract, Andrei's was compensated by the highest standards, but he constantly demanded that his royalties be increased, as he was now dreaming not of a modest apartment like Fellini or Iosseliani were satisfied with, but a villa with a swimming pool.

Larisa, who had devoted so many years to glorifying her husband, complained that everything had gone to his head. He was extremely harsh and disrespectful even to those who were well disposed toward him. When visiting the arts council in Covent Garden, Tarkovsky was not embarrassed to tell Dvigubsky where to get off, loudly and in Russian, because he had not satisfied Tarkovsky in something. He demanded that he immediately leave the meeting and not dare to come out to bow after the performance as the stage manager. He even made a condition to Claudio Abbado that he should not invite Nikolai to the premiere's after-party and announced categorically, "It's either him or me."

Chapter 10.
A GUEST IN EXILE

I.

After the Cannes Film Festival, Tarkovsky was supposed to return to Moscow as Goskino demanded. He was promised that a visa would be reissued, but no necessary steps were taken. Tarkovsky behaved in a highly loyal fashion, not permitting himself to make any negative statements about the USSR. However, fearing that once back in his home country, all doors would be closed to him, he made the decision to stay in the West as long as possible, and at the same time not deprive himself of the possibility of returning. He sent an inquiry about his son's visit to all Soviet authorities and a request to extend his visit abroad for another three years, as he believed that a patriotic film, full of nostalgia for his distant homeland, could change the attitude which prevailed in Moscow toward him. However, there was no response to his letters and requests.

Larisa gave an angry interview: "My husband is a Russian artist, a master of his craft, who has never engaged in politics. I am convinced that everything which has been happening to us — the stoppages, the cancellations of film screenings — is a result of intentional action. As a result we have no choice, either die in our homeland or work here! … Andrei has glorified Russian art and in the 20th century he is being denied a reunion with his son and an elderly woman who needs taking care of…"

A hard life began for the director. There was no money for the new film. Invited by many cultural organizations, Tarkovsky came to West Berlin at the end of 1984. He gave lectures there and participated in discussions. His friends arranged a scholarship for him from the Berlin Art University amounting to one thousand dollars a month. The Tarkovskys lived in the suburbs, in the district called Glienicke, far outside the city, which had a depressing effect on Andrei. He was especially depressed by the wall that was dividing the city. "Berlin is a completely ruined city," he noted in his diary. "There is such a feeling in the air, an atmosphere as if the war never ended here."

Tarkovsky saved himself by frequently visiting museums: Dahlem, Charlottenburg Castle. The latter turned out to be a suitable location for shooting *Hoffmaniana*, the screenplay which he had tried to push through several times in Moscow, but even here he could not find the people who could help him to realize the project.

First however, he wanted to realize the idea that had occupied him for many years — to make a film based on a screenplay of his that he had begun writing in November 1983. Andrei hoped that the new film would finally change his situation and he would win the Grand Prix in Cannes that he so longed for. The title of the screenplay was *The Sacrifice*. Andrei was constantly troubled by his unstable situation abroad, but Moscow was silent and disregarded all his inquiries. One day the director of Mosfilm visited Andrei's father, Arseny Alexandrovich. He would be going on a business trip to Italy and could hand over a letter from his father to Andrei. After a while Arseny Alexandrovich received a reply from Andrei which seemed addressed not as much to his father, as to the Central Committee or the KGB. Andrei of course had no doubt that his entire correspondence was being checked by the authorities and reported to higher-ups.

"Dear father, I am very sad to hear that you've been feeling as if I've chosen the role of an 'exile' and that I am all but abandoning my Russia... I do not know for whom it is advantageous to interpret in such a way the difficult situation in which I have found myself thanks to many years of persecution by the management of Goskino and, particularly its President, Filipp Ermash. Maybe you have not counted, but in my over twenty-year career in Soviet cinema, I have been hopelessly unemployed for around 17 years. Goskino did not want me to work! I was being bullied all this time, and the last straw was the scandal in Cannes in connection with the dishonorable acts of Bondarchuk, who, as a member of the festival's jury and incited by his superiors, tried (though in vain) to do all he could so that I would not receive an award (I received all three of them) for the film *Nostalghia*. I find that film extremely patriotic and many of those thoughts that you bitterly cast in front of me as a reproach, have been expressed in that film..."

This letter did not reflect the true situation, however. The silence of the authorities and especially of the odious Ermash toward all of his delicate requests and pleas drove Tarkovsky mad. He hoped that his name would mean something and that his homeland would not dare to spurn him. Nonetheless, they did spurn him and this humiliation affected him more than any torture. The Tarkovskys were increasingly certain about not going back.

In Moscow, Olga Surkova, at Andrei's request, met Arseny Alexandrovich in order to cautiously inform him about his son's intention to stay abroad. He listened to what she said with refined reservedness, only his lips slightly twitched and a pain which he did not wish to reveal glimmered in his eyes. But, while he was saying goodbye to her, Arseny Alexandrovich burst into tears on Olga's shoulder.

Olga's devotion to Tarkovsky was facing a serious trial. She long watched with grief at what was happening inside Andrei. After Cannes he refused to be interviewed without payment, he constantly complained about his financial straits and raged against the tight-fisted "bourgeoisie". A totally unexpected thing happened too: Andrei removed Olga's name from the book that they had written together back in the USSR.

Olga Surkova managed to put the manuscript of the *Book of Concordances*, which nobody wanted to publish in the Soviet Union, into order. Now it was possible to publish this extensive text consisting of Olga's interviews with Andrei abroad, the dialogues were accompanied by excerpts from his diaries and Surkova's commentary. The book had two co-authors and it assumed an even division of the royalties. However, Tarkovsky now decided to publish the book under only one name — his own. And he did not feel any remorse at this whatsoever, for after all, he was in a difficult financial situation.

2.

In the summer, the Tarkovskys lived in the "tea house" in San Gregorio. The locals remembered the polite, withdrawn man, who always greeted anyone who passed by. Andrei became friends with a skilled stonemason. He would sometimes go with him into the mountains to pick flowers or blackberries. The forest clearings with bees buzzing over the flowers so greatly resembled the ones in Zavolzhye from his childhood. And if one lay on the grass and looked into the sky, he could almost return to that childhood… Andrei tried to remember how he saw the world in those days. But then his disheveled companion would come to him and sit down, trying to say something, compensating with gestures for their lack of a shared languages. They even managed to discuss plans for the renovation of Andrei's little house, scrawling on sand. Andrei shared his dreams about founding an amateur village orchestra and wanted to design suits for the musicians.

Tarkovsky saw a future in this little village nestled at the foot of the castle. To become one of the people and a bit of a landlord, inhabiting the ancient chambers — not bad, eh? Then the Soviet leaders would be kicking themselves! He was absorbed by dreaming, however, for due to his reserved personality, the Russian master did not aim at socializing with local people and spent his time mainly in the "tea house" garden.

Here, under the old trees, there was garden furniture woven out of willow trees and here the most painful subjects were discussed. After all, Andrei, who believed that he was under official disfavor, was quite seriously afraid of being killed or abducted by the KGB. But for the time being he did not want to share his fears with his wife, especially on such a quiet and peaceful evening. Overripe peaches dropped heavily onto the grass, the breeze brought the fragrance of the thick wall of yellow flowers. Far away on a hillside one could hear the sound of a pipe — a shepherd gathering his herd. What KGB agents could lurk here? It was preposterous! Andrei was rarely in a relaxed state. He drank his coffee in the garden, watching the sun go down behind the hillock, gilding the ancient castle and glaring blindingly in the narrow window panes.

"If fate makes me this gift, I must organize a film academy for the best directors from around the world in these interiors," he squinted, resembling the baby they once called Lynx. "Just imagine, masters from all over the world will come here to pick up spirituality. I will hold seminars twice a year, no, rather every three months."

"Will you come here from Moscow?" Larisa grinned as she mixed cottage cheese with sour cream in a saucer. "They won't let you go!"

"Maybe something will change in Russia."

"Oh, what can change with those monsters? The time has finally come to spit in their faces and strive to secure a status here. Enough of sitting around, mumbling about your loyalty."

"Lara, I worry about our loved ones, who we will have to leave as hostages."

"They cannot refuse to give us my mother and son back!"

"I am especially worried about my father. He isn't young any more, he won't survive prison."

"Why are you blowing up your fears? You're like some Count of Monte Cristo! They have long since stopped imprisoning the parents of those who fled abroad. And losing their job and Party membership card does not threaten a retired person anyway." Larisa spread the cottage cheese mask that she had prepared on her cheeks (the goods they bought in the village were of the finest quality).

"You're starting to resemble a kabuki actor. First the make-up. The process takes several hours and they put burning seeds into the eyes of the actors playing the roles of evil men to make them red. Such naturalism together with complete convention! Each performance is a challenge for an actor."

"And you are only able to utter manifestos, and completely incapable of actually doing something. Although…" she burst into sarcastic laughter. "Meeting your wife who flew from Moscow, in the company of your mistress — that is real heroism! Did you at least realize that it was cold-hearted of you, Andrei? You not only didn't you try to hide that you had been having an affair with Donatella Baglivo, but also you openly flaunted this disgrace in front of your wife!" Larisa, following her well-practiced knack for making scandals, was ready to demonstratively burst into tears. She was however prevented from doing so by her mask and the main subject to which she was directing the conversation. She lost her temper when mentioning his mistress, but she had the right to get angry!

"You didn't hide much either…" Andrei dared to take a step toward a fight. The mood was spoiled immediately — he angrily sprung up from his chair, shaking the woven table. A glass bowl fell onto the grass. "You always cold-heartedly manipulated me!"

"Great!" Larisa splashed her plump hands. "Go on, maybe you'll hit me too!" She stood up and put her hands on her hips. She looked big and strong compared to her husband, who was thin like a teenager. She looked him over from top to bottom with contempt. "You've become emaciated from your stress and women. And you've bit your lips up from anger!"

"Lara, be quiet!" He froze, looking at the thicket of the orchard with eyes open wide. "There's someone out there!"

"Let him be! The country people got used to picking fruit in that abandoned lot. Your friend could have at least put up some fence."

"No, it's something completely different." He sat down and lowered his voice to a whisper. "Larisa, I've noticed that I'm being watched! I think that the KGB have decided to kidnap me and take me back to Moscow. They are afraid of an international scandal!"

Larisa stood still with her mouth open, devising a sufficiently sharp riposte. But as she realized that fear made her husband even more helpless, she changed her tactics:

"Well, what do you think? They are capable of everything. Even the most radical measures! You don't watch enough mysteries. A jab from an umbrella in the crowd is enough to make a person die supposedly of a heart attack."

"Can they really eliminate me?"

"We ought to be more careful. We'd better go inside the house. Make up your mind already!" Larisa pushed her husband toward the door. "Or they will really jab you with a needle in a crowd, and make me a widow."

3.

Well-versed people explained to Tarkovsky that his situation could be changed and the decision of the authorities could be influenced only with the help of pressure from the press and world public opinion. Andrei made the decision to give a public speech out of desperation. He agreed to a press conference that was organized in Milan by Vladimir Maximov with the help of a certain political party hostile to the Soviet Union. Tarkovsky's situation extremely worried this battle-hardened fighter for social justice. Maximov used his skills of persuasion to explain to the well-known outcast that it was necessary to take serious steps and break with the country that had long tormented him.

On the morning of June 10, 1984 a taxi was sent to drive the couple to the airport. It was a desperate move for Tarkovsky, who had put himself into a state, imagining KGB schemes. All the way he was afraid of being abducted and he looked like a hunted, prematurely aged boy.

Maximov, together with Irina Ilovayskaya, the editor-in-chief of *Russkaya Mysl* (Russian Thought), Mstislav Rostropovich and Yuri Lyubimov expected him at the hotel in Milan. Andrei was furious. Pointing to Lyubimov, he whispered loudly to Maximov in the restroom, "Why is he here? He manages to butt in everywhere with his dissident jokes. Why should I mingle with him? I'm not a dissident and I can't stand his theatrics!" He wrung his hands tragically, "Oh, why, why all that…"

The press conference assumed there would be a significant intervention of public opinion in the fate of this director who had been rejected by his home country. After an indignant speech by Maximov, it was Rostropovich's turn to speak:

"I was driven out of my home country ten years ago because I signed a letter defending Aleksandr Solzhenitsyn. Many great artists have been subject to persecution in our country. The cultural level of our government is so low that they are simply unable to appreciate genuine art… It is no coincidence that Tarkovsky found his new path in Italy, the country of great cultural traditions. I wish my great friend success! And I am convinced that through his sufferings, this man will make his country famous many times."

Tarkovsky stood up in the glare of the camera flashes with clenched teeth. He was determined not to hold back his feeling of being insulted. "I am experiencing a great shock today and I would like to explain the reasons for which I am forced to stay out of our country. Goskino has created such conditions for me that in 24 years I have made only six films, and I could not make the films I wanted to the most — my most interesting proposals were turned down. These huge periods of unemployment became a question of survival for my family. I dare to think that with all my films, I have benefited Soviet cinema to some degree. Nevertheless, none of my films have received any prize inside the Soviet Union and have not been presented at any domestic film festival from the very moment when Filipp Ermash became the President of Goskino. I have been simply crossed out from the list of filmmakers able to work…"

He spoke for a long time, not passing over any details. He remembered his fiftieth birthday too, "deliberately" overlooked by the officials, the refusal to issue him permission to travel abroad, and Bondarchuk's participation in the jury of the Cannes Film Festival with the purpose of "slaughtering" *Nostalghia*. He explicitly put an end to his loyalty.

"From all this, I understood that they hated me. All my letters to the Central Committee remained without reply. I wrote to Andropov and to all institutions — to the Consulate in Rome with a request to extend my visa for three years — with no reply. If at least one person had answered me, I would not have let what is going on today happen: they pushed me away and we decided not to come back, though this was a very difficult statement to make. For me it is a tragedy to leave my home country."

To the question made by a reporter, "What country will you go to live in now?" Tarkovsky replied, "For us the most important part was making this decision. Nothing else matters anymore."

In the winter of 1984–5 he again traveled to that exhausting city for the Berlin Film Festival. He went there hoping for the honors he deserved, but everyone was excited about something else there and Tarkovsky received little attention. He was offended, as he thought that he completely deserved to be the central figure at any film festival.

Tarkovsky not only opposed commercial art, he was a natural antagonist of it. He despised this phenomenon more than anything in the world as a threat to what was most precious and holy for him: the high art of cinema. Here however, they prized directors who managed to win a wide audience, and the principles of *auteur* cinema could not compete with those of commercial cinema — they coexisted on an equal basis, which in itself irritated Tarkovsky. Now, from the example of *Nostalghia*, he began to understand that the charges of elitism toward his films were not at all an invention of Soviet film officials. And elitist *auteur* cinema did not bring a profit! Once Fellini told him about that, but Tarkovsky believed that the laws of commerce would not apply to his sensational films. He rejected commercial art, but he was desperate for significant remuneration, completely unable to combine these two aims. One viewer, after she slept through an entire showing of *Nostalghia*, asked him, "Andrei, couldn't you make your films more cheerful? Then they would be more interesting to watch!" That already sounded like an insult, which he could hardly endure.

4.

In the following year Tarkovsky visited Stockholm to discuss a script at the Swedish Film Institute. The whole matter depended on money — the film needed a producer. The announcement of the film touched on exactly those issues which inspired Western public opinion to fight for nonconformity: "The film will deal with the following: if we don't want to live like parasites on the body of society and feed on the fruits of democracy; if we don't want to become conformists and idiot consumers, then we should give up a great deal… Only when you know that you're ready for self-sacrifice, you can succeed in influencing the course of your life as a whole. The price is usually our material wealth. You must do as you say, so that the principles you declare are no longer jabbering and demagogy."

It was clear to everyone that Tarkovsky's name guaranteed quality, his ideas guaranteed recognition from the public and critics, but neither was able to guarantee commercial success. Tarkovsky's financial straits and the wide respect for him urged Western producers to help Andrei begin work on his new film. Anna-Lena Wibom from the Swedish Film Institute was appointed the main producer. She was the one who had slept through the showing of *Nostalghia* and expressed to Tarkovsky her wish that he make his films a little bit more cheerful. She managed to engage Germany, Great Britain and Italy in the financing of the new film. But even drawing on multiple sources, they managed to collect only very limited funding for the film. Andrei decided to shoot the film on the island of Gotland. Tarkovsky's statement at the press conference regarding his decision to remain abroad did not evoke the reaction expected from the Soviet authorities. As usual, there was no reaction to the requests of the Tarkovskys concerning the visit of their son and Andrei's mother-in-law. On November 10, 1985 Tarkovsky wrote in his diary: "In Rome Larisa and I visited the Ministry of Foreign Affairs. They want to help us. How? We've been asked to wait for a week, while they consider the necessary steps to be taken for inviting our relatives. Bad news arrives from Moscow. Terrible days, terrible city. God, do not forsake me!"

Chapter 11.
THE SACRIFICE, FROM SERMON TO OFFERING

I.

Ahead was a new film, of course — the most important one, in which it was necessary that he express every issue he felt urgent, ideas of extreme importance for humanity, and to make it in such a way that nobody would ever say that he could not surpass *Andrei Rublev*. Indeed, *Andrei Rublev* had entered the top hundred films in the world, yet Tarkovsky, despised by his home country and having lived for years with his hands tied, could still do better. The most important was that he now knew what he should say, no, shout to the world! And he was convinced that cinema was the most powerful means of influencing mankind.

Tarkovsky's statements in the press concerning the new film clearly determined his standpoint. He expressed his thoughts about the inevitable global catastrophe repeatedly and insistently. "We are living in the most important period in the history of our planet and we must realize that this is a breakthrough era. A lot depends on people themselves. Now is a crucial time, we must act and understand why it is necessary. And I want to emphasize that the primary task of art is to solve the spiritual crisis that rules over the whole world.

There should be something in society that stimulates spiritual growth, which develops a sense of their own self and leads them to aspire to individuality and humanity in people. The mission of art — the most selfless of all types of human activity — is to execute this function."

In his diary Tarkovsky wrote: "Nowadays humanity can be saved only by a genius. No, not a prophet, but a genius who formulates a new moral standard. But where is he, this messiah?" The answer was quite obvious: Tarkovsky saw himself in the role of the messiah, truly free from material stimuli, an artist at the highest level of morality.

"My film is called *The Sacrifice*. Shouldn't the readiness for sacrifice be the natural state of the soul? The plot is simple: a man finds himself at the outbreak of nuclear war. After he manages to find seclusion, he prays that time would turn back and that this would not happen. At some point he falls asleep and when he wakes up, he begins to have doubts about whether he has dreamed the terrifying news. Nonetheless he feels obliged to fulfill the promise he made to God, to renounce all falsehoods and burn down his beloved house. When he sets the house on fire he is considered a madman and is placed in an insane asylum. It remains unclear to him, however, whether his family and friends are right, or whether it is he who is right and who has saved the world at the cost of his own life. I want to speak to the importance of personal responsibility and personal faith in a man capable of taking personal responsibility for the fate of the world, in order to counterbalance the societal irresponsibility that rules everywhere today."

It is surprising how he could believe his own words and what importance he gave to silence. Ivan the partisan keeps quiet among the others, Rublev takes a vow of silence while the jester has his tongue cut out, the son of the protagonist in *The Sacrifice* is silent because he takes a vow of silence in his own way, and, finally, the last lines of Tarkovsky's last film are uttered by this same boy who begins to speak: "In the beginning was the word."

In the spring of 1985 Tarkovsky with his wife and crew set off for the island of Gotland where they were to shoot *The Sacrifice*. Sven Nykvist became the cinematographer for the film. He had been

Ingmar Bergman's regular cameraman and could create the mystical combination of dreams, fantasy and reality which Tarkovsky needed. The main role was given to Erland Josephson, who had played Domenico in *Nostalghia*, and was considered the best candidate for the part of "the savior of the world" from the species of half-crazy fanatics. The nature of Gotland, resembling the environment of the Russian North, made it easier for Western audiences to get into the film and brought it closer to Bergman's work. In turn, the old house with chairs on thick grass reminds Russian audiences of life in a Chekhovian manor. The shooting took place on clear northern nights, as the daylight seemed to Tarkovsky too bright, too optimistic.

The plot of the film, absurd from a logical point of view, follows naturally on the motifs of *Stalker* and *Nostalghia*. Tarkovsky's preferred strategies for patterning his fiction, his ethical and plot motifs bring *The Sacrifice* into the single canvas of his entire body of work.

The background of the film's plot consists of family relations, fatherhood, childhood and the home. Mr. Alexander (the protagonist of the story) is a kind of Father, Teacher, Prophet, Messiah — a man living outside of the world and therefore capable of foresight, of seeing worldly sins in his mind's eye. An eccentric and fanatic, he treats self-sacrifice as the sacred duty of mankind.

The film begins with a long, infinitely wide set where little human figures swarm around a dry tree. An old painting is shown through the credits, in which an old man hands a vessel to an infant lying in the arms of the Madonna — this is Leonardo da Vinci's *Adoration of the Magi*, preserved in the Uffizi Gallery. Intensifying the mood of inspired concentration, Bach's St. Matthew Passion turns into seagull squawking and the sound of the sea. This prelude precedes a landscape of a green field under a gray sky with a road winding along a leaden seashore behind the credits. A man on a bicycle named Otto appears on the road; he is an odd character, somewhat related to Domenico from *Nostalghia*. All of this is presented with an ambiguous slowing of the pace, aimed to bring the audience into the seriousness of the proceedings.

The prelude has already established the source of the motifs: the infant receiving his extraordinary and terrifying destiny from the hands of one of the Magi. This acts like an epigraph for the whole film: *His* sacrifice for the sake of mankind and the Ascension that defied death. A reproduction of the *Adoration of the Magi* hangs in Alexander's study. During the film, people's faces keep reflecting in the glass frame of the painting as if intersecting Leonardo's picture and recalling the infant before whom figures are kneeling as the future sufferer and savior. Alexander has bought a house, where his son, nicknamed Little Man, was born and where he now lives with his entire family. Here a complicated bundle of family relations is entangled.

Alexander's two women — an Englishwoman, Adelaide, and an Italian, Eugenia — are exotic, extravagant, and overtly mentally abnormal. They turn the protagonist's life into a bundle of pain and resentment, and the storyline into a strained blend of murky episodes. This peculiar domestic atmosphere is intruded upon by a foreign element: Otto, a marginal character. Two simple-minded housemaids also appear: Maria and Julia. They come from the village and sympathize with the strained atmosphere of the family. The bad home, the strange family, the odd relationships between them — one can easily lose their mind; or, losing their mind, dive into the depths of the spirit, foreseeing disasters and catastrophes. The presence of the unexplained, like in *Stalker*, is marked by strange sounds which cause glass objects in the house to tremble, namely the dishes in the sideboard and the windowpanes. This sound accompanies shifts in reality: it is as if Alexander's dream continues to develop the drama within the family and imperceptibly intertwines with reality. The protagonist listens to the radio and hears an announcement that a nuclear war has begun. He is shocked and for the first time in his life turns to heaven with a prayer, "because this war is the ultimate war, and after it there will be no victors and no vanquished; no cities or towns, no grass or trees, no water in the wells or birds in the sky..." In a daze of self-sacrifice, Alexander promises to God that he will give up everything — his family, his beloved son, become mute — if only everything would be like it was before.

Again there is a hallucination, a dream within a dream, in which Otto appears and suggests a path forward for Alexander: go to the neighboring house and sleep with the housemaid Maria. This act, he claims, is the only way to save the world.

When Tarkovsky was still in his native Russia, he planned to make a film in which a man is cured of cancer after spending a night with a witch. The motif of salvation turned into a parable about a man who saves the world through self-sacrifice. In spite of the oddity of the suggestion, Alexander takes a gun and rushes to the neighboring house on Otto's bicycle. The episode at Maria's place is no less peculiar, both in the context of self-sacrifice, and for the reinforcement of the main theme. An elderly man, completely untroubled by lust, explains to the simple woman why he must go to bed with her. The explanation is unconvincing and Maria is afraid of the madman. Only after he presses the gun against his temple does he manage to obtain charity from her by begging. At that moment, like in *The Mirror*, their reciprocal self-sacrifice makes them rise in the air over the bed. Ascension? Still the same sound is heard, increasing in strength, marking the shift in reality.

Alexander wakes up in his study and cannot understand what was a dream, and what has happened for real. The director leaves both options unclear. The family breakfast on the grass is so ordinary in its detailed mundaneness. But even this does not convince Alexander of the unreality of his visions. He begins preparations for a prompt fulfillment of his vow. He dresses in a robe with a Taoist symbol on the back and sends everybody out to have a walk. He then brings the furniture to the terrace and sets fire to all his possessions. It readily catches fire. The camera could not bear the omnivorous blaze.

In the six minutes of the scene the house burnt down completely. Tarkovsky intended that the fire serve as the backdrop for the arrival of the ambulance which would take Alexander away to the asylum. The idea of staging a fire was unacceptable for Tarkovsky — everything had to be real, especially that sacrificial fire. They were forced to rebuild the house in a few days and set it on fire once more. The second time they managed to film the entire scene of Alexander's beloved house going down in real flames. Nobody knows who called the ambulance that rushes to them. The serious men from the ambulance restrain the protagonist and drive him away to the mighty sound of Bach. Adelaide, growing faint, necessarily sinks into a puddle.

Following this elevated and ridiculous ending, as if parodying itself, like in *Ivan's Childhood* an epilogue appears: a dry tree under which lies the boy who has just watered it. The camera rises slowly. The dry tree, through the branches of which one can see the sea and the sky, bursts into flower.

The main plot of the sacrifice devised by Alexander is interwoven with another plot line, his relationship with his son. Alexander is not an average man. He is an educated intellectual with a great sense of the spiritual. The prototype for Alexander was, of course — though reconsidered within the main plot of the film — Arseny Tarkovsky. Alexander is an essayist, art theorist and university lecturer. One day, during a walk with his son, he sets a dry trunk into the ground and tells his son a parable about a monk who watered a dead tree for five years until it finally bloomed, because spiritual focus and sacrifice are always rewarded from on high. The boy, who has recently had a throat operation, cannot answer. He can only listen to his father's words, deep in thought about what has been said.

As Tarkovsky explained to Erland Josephson, "The film continues the direction of my previous work. However, here I tried more to join the episodes with their poetic meaning. Therefore, the narration has taken the form of a poetic parable, though there is a lot of autobiography in it. And the house built by the sea is the story of our house in the countryside. And all the characters in this film are from our lives. The boy is me... The protagonist of this film loves his son very much and constantly talks to him of different, quite serious subjects, the meaning of which the boy does not even understand... In general, my father and I had similar conversations — when I was still little and we would often go for walks together. (...) The memory of this has remained with me all my life, those walks, when he talked to me."

The conversation between Alexander and his mute son turns into a complete monologue from the father's side. And it seems that these are the best scenes in the film. There they are, the two of them, the big and the little, sitting on the grass in a pine grove, resting after a walk. "Don't be afraid," the father convinces him, expressing his own thoughts. "There is no such thing as death. No, there's the fear of death and that is an awful fear. Sometimes it even makes people do things they shouldn't. But how different things would be if only we could stop fearing death!"

The shooting of *The Sacrifice* took five weeks. All this time Tarkovsky intently followed every detail that entered the frame. The cinematographer Sven Nykvist was at first annoyed that the Russian director kept looking through the camera. Later he understood that this demanding master could not work any differently. Tarkovsky spent the weeks over which he shot the film on his feet and even energetically jumped rope during breaks. He did not suspect that he was already seriously ill. The blooming tree, revived by the effort of faith, is a symbolic finale to Tarkovsky's entire career, as are the credits: "This film is dedicated to my son Andryusha, with hope and confidence." The dedication shows that this film was meant to be a spell, a magical act capable of influencing reality, altering it. The showing of the film coincided almost exactly with the disaster at Chernobyl. The Western press began to say that Tarkovsky had foreseen nuclear war and his film warns about this danger.

The Sacrifice qualified in 1986 to be entered in competition at the Cannes Film Festival, as a film produced by the Swedish Film Institute with the cooperation of the French Ministry of Culture. The cinematographer, Sven Nykvist, received a special award for the best artistic achievement, and the film took the FIPRESCI award and the Prize of the Ecumenical Jury. Still not the Grand Prix? One might say that this time Tarkovsky's refusal to emotionally win over the audience did not turn out well and left even experienced connoisseurs of his style underwhelmed. The explicitly constructed plot makes the viewer uneasy with its excessively didactic nature, intensified by the remarkably slow pacing. The ability to express the unexpressed is a difficult way of talking to the audience. Tarkovsky's techniques were still based on Bresson's ideas of cinematographic style that he had adopted in his youth, but times had changed and the new claims had been made. Ingmar Bergman wrote, "I find Tarkovsky the greatest, because he brought a special language to cinema, which allows him to capture life as a dream." However the language allowing him to show "life as dream" at that time ceased to completely absorb Bergman himself. The renowned Swedish director stopped making films, as he had come to the conclusion that the aesthetic he had developed was only an offshoot of cinema, and not the only main direction of the art. Tarkovsky required great bravery to go on — despite the innovations in commercial cinema (which often proved very effective at speaking to audiences) — and develop the principles that led to a dead end: detachment, coldness, the ambiguous meaning of the slow pacing. Even with a great inner piercing the strength of the impact on the audience would be significantly lost. In *The Sacrifice* he reached the final point, developing the messianic motif from confession to sermon, and from sermon to offering. The film became a logical conclusion of this journey.

Tarkovsky's films with their dreams, which demolished the disturbing reality of our world, with their discrepancy between the pregnant visual figurativeness and their trivial text, with their multilayered metaphors, vaguely pointing to something of great importance, elevating the viewer over the prose of life, all this formed his unique *auteur* style. Tarkovsky's style, like an imprint of his unique personality, cannot be imitated (using only external techniques would be a mere mimicking of his art). Individual elements of Tarkovsky's film language have become, for better or worse, almost inevitable tools in filmmaking after him. Tarkovsky's inventions are present in nearly every good contemporary film.

Tarkovsky's last film received a mixed reception from foreign viewers. First he was attacked by pro-Soviet critics, who had been "instructed from above". Now it was the turn for those who earlier had been ready to crown him with laurels. Viewers who did not lack common sense and fault-finding critics found Alexander's attempt to save the world ridiculous or even insane. As one English film expert observed caustically, "By his act he destroys his family almost as radically as the war." An article appeared under the title "The story of a madman or an apocalyptic vision?"

Tarkovsky refuted the critics in the press, repeating again and again that the ambiguity in the structure of the film is deliberate and that "bad dreams and visions reflect the state of the world and the protagonist's own life."

The autobiographical nature of all Tarkovsky's films, which he insistently underscores, consists not only in episodes and motifs from his personal life. The evolution of his work, from the naive and unexpected *Ivan's Childhood* to the pretentious and confessional *The Sacrifice*, accurately maintain the director's course of development, or rather the stability of his primary impulse — the determination by the power of his will to vanquish the cruel Zone, the territory of the spiritless, the reign of material forces. Tarkovsky's protagonists, the bearers of the *auteur's* "I", are incapable of experiencing the joy of living either in Moscow, or in Italy, or on a space station, or in 15th-century Russia or Sweden at the turn of the 20th century. In his Rome diary of 1984 he wrote: "I cannot live in Russia and I cannot live here either!" This is not only the cry of someone forced to emigrate, but also the unaltered impulse of Tarkovsky's artistic work, his dominant psychological state — gloomy, apocalyptic. He was born with this disposition and tried to express it with all the powers of the gift given to him from above.

Little Lynx, what did you cry about day and night in your cardboard cradle? What was revealed to you in the eternal dwelling of souls from whence you came into this world? The pain of the insults to come, the despair at being misunderstood? Was the infant frightened by the roar of wars assailing the earth? Was he blinded by the false glitter of gold that overwhelmed the man who had forgotten his calling?

Or maybe, you saw in the dim haze of your fate a terrifying, sadly ominous end?

Chapter 12.
FAREWELL

I.

The Sacrifice was the only film that Tarkovsky would make entirely abroad. It was also his last film and it resounded as his last will.

He was on his last legs as he worked on this film. Five weeks of constantly tense shooting took a lot of energy out of him. When he came back to Rome from the island of Gotland, he was already seriously ill.

While still in Berlin, Andrei started having a hacking cough which he shrugged off, blaming everything on the bad aura of the destroyed city and the tuberculosis that he had experienced as a young man. He did not have time to be ill. He was about to begin editing and adding sound to the film and this task lay heavily on his soul: for four years he had been struggling in vain for the right to see his son and the elderly Anna Semyonovna. The situation had not changed even after his desperate announcement that he would stay abroad.

When he came to Florence to work on the editing of *The Sacrifice*, he had a slight fever that would not let up and this began to worry him. He was tormented by fatigue and chills, just like a lingering cold.

November 18th, 1985   "I am ill. Bronchitis and something funny in the back of the head and the muscles, which puts pressure on the nerves and causes strong pains in my neck and shoulders. Nonetheless, I must be adding sound to the film now."

The mayor of Florence, who was an admirer of the Russian maestro, gave him and his wife a cozy apartment. Nonetheless, he could not find peace. He could not enjoy his own home in this magical city, full of shadows of classic Russian writers who lived and worked under a canopy of pine trees: Dostoevsky, Gogol, and Turgenev… He did not have time to delight in the charming scenery, for he had to finish the film.

NOVEMBER 24TH   "I'm ill, quite seriously even. There is terrible tension between me and the producer because of the film's running time (2 hours and 10 minutes)."

NOVEMBER 30TH   "The doctors are concerned about my state. I had to have a general blood test and an X-ray."

DECEMBER 11TH   "What's wrong with me? The next stage of tuberculosis? Pneumonia or even cancer? In a dream last night I saw Vasily Shukshin. People were playing cards and someone said, 'It's time to settle scores'. They meant that the game was over and it was time to tally the result."

He always remembered and interpreted his dreams. He wove many of them into his films. But the film about dying would not come to be.

DECEMBER 13TH   "It's a black Friday today indeed. I've been to the doctor at the clinic… They took a biopsy from the mysterious tumor on my head… I should have got life insurance in Italy, but I guess that now it would be very difficult to do so."

Tarkovsky was afraid that he had some serious disease, but he did not want to believe that it might be terminal. He was going to live, work, make films, and renovate the house in San Gregorio or even… What if the dust-covered halls of the castle were waiting for him? What if *The Sacrifice* snatched the Grand Prix from the obstinate jury at Cannes?

DECEMBER 15TH "A man lives knowing that sooner or later he will die, but he doesn't know when. That is why he pushes this moment away for an unspecified time and that helps him to live. But I know that and nothing will help me to continue living. The most important thing is Larisa. How should I tell her? How can I do inflict this terrible harm on her with my own hands?"

The verdict was handed in: cancer. But this illness does not necessarily lead promptly to death, right? There are cases of recovery. And how can you believe that it is you — the genius, the extraordinary man, who has been predestined for the worse kind of fate? Tarkovsky dreamed about Pasternak and the oracle at the séance. "He knew that I would make only seven films in total, but he didn't count *The Steamroller and the Violin*, which actually shouldn't be considered."

He needed someone experienced to convince him at once that his illness was treatable. He was afraid to ask the doctors, so he called his Italian friend, the cameraman Franco Terilli, saying "Come to Florence immediately!" Terilli found Andrei lying in bed. After Tarkovsky asked Larisa to leave him alone with his guest, he beckoned Franco to come closer. "Don't be afraid of what I have to tell you," Andrei spoke in almost a whisper. "I am not afraid. They called me from Sweden. I have cancer. I have very little time left to live."

Terilli was shocked. He had heard about Andrei's illness, but when he had visited during the film shoot, the director had looked so young and full of energy!

"Maybe it's a mistake…" his friend said, exaggeratedly denying Tarkovsky's news. "I saw you not long ago in Gotland jumping rope!"

"But now… I scream in pain at times."

"Even if the diagnosis is correct, it's not over yet. I know many people who have beat cancer and then forgotten about their illness."

Andrei's thin, pale lips stretched into a smirk. From his mouth to his temples and chin, deep wrinkles ran across his gaunt face, with an effect of something like an indigenous mask carved from wood.

Attentive to faces like every cameraman, Terilli noticed that he had never seen such wrinkles before.

"You're looking at these wrinkles?" he asked, touching his cheek with a finger. "They are hereditary, just like my father's."

"Is he alive?"

"I wish I could see the old man, God help me," Tarkovsky turned toward the wall. Terilli thought he glimpsed a tear.

"No, Franco! I'm not crying for myself," Tarkovsky turned his brightened face back to his friend and said calmly and solemnly, as if reciting a spell, "I'm not afraid of death."

The Tarkovsky family celebrated Christmas of 1985 in their apartment in Florence.

"What a magnificent city!" Larisa was setting the table next to a fluffy artificial Christmas tree. "It has provided us with a furnished apartment free of charge… It even feels like we're home again!"

"Only the Christmas tree is made of plastic."

"Who knows how you might react to real fir with your allergies."

"You'd better take away the garlic sauce. That smell makes me nauseous… And what do my allergies have to do with it anyway?" Andrei lifted himself to answer the ringing telephone. Larisa handed it to him. He spoke briefly and then said to his wife, "It was the mayor. He congratulated me and told me how glad he was that we live in this city."

"One could hardly stand your jabbering."

"I did learn to say *pronto* and *si*. To his question about how I feel, I answered 'good'." He handed the phone back and put his head in his hands: "It's an awful feeling — weakness and nausea. But what matters most is the film! It is my most important film. I must finish adding the sound!"

"Andrei, dear, let's be reasonable. Nobody knows when you will get the money for *The Sacrifice*. You don't have medical insurance and the treatment requires a huge amount of money, 40 thousand francs. The tests alone have already cost 16 thousand!"

"What do you suggest? Maybe I shouldn't undergo the treatment? Or should I give up adding sound to the film?"

"On the contrary, you must be treated by a great specialist. You should call Marina Vlady. After all, she became very concerned about your health when she learned about your illness from the press. Her husband is the best oncologist in France!"

"It would be impolite after I didn't give her a part in *The Mirror*."

"This is what you remembered! Back then you didn't care about being kind. You cared about Terekhova more than anything else in the world."

"Oh, stop saying such silly things all the time. Your voice alone makes me feel sick…" He lay down on the sofa and turned away to face the wall.

Larisa ran into the other room, crying demonstratively and desperately. The bed creaked as her body fell onto it.

Larisa would recount with admiration: "When she found out about Andrei's miserable situation, Marina asked him to come to her immediately. Without needless words she took out her checkbook and wrote a check for the necessary amount. Later Marina Vlady's husband, Prof. Leon Schwartzenberg, became Andrei's medical adviser." Marina recalls, "He called me and asked to connect him with Prof. Schwartzenberg. I responded to his request right away. He was in great pain, he was exhausted. The cancer had spread too far. It had metastasized into his bones. On the day after his arrival he was admitted into the clinic… The treatment helped him in the sense that he no longer suffered from pain and could finish editing the film, which took several weeks… And then that story began with his son's visit. For four years he had desperately struggled to arrange the visit of his son and the grandmother. I talked to the Soviet ambassador. I gave him the letter from Prof. Schwartzenberg, describing the condition of Andrei's health. At the same time, President Mitterand wrote, I think, to Gorbachev, and after just a while we found out that his son had received permission to come to France".

In May, the Cannes Film Festival took place. Andrei was getting chemotherapy and felt alien to this world. Nausea, fatigue, an emaciated face under a bald scalp… He left locks of his famous pitch-black hair on the pillow. He had to have the rest of it shaved off. He was not tormented by thoughts about the Grand Prix slipping past him again. He already felt as though he was on the other side of reality.

However, after the most intensive chemotherapy treatment, Andrei's state significantly improved and on June 11, 1986 he left the clinic. Marina Vlady accommodated the Tarkovskys at her place. For a while the home of Marina Vlady became Andrei's home. Sometime later ("following the advice of an unwise friend", as Marina Vlady remarks) he left Paris and went to West Germany to undergo the next course of treatment in a popular clinic there. Unfortunately, the popular clinic did not help, although Andrei had a great deal of hope that it would. He eventually returned to Paris and he spent the last months of his life there.

"He believed that he would recover," Larisa Tarkovskaya recalled. "For some reason he believed that God would help him. He was especially heartened when his son arrived…"

"Father asked me about everything that was going on in Moscow," recalled 16-year-old Andrei who had come to Paris with his grandmother. "He was worried about our house in the countryside and kept planning to renovate it. It appeared to me that he missed his native country a lot… He made the effort to keep up a manly façade, in order to set an example for my mother, who suffered no less."

Andrei junior returned home still not having heard from his father that he had so little time left. When his son called him for the last time in Paris from Moscow, his dying father told him: "Nothing special has happened. Everything's going to be fine."

On the cover of his diary which Andrei started writing on January 10, 1986 and which he called his *Martyrolog*, a light sailing boat is gliding on the waves. On that day the doctors had said that he had only three weeks left to live. "Does death frighten me?" Andrei reflected in a documentary on his work by Donatella Baglivo. "I think that death doesn't exist at all. There is only an act of some sort, painful, in the form of suffering. When I think about death, I think about physical suffering, but not about death as such. And death, in my view, simply doesn't exist. I don't know… Once I dreamt that I had died and it was similar to truth.

I could feel such liberation, such unimaginable lightness that, maybe, it was this feeling of lightness and freedom that had given me the impression that I was dead, that is, I abandoned all ties with this world. Anyway, I don't believe in death. There is only pain and suffering, and people often confuse death and suffering. I don't know. Maybe, when I face it directly, I will get scared and I will reason differently… Hard to say." The film was finished when Andrei was not ill yet or he did not know about his illness. But even after he found out that he was on the verge of death, he did not change his way of thinking. He asked to be taken to Italy, to a little seaside town, Cala Piccola. These were strange days — days of farewell to the sunny world which he always despised. He never managed to grow fond of such a banal, picture-perfect warm sea. He lay alone in the tower room. He would, with pleasure, but seldom, receive his son and the mason with whom he discussed the construction of the house in San-Gregorio. Downstairs, on the sunny terrace, an atmosphere of holiday rest prevailed. Friends and children uproariously enjoyed the sea, pretending that nothing extraordinary was happening, that he was not lying in bed staring into the ceiling, a skinny "teenager" with a bandana tied over the bald skull. This was the world-famous director who had given the world Ivan, Andrei Rublev, the Stalker, Chris Kelvin for eternal remembrance. Somewhere, in other places, friends collected money for the terminally ill Tarkovsky. He would listen to the noise coming from downstairs, grasp the rolling of the waves, struggling to bring back the "Bright, Bright Day", and the silvery poplar, and the garden in Yurtsevo, withering in the heat of July… He did not dig up the chest that he took from the Simonovo church when he was little… He didn't keep his promise after all. And there much more that he wanted to do, but he would not be able to now…

"Andrei, dear, it's time for your second injection," Larisa came in, sat next to him and filled the syringe. She didn't even ask; she could see from the fact that he had bit his lips bloody that morphine did not help him much anymore. "You'll fall asleep soon." He did fall asleep briefly, but soon he howled with surging pain. The injections brought only temporary relief. He had to return to Paris.

On December 5, 1986 Tarkovsky wrote in the *Martyrolog*, "Yesterday they didn't give me the third round of chemotherapy. I feel awful. I can't even think about getting out of bed or even lifting myself a bit. Schwarzenberg doesn't know what to do, because he doesn't know where those terrible pains come from. The film is proving successful in England, in the USA. Incredibly good response. The Japanese are organizing some assistance fund, but it must be explained to them, why such a famous film director is so poor."

His hospital room was not so big, but it had a large window. Larisa would visit him every day. His friends would sit silently in the corner and leave quietly. Someone put his favorite stones which he had picked up on the shore of the island of Gotland on the windowsill. The everlasting companions of such a perishable man… Pain, fear, the bitterness of dying… This is what he was afraid of. And death, there is no death…

"About ten days before he passed away," Franco Terilli recalls, "Andrei sent me a piece of paper with a drawing of a wine glass and a rose on it from Paris. He already had difficulty writing. A few days before he died I received a phone call and was asked to call Andrei the next day — he wanted to tell me something very important. He lifted the receiver but did not say a word. I understood that he wanted to say goodbye to me with silence."

In a documentary that he made to commemorate Andrei, his Italian friend Ebbo Demant, documentary director, tells the story of how Andrei gave him a piece of paper on which he had drawn his own grave. An eye is watching out of a tree root. The picture greatly resembles a drawing from his childhood preserved by his sister where Tarkovsky had drawn himself hiding among the roots of a huge tree.

Martyrolog, December 15. "Paris. Hamlet. All day in bed, not getting up. Pains in the lower part of the stomach and the back. Nerves too. I can't move my legs. I'm very weak. Am I really *going* to die? What about Hamlet? But now I don't have strength to do anything. That's the question…"

What did flash through his mind in his last moments? No, he did not cry like the infant Lynx. Life had ceased to frighten him, just like death and the hereafter did not scare him. Clear and measured, in the voice of his father, the unforgettable lines that Arseny Tarkovsky had written for Viktor Berkovsky's song *"Vot i leto proshlo"* (Now the Summer is Over) pulsated in his temples:

> *Now the summer is over,*
> *Like it never was at all.*
> *It's warm in the sunshine*
> *But that wasn't enough.*
> *Everything that came to pass,*
> *It fell right into my hands*
> *Like a pointy leaf.*
> *But it wasn't enough.*
> *Neither evil nor good*
> *Was lost in vain,*
> *Everything was brightly ablaze.*
> *But it wasn't enough.*
>
> *Life took me under its wing,*
> *Sheltered me and kept me safe.*
> *I was truly lucky,*
> *But that wasn't enough.*
> *Not a leaf was burnt,*
> *Not a branch broken…*
> *The day is clear as glass,*
> *But it wasn't enough.*

On December 29 Andrei Tarkovsky passed away. Perhaps, not believing in death, he simply crossed the threshold to some other reality, the one that had so often inspired him? Hundreds of people came to the courtyard of the St. Alexander Nevsky Orthodox Cathedral where the burial service for Andrei was read. Having taken up a position on the porch with his famous cello, Mstislav Rostropovich played the solemn and stately *Sarabande* by Bach. The Sainte-Geneviève-des-Bois cemetery in the suburbs of Paris became Tarkovsky's final resting place. Paris was celebrating the New Year, nobody from the magistrate or the mayor's office was in town. A grave, which nobody had taken care of for a long time, was found with great difficulty. It was the grave of Yesaul Grigoriev.* In spite of the light snow, the widow stepped forward to the grave wearing a huge hat and black veil and threw white roses onto the coffin as it was being lowered.

In 1994, Tarkovsky's remains were moved to his own place, specially provided by the mayor. Ernst Neizvestny made the headstone with the inscription "To the man who saw the Angel".

---

* By a strange coincidence, it was Yesaul Grigoriev who killed the younger brother of Arseny Tarkovsky during the Russian Civil War. Andrei's uncle was 19 then. Or maybe it was some other Yesaul. There are many Grigorievs in the world, aren't there?

Appendix A.
Afterword:
"I don't believe in death"

Tarkovsky left this world without renouncing his Soviet citizenship or asking for political asylum. After his death, however, his widow received the recognition she had longed for: she was granted honorary French citizenship accompanied by a sufficient pension.

The Russian film industry let out a sigh of relief, established the Andrei Tarkovsky Memorial Prize and posthumously awarded him the Lenin Prize. Honors were paid, their conscience was clear. The Soviet government did everything to turn Tarkovsky into the symbol of a martyr.

When he heard about his son's death, Arseny Alexandrovich was shocked: "There is nothing worse than to bury your own child." He would never see his son again.

Andrei Tarkovsky's son Arseny became a surgeon. He loved his grandfather, after whom he was named, very much. In the last years, the elder Tarkovskys lived in a veteran's home in Matveyevskoe. The younger Arseny, who had graduated from a medical university, often visited them and when his grandfather fell ill, he would sit by his bed. He was also there on the last night, when Arseny Alexandrovich was already unconscious…

Tarkovsky's younger son Andrei now lives in Florence, in the house which the city gave his father when he made the decision not to return to his home country. The Andrei Tarkovsky Archive was located in that same house.* In the preface to the *Martyrolog*, Andrei Andreyevich Tarkovsky would write, "My father often repeated one phrase to me, that Man has not been created to be happy, that there are more important things than happiness. The quest for truth is a painful path. For a Russian artist, this path often becomes the Way of the Cross."

Andrei Tarkovsky was one of the greatest directors of the 20th century. He created his own film language, he was a philosopher, a personality on a cosmic scale.

Irrespective of the aims of the director himself, the Tarkovsky phenomenon remains a potent symbol not only for Russian (Soviet) filmmaking, but also for society as a whole. He embodies the image of the Russian artist for the West, and for Russia the image of the rejected Messiah. Tarkovsky is a symbol of the Soviet intelligentsia as a class, with its ambitions and its divisions, its energy, its helplessness and its belief in its own destiny. He did not choose his fate; the fate chose him and determined what would befall him: a life on the cross, in the name of sacrifice, in the name of his cause — and naturally in the name of the resurrection. This is a resurrection of all the good things of which one's life consists: brotherly love, earthly existence, spiritual growth.

Tarkovsky's role in Russian culture is unique. He tried to build upon a system of moral values, distorted by the totalitarian regime and by the "rotten" West, his own code of commandments for a new world man. Precepts of spiritual transformation and messianic service for saving the world, these were the grounds of Tarkovsky's philosophy. Faithfulness toward one's calling, an uncompromising opposition to one's various circumstances and the hope for miracles were the central theme of his films and at the same time the central theme of his life.

What does Tarkovsky mean to us today, almost half a century after his astonishing wave of innovation, in a disturbing time when accelerating technological progress increasingly fills our lives with

---

* This archive was subsequently sold at auction at Sotheby's in November of 2012 for 1.5 million British pounds to officials in Russia's Ivanovo region — Christopher Culver.

action, and art becomes part of the everyday rhythm? No one works on paintings for long years any more, composes a symphony until their hair turns gray or hunches over a weighty novel that reveals in enormous detail the course of history and human existence. Both artists and audiences have undergone a clear division into elitist and mass ones. Cinema for the general public has become a thickened syrup of sheer action. Cinema for genuine connoisseurs is persistently moving in the direction set forth by Bresson, Bergman and Tarkovsky. The latter blazed a trail, but he warned about imitation. It is particularly this profound inner essence, as utterly individual as one's fingerprints, that protects his films from being copied. These days, the unique atmosphere of Tarkovsky's films, the work of a director who insistently denied viewers even the slightest bit of entertainment, has become either a museum or a shrine. It is fare for gourmets, masochists or a chosen few who are still hungry for spiritual improvement.

"There are artists toward whom you clamber up, like on a glass mountain and you feel how you slip down, not being able to reach the heights of *their* thinking." Such a glass mountain, as described by Andron Mikhalkov-Konchalovsky, describes the standpoint and the essence of Andrei Tarkovsky. His films often soared high. One can and should rise to meet them, throwing off our everyday vanities, the habit to live without care for our mundane sins, the pursuit of worldly possessions, of creature comforts. It will be an arduous journey, and hardly anyone who reaches the summit will come closer to the director's message. There, in the rarified air of ideas, there is often a lack of human warmth and sensitivity, so necessary for achieving the crucial interaction between artist and audience: the sense of a deep spiritual participation, a penetrating unity, where the world created by the artist is contained in your own world.

Today Tarkovsky is easily accessible: books about him are regularly published, retrospectives of his films run all over Russia.

Over the years Andrei Tarkovsky's relatives, colleagues and scholars studying his work have come to the town of Yuryevets in the Ivanovo region, where he was born and spent his childhood.

In 2007, which would have marked the director's 75th birthday, the International Film Festival "Zerkalo", named in honor of Andrei Tarkovsky, was founded by the Government of the Ivanovo Oblast with the support of the Administration of the President of the Russian Federation, the Ministry of Culture, the National Film Foundation of the Russian Federation and the Union of Cinematographers of the Russian Federation.

The Governor of the Ivanovo Oblast, Mikhail Men (son of Alexander Men), was appointed Chairman of the Organizing Committee of the Festival. The director's sister, Marina Tarkovskaya, became one of the inspirations for and organizers of the Festival. Since 2010 the President of the Festival is Russian director and People's Artist of the Russian Federation Pavel Lungin.

The extensive program of the festival includes: the International Competition of Fiction Films, special screening, retrospectives, reviews of animated films and student films. Each year about 150 films are shown at the Festival, over 50 master classes are held and the Festival draws around 25 thousand people.

In May 2011, the 5th annual Tarkovsky Film Festival took place in Ivanovo and the region.

In 1993, the Andrei Tarkovsky Foundation established the annual Andrei Tarkovsky Prize, which is awarded at the Moscow International Film Festival to the best film within or outside the competition program.

Does he know about that? Has he become an impartial judge of the course of his life, his human weaknesses? Is he fully satisfied with the growing recognition? No one knows, but one would very much like to believe it.

* * *

Glagoslav Publications Catalogue

- *The Time of Women* by Elena Chizhova
- *Andrei Tarkovsky: A Life on the Cross* by Lyudmila Boyadzhieva
- *Sin* by Zakhar Prilepin
- *Hardly Ever Otherwise* by Maria Matios
- *Khatyn* by Ales Adamovich
- *The Lost Button* by Irene Rozdobudko
- *Christened with Crosses* by Eduard Kochergin
- *The Vital Needs of the Dead* by Igor Sakhnovsky
- *The Sarabande of Sara's Band* by Larysa Denysenko
- *A Poet and Bin Laden* by Hamid Ismailov
- *Zo Gaat Dat in Rusland* (Dutch Edition) by Maria Konjoekova
- *Kobzar* by Taras Shevchenko
- *The Stone Bridge* by Alexander Terekhov
- *Moryak* by Lee Mandel
- *King Stakh's Wild Hunt* by Uladzimir Karatkevich
- *The Hawks of Peace* by Dmitry Rogozin
- *Harlequin's Costume* by Leonid Yuzefovich
- *Depeche Mode* by Serhii Zhadan
- *Groot Slem en Andere Verhalen* (Dutch Edition) by Leonid Andrejev
- *METRO 2033* (Dutch Edition) by Dmitry Glukhovsky
- *METRO 2034* (Dutch Edition) by Dmitry Glukhovsky
- *A Russian Story* by Eugenia Kononenko
- *Herstories, An Anthology of New Ukrainian Women Prose Writers*
- *The Battle of the Sexes Russian Style* by Nadezhda Ptushkina
- *A Book Without Photographs* by Sergey Shargunov
- *Down Among The Fishes* by Natalka Babina
- *disUNITY* by Anatoly Kudryavitsky
- *Sankya* by Zakhar Prilepin
- *Wolf Messing* by Tatiana Lungin
- *Good Stalin* by Victor Erofeyev
- *Solar Plexus* by Rustam Ibragimbekov
- *Don't Call me a Victim!* by Dina Yafasova
- *Poetin* (Dutch Edition) by Chris Hutchins and Alexander Korobko

- *A History of Belarus* by Lubov Bazan
- *Children's Fashion of the Russian Empire* by Alexander Vasiliev
- *Empire of Corruption: The Russian National Pastime* by Vladimir Soloviev
- *Heroes of the 90s: People and Money. The Modern History of Russian Capitalism* by Alexander Solovev, Vladislav Dorofeev and Valeria Bashkirova
- *Fifty Highlights from the Russian Literature* (Dutch Edition) by Maarten Tengbergen
- *Bajesvolk* (Dutch Edition) by Michail Chodorkovsky
- *Dagboek van Keizerin Alexandra* (Dutch Edition)
- *Myths about Russia* by Vladimir Medinskiy
- *Boris Yeltsin: The Decade that Shook the World* by Boris Minaev
- *A Man Of Change: A study of the political life of Boris Yeltsin*
- *Sberbank: The Rebirth of Russia's Financial Giant* by Evgeny Karasyuk
- *To Get Ukraine* by Oleksandr Shyshko
- *Asystole* by Oleg Pavlov
- *Gnedich* by Maria Rybakova
- *Marina Tsvetaeva: The Essential Poetry*
- *Multiple Personalities* by Tatyana Shcherbina
- *The Investigator* by Margarita Khemlin
- *The Exile* by Zinaida Tulub
- *Leo Tolstoy: Flight from Paradise* by Pavel Basinsky
- *Moscow in the 1930* by Natalia Gromova
- *Laurus* (Dutch edition) by Evgenij Vodolazkin
- *Prisoner* by Anna Nemzer
- *The Crime of Chernobyl: The Nuclear Goulag* by Wladimir Tchertkoff
- *Alpine Ballad* by Vasil Bykau
- *The Complete Correspondence of Hryhory Skovoroda*
- *The Tale of Aypi* by Ak Welsapar
- *Selected Poems* by Lydia Grigorieva
- *The Fantastic Worlds of Yuri Vynnychuk*
- *The Garden of Divine Songs and Collected Poetry of Hryhory Skovoroda*
- *Adventures in the Slavic Kitchen: A Book of Essays with Recipes* by Igor Klekh
- *Seven Signs of the Lion* by Michael M. Naydan

- *Forefathers' Eve* by Adam Mickiewicz
- *One-Two* by Igor Eliseev
- *Girls, be Good* by Bojan Babić
- *Time of the Octopus* by Anatoly Kucherena
- *The Grand Harmony* by Bohdan Ihor Antonych
- *The Selected Lyric Poetry Of Maksym Rylsky*
- *The Shining Light* by Galymkair Mutanov
- *The Frontier: 28 Contemporary Ukrainian Poets - An Anthology*
- *Acropolis: The Wawel Plays* by Stanisław Wyspiański
- *Contours of the City* by Attyla Mohylny
- *Conversations Before Silence: The Selected Poetry of Oles Ilchenko*
- *The Secret History of my Sojourn in Russia* by Jaroslav Hašek
- *Mirror Sand: An Anthology of Russian Short Poems*
- *Maybe We're Leaving* by Jan Balaban
- *Death of the Snake Catcher* by Ak Welsapar
- *A Brown Man in Russia* by Vijay Menon
- *Hard Times* by Ostap Vyshnia
- *The Flying Dutchman* by Anatoly Kudryavitsky
- *Nikolai Gumilev's Africa* by Nikolai Gumilev
- *Combustions* by Srđan Srdić
- *The Sonnets* by Adam Mickiewicz
- *Dramatic Works* by Zygmunt Krasiński
- *Four Plays* by Juliusz Słowacki
- *Little Zinnobers* by Elena Chizhova
- *We Are Building Capitalism! Moscow in Transition 1992-1997* by Robert Stephenson
- *The Nuremberg Trials* by Alexander Zvyagintsev
- *The Hemingway Game* by Evgeni Grishkovets
- *A Flame Out at Sea* by Dmitry Novikov
- *Jesus' Cat* by Grig
- *Want a Baby and Other Plays* by Sergei Tretyakov
- *Mikhail Bulgakov: The Life and Times* by Marietta Chudakova
- *Leonardo's Handwriting* by Dina Rubina
- *A Burglar of the Better Sort* by Tytus Czyżewski
- *The Mouseiad and other Mock Epics* by Ignacy Krasicki
- *Ravens before Noah* by Susanna Harutyunyan

- *An English Queen and Stalingrad* by Natalia Kulishenko
- *Point Zero* by Narek Malian
- *Absolute Zero* by Artem Chekh
- *Olanda* by Rafał Wojasiński
- *Robinsons* by Aram Pachyan
- *The Monastery* by Zakhar Prilepin
- *The Selected Poetry of Bohdan Rubchak: Songs of Love, Songs of Death, Songs of the Moon*
- *Mebet* by Alexander Grigorenko
- *The Orchestra* by Vladimir Gonik
- *Everyday Stories* by Mima Mihajlović
- *Slavdom* by Ľudovít Štúr
- *The Code of Civilization* by Vyacheslav Nikonov
- *Where Was the Angel Going?* by Jan Balaban
- *De Zwarte Kip* (Dutch Edition) by Antoni Pogorelski
- *Głosy / Voices* by Jan Polkowski
- *Sergei Tretyakov: A Revolutionary Writer in Stalin's Russia* by Robert Leach
- *Opstand* (Dutch Edition) by Władysław Reymont
- *Dramatic Works* by Cyprian Kamil Norwid
- *Children's First Book of Chess* by Natalie Shevando and Matthew McMillion
- *Precursor* by Vasyl Shevchuk
- *The Vow: A Requiem for the Fifties* by Jiří Kratochvil
- *De Bibliothecaris* (Dutch edition) by Mikhail Jelizarov
- *Subterranean Fire* by Natalka Bilotserkivets
- *Vladimir Vysotsky: Selected Works*
- *Behind the Silk Curtain* by Gulistan Khamzayeva
- *The Village Teacher and Other Stories* by Theodore Odrach
- *Duel* by Borys Antonenko-Davydovych
- *War Poems* by Alexander Korotko
- *Ballads and Romances* by Adam Mickiewicz
- *The Revolt of the Animals* by Wladyslaw Reymont
- *Liza's Waterfall: The hidden story of a Russian feminist* by Pavel Basinsky
- *Biography of Sergei Prokofiev* by Igor Vishnevetsky

  More coming . . .

9 781782 671015